KT-442-154

Gaining Ground: Law Reform for Gypsies and Travellers

Edited by Rachel Morris & Luke Clements

University of Hertfordshire Press

UNIVERSITY OF PLYMOUTH

Item No. 900 4054837

Date - 9 FEB 2000 B

Class No. 342. 0873 GAI

Contl. No.

LIBRARY SERVICES

First published 1999 in Great Britain by
University of Hertfordshire Press
Learning & Information Services
University of Hertfordshire
College Lane
Hatfield
Hertfordshire AL10 9AD

© Traveller Law Research Unit, Cardiff Law School

ISBN 0 900458 98 4 ✓

Designed by Geoff Green, Cambridge CB4 5RA

Cover photograph
Michelle Johns/The Rural Media Company
Text photographs
Stefano Cagnoni Photography, London

Printed in Great Britain by
J. W. Arrowsmith Ltd.

Contents

Part II: Voices for reform

Appendices

Preface

WITHDRAWN
FROM
UNIVERSITY OF PLYMOUTH
LIBRARY SERVICES

The Traveller Law Research Unit (TLRU) of Cardiff Law School, the University of Wales Cardiff has, since March 1995, provided a service for Travelling people in England and Wales. An early initiative of the Unit was the Telephone Legal Advice Service for Travellers (TLAST).[a] Because of the various traditional impediments to Travelling people in accessing lawyers, not least their often isolated locations, the project provided Travellers with access to specialist legal advice by telephone.[b] This successful initiative eventually created a network of specialist advisers throughout the UK who are prepared to provide user-friendly advice and representation for Travelling people.

In addition to the provision of legal and practical advice and information, the Unit has published Directories of 'Traveller-friendly' legal practitioners and other Traveller-related service providers which are not only useful sources of information but have proved to be invaluable networking tools for planners, lawyers, academics, community development workers, religious organisations, local government officers, health and social services workers, educators, Travellers, and Traveller and equality organisations.

In March 1997 the Unit organised a highly successful Conference with specialist speakers from the Republic of Ireland, Scotland, Northern Ireland and England and Wales. The Conference provided a forum at which imaginative and practical proposals for Traveller law reform were discussed by over 90 Traveller-related organisations including local authority personnel, teachers of Travellers, Health Visitors, legal practitioners, planners, Church officers, police officers and individuals. What emerged from the Conference were proposals for the development of specialist working groups, to meet with a view to providing a common platform to lobby for Traveller law reform. Following upon the Conference, a consultation process was initiated which involved 40 organisations and which generated further discussion and proposals for practical

---

a TLAST was funded for three years, until April 1998, by the Nuffield Foundation and the Joseph Rowntree Charitable Trust, while Cardiff Law School covered infrastructure costs.

b A particularly positive development for Travelling people over the last 5 years has been the widespread availability of mobile telephones.

reforms; these were incorporated into a 100-page Conference and Consultation Report.[c]

At the 1997 Conference, speakers from Eire outlined the successful programme adopted there to improve provision for Travellers and outlaw discrimination. As a direct result of the programme, last year the Oireachtas passed the Traveller Accommodation Act 1998, which sets up a framework whereby 3100 new units of accommodation will be built to meet a five-year target, using existing housing association mechanisms and consultative committees on which Travellers are represented. The new ethos of equality and anti-discrimination personified in the new law and policy relating to Travellers in the Republic of Eire will take a long time to trickle down to the level of local prejudice and hostility. Those charged with the implementation of the 1998 Act appreciate that there is no 'quick fix' in healing the rifts between Travellers and the settled community. Nonetheless, the Act 'gives a clear political message that Irish society can no longer tolerate the deplorable living conditions that have for too long been foisted onto Travellers.'[d]

Commencing in March 1998, meetings were arranged with members of the TLRU network who had expressed an interest in being actively involved in promoting reform of the laws that affect Travelling people in the UK. The meetings continued through to July and were attended by a wide variety of people, as individuals or as representatives of organisations. Entitled 'Traveller Working Groups', the meetings convened considered in greater detail the subject areas of education, accommodation and site provision, eviction and criminal justice, planning and health and social services. Those present at these meetings and others interested to be part of the 'platform' toward reform were asked to put forward their ideas for practical, affordable and realisable reforms; to offer what time and expertise they could to detail and formulate reform proposals; to build on areas where there was consensus on necessary reform; to provide research results and other information useful to the process; and to broadly consult with Travellers to ascertain whether those ideas brought to the table had support and were comprehensive.

The ideas put together by these groups were considered at the 2nd Conference on Traveller Law Reform, held on Wednesday 17th February 1999 at Friends House, Euston, London, and further refined.[e] The end results are contained in this book. What connects them all is the recognition that Travelling people not only experience a scandalous level of prejudice and discrimination in all areas of their lives, but that this treatment appears to be deemed acceptable by all levels, even the highest levels, of British society.

The Traveller Law Research Unit acknowledges that meetings were held in England and there was a great deal more input from England than from Scotland, Wales or Northern Ireland; therefore the outcome may seem unduly Anglo-centric. Efforts have been made to ensure that wording and references acknowledge regional differences wherever possible. Where the word 'national' is used in Part I of this Report, it refers to the whole of the United Kingdom (unless otherwise stated).

---

c Luke Clements and Penny Smith, editors (1997) *Traveller Law Reform: Conference and Consultation Report*, TLAST/The Traveller Law Research Unit of Cardiff Law School.

e Letter from David Joyce, National Accommodation Officer, the Irish Traveller Movement, to the Department of the Environment in Ireland, commenting on the Traveller Accommodation Bill, 15th April 1998.

The 1997 Conference Report outlined many of the different legal provisions that apply in these countries; for instance that the Caravan Sites Act 1968 never applied to Scotland, and that although Part II of the Act was repealed in England and Wales in 1994 it remained in force in Northern Ireland. Whilst there are substantial differences between the common law and legislative provisions which related to Travellers in Scotland, Northern Ireland, England and Wales, the main problems of exclusion lack of respect and discrimination are common to all. The need therefore is for United Kingdom wide law reform; Travellers inevitably move between the various nations that make up the United Kingdom and have a right to respect wherever they reside and a right to expect the law to be consistent in how it impacts upon their way of life.

Part I of this book outlines each of the legal themes which have been considered and the reform proposals put forward as a result. Not all proposed reforms require legislative amendment or development; it has been recognised that changes in policy and practice may be more effective harbingers of change in some areas that the law. Part II contains pieces written by people who attended the Traveller working groups and 2nd Conference on Traveller Law Reform, and whose practical or professional experience has spurred them to write in more detail about some of the areas of the lives of Travelling people which need reform, and what shape that reform might need to take. The appendices contain information relevant to law reforms and the Traveller law reform process.

We are grateful to the kind and generous hosts of the Traveller Working Groups, and to those individuals and organisations who took the time and trouble to attend and contribute to them. A list of Working Group participants can be found at Appendix 1.

Clara Connolly (formerly at the CRE), Russell Campbell at Shelter, Francine Bates at the Carers National Association, and Jerry Ham at the Groundswell Project, assisted with venues and refreshments for the Accommodation and Site Provision Traveller Working Group meetings. Dr Derek Hawes (now retired) at the School for Policy Studies at the University of Bristol hosted and helped to organise the Health and Social Services meetings. Chris Johnson, Des Smith & Chris Esdaile (formerly at McGrath & Co. Solicitors; the Traveller Advice Team – including Chris and Chris – have now relocated to the Community Law Partnership in Birmingham) hosted the first Planning and Criminal Justice Group and all subsequent Eviction and Criminal Justice Sub-Group meetings. The Planning Traveller Working Sub-Group held all subsequent meetings at the Chambers of Alan Masters, 10/11 Grays Inn Square, London.

A number of those attending the Traveller Working Groups have written items for inclusion or which have been included in this Report, and we are greatly in their debt: Diana Allen, Penny Ballinger, Dr Malcolm Bell, Philip Brown, Sarah Cemlyn, Michael Cox, Sarah Cox, Stephen Field, Bill Forrester, Paul Goltz, Debbie Harvey, Liz Hughes, Chris Johnson, Dr Donald Kenrick, Michelle Lloyd and Richard Morran, Alan Masters, Trish McDonald, Annie Murdoch, the National Association of Teachers of Travellers, Jim Spiller, Rodney Stableford, The Land Is Ours, Tony Thomson and Richard Trahair.

We are also immensely grateful to Lord Avebury and Hugh Harris for allowing us to include their conference speeches in this Report.

Other participants of the 2nd Conference on Traveller Law Reform who should be thanked for their time and effort are:

- Chairs and notetakers of conference workshops: Kanta Wild-Smith, Liz Hughes, Chris Johnson, Sarah Cemlyn, and Alan Masters – who also spoke during the morning session of the conference, Susan Alexander, Bill Forrester, Anthea Wormington, Terry Holland, Debbie Harvey, Karen Ryan, Sandra Clay, Jim Spiller and Rodney Stableford.
- Assistants Jennie Waring, Camilla Berens, Jake Bowers-Burbridge, Lisa Lowe, Karen Ryan and Tim Wilson.
- The staff of Friends House.

Special thanks to the Joseph Rowntree Charitable Trust and Cardiff Law School for financial and administrative support enabling the Traveller Law Research Unit to facilitate this law reform process.

Foreword by Lord Avebury

Remarks by Lord Avebury, opening the Second Conference on Traveller Law Reform 1996

I was delighted to be asked to open this second conference on Traveller Law Reform, at a time when decisions not only on the law applying to travellers, but of administrative ways of tackling their social exclusion are becoming ever more urgent. Your first conference was nearly two years ago, in March 1997, just before the present government came into power. The aim was to provide a forum at which imaginative and practical proposals for Traveller law reform could be raised, and you were successful in attracting local authorities, teachers, health visitors, legal practitioners, planners, Church workers, police officers, Travellers and Traveller organisations. That led to consultations and further discussion, culminating in the report 'Traveller Law Reform: Conference and Consultation Report' edited by Luke Clements and Penny Smith.*f*

The conference also gave birth to a number of specialist working groups, which began to meet in March 1998 with a view to providing a common platform to lobby for Traveller law reform. Now, as the government approaches the beginning of their third year, we shall be focussing today on the work of these groups, which have formulated proposals for reforms covering planning, eviction, education, health and social services, accommodation and site provision and the media. These are in the draft report now before you.

At the 1997 conference you also looked at the successful policies adopted in the Republic of Ireland to improve provision for Travellers and eliminate discrimination. They have adopted a five-year programme for meeting the accommodation needs of travellers, under which the housing associations are providing 3,100 new units. This is

f See footnote *c*.

in stark contrast with our own approach, in the Criminal Justice and Public Order Act 1994, which abandoned the idea of any involvement of official agencies in meeting the needs of travellers. They are left to fend for themselves under Circular 1/94, taking their chances with a planning system to sink or swim that is heavily weighted against them.

From the time of the 1968 Caravan Sites Act onwards, there was at least a presumption that it was in the public interest to ensure that Gypsies and other travellers had sites where they could stay, and that if we solved their accommodation difficulties, it would become easier to address their multiple social handicaps. By repealing the duty of local authorities to provide accommodation for Gypsies, in the Criminal Justice and Public Order Act 1994, one of your Working Groups argues, it is implied that travellers are not equal to settled people, and the use of an Act with this title implied that the question was something to do with criminality and order, a connection which is very offensive to travelling people. That legislation decisively shifted the centre of gravity of discussions about Gypsies, from the need to make provision for their accommodation, to the question of controlling unauthorised encampments, and there is even a lack of interest in testing the assumptions on which the 1994 Act was predicated.

We are back to where I came in when I first entered the Commons 37 years ago. Then, as now, the Gypsies had to make their own way through the planning system. It was the late Norman Dodds, Member for Erith and Crayford, who suggested the development of a network of public sites. The gradual extension of the built-up area of greater London – which of course didn't yet exist as a political entity at that time - meant that some of the Gypsies' traditional stopping places were disappearing under the advancing tide of bricks and mortar, in his constituency and in mine of Orpington as well. Norman died in 1965 before any government would look at his ideas sympathetically.

The following year, 1966, the first ever government survey of Gypsies' patterns of living was published under the title Gypsies and Other Travellers, and this showed that only a very small fraction of the Gypsy families then were living on authorised sites. When I drew a place in the ballot for Private Members' Bills in 1968, I agreed with Dick Crossman, then Minister of Housing and Local Government, to pilot a Bill for two purposes: one half dealt with the rights of people on all caravan sites not to be evicted without a court order, and the other placed an obligation on local authorities to provide sites for Gypsies residing or resorting to their areas. In return, local authorities which made adequate provision were to be given additional powers to deal with unauthorised encampments within their area.

For a variety of reasons, the 1968 Act took much longer to work than we expected it would at the time. First, the government delayed the coming into force of the Act because of financial constraints. Second, the duty to provide was laid on the county councils, but the districts had a right of objection to any proposal, which they almost invariably exercised. The counties were not keen on having rows with their districts, and were reluctant to make proposals which they knew would be unpopular with the localities concerned, whatever the benefits over the longer term. Under the Bill, the Minister did have a power to give county councils directions about the number of sites they should provide, but this was exercised in only three cases over the 30-year life of the Bill.

When Sir John Cripps reviewed the workings of the Caravan Sites Act in 1976, he noted the reasons why it was taking longer to solve the problem than we had expected, and the main obstacle was the determined local opposition to every proposal made to establish a site anywhere. Sir John recommended that the government and local authorities should agree on a national plan specifying the number and location of sites, but this was sidelined as being too dirigiste.[g] That was the best chance we ever had of accelerating the implementation of the Caravan Sites Act, and it was most unfortunate that it failed through lack of political will.

All the same, the local authorities were addressing the need slowly but surely over the years, helped by a much smaller contribution by the private sector. The number of mobile homes on unauthorised sites began to decline, in spite of a rapid increase in the size of the traveller population, and if the last government hadn't sabotaged the whole scheme, unauthorised encampments would have virtually disappeared within the next ten years.

There was another negative consequence. In the summer of 1994, when the Act was repealed, 62% of local authorities were still not designated, meaning that they had not yet provided enough sites to satisfy their legal obligations. The areas which neglected their duties were then let off scot free, and were given the powers that others had worked hard to provide for themselves.

The Tory government's argument for repealing the 68 Act was that there was a hard core of 4,000 caravans on unauthorised sites, which had persisted since 1981, and therefore even fewer sites should be provided, in the hope that in some miraculous way, private enterprise would increase to the level where it not only made up for the loss of local authority provision, but also dealt with this shortfall. So that you can see I am not making this up, let me quote Earl Ferrers, the Tory Minister who was in charge of the Criminal Justice Bill in the Lords:

> "That system" - referring to the scheme of the 1968 Act – " has been in operation for 24 years, and the fact is that levels of unauthorised camping – in terms of numbers of gypsy caravans on unauthorised sites reflected in the January counts carried out by local authorities in England and Wales – have hardly changed since then… The Government had to decide to do something. We decided to look again at the policy of public site provision against the backdrop of unabated levels of unauthorised camping… The conclusion we reached, after extensive consultation, was that local authority site provision was not likely ever to meet that apparently growing demand for sites… it is the Government's view that public provision has now reached a satisfactory level and that further provision should be made by the gypsies themselves through the planning system."[h]

At the time this illogical case was being made, the number on unauthorised sites had already been falling, partly because of a fortuitous and unpredicted drop in total numbers which continued for the next two years. This meant that the harmful consequences of shutting down the main providers of accommodation for Travellers were not immediately felt, and still haven't been fully apparent. Although the total number of caravans started to rise again slowly in the last two years for which the figures are available, it has still not reached the 1993 peak last January. The other factor which has delayed the reckoning is that when the 1994 Act was passed, there were still some 100% grant schemes in the pipeline, all of which presumably have now been completed. From now

---

g Sir John Cripps, Accommodation for Gypsies; A report on the working of the Caravan Sites Act 1968, HMSO, 1977.

h Official Report, House of Lords, July 11, 1994, Col 1 541-2.

onwards, any further provision required either to meet the needs of an increasing population, or to accommodate Gypsies returning from a settled way of live to caravan dwelling, have to be provided by the Gypsies themselves.

One new factor in the equation is the arrival of Romany asylum-seekers from south-east Europe. Despite the hysteria in parts of the tabloid press, the numbers have been quite small, yet even a few hundred presented difficulties.[i] Because it was the policy during the Communist era to forcibly resettle the Roma in fixed accommodation, it seems that any of those who do gain asylum – and recently, the Refugee Council tell me, 17 Slovak Romanies were successful on appeal – will not increase the number looking for asylum in this country.

One consequence of the legislation may have been to encourage travelling people to move into houses, and that may have been the reason for the reduction in the count in the three years from 1993 to 1996. The authorities have never taken any interest in the reasons why Gypsies decide to live in houses, or to move out of houses into caravans, even though the sum of all those decisions can have a significant effect on the demand for sites. The study of unauthorised camping by the University of Birmingham for the DETR published last October says that the approach must be seen within the context of related policies on planning and site provision, housing and traveller education and health.[j] One element in this is surely whether local authorities and housing associations are sympathetic to applications by Gypsies for accommodation in permanent dwellings, yet in answer to a Question, whether the government would ask local authorities in England and Wales to keep records of Gypsy families moving into, and out of, council housing, the Minister Helene Hayman answered:

> We have no plans to do so. Gypsy families have exactly the same rights of access to council housing as anyone else, and we see no need to ask local authorities to keep such records.[k]

It was pointed out that it would need very little effort to log the number of families changing their mode of living, and that anecdotal evidence from the Bromley Gypsy/Traveller Community Project showed that there was substantial movement in both directions, with a net flow off the sites and into housing. Residents at the Cottingley B site in Leeds had indicated that they would like to see community housing initiatives planned by housing associations and Gypsies working together.[l] The Minister, Nick Raynsford, then said he would give further thought to the suggestion, though he was concerned about what he called 'an additional burden on some local authorities who may not keep such information readily to hand'.[m]

The counts are presenting a misleading picture of the relative contributions of the public and private sectors, because when a public site is handed over to a Housing Association, it is reclassified in the figures. The Minister confirmed that the two sites in the London Borough of Bromley which were transferred to the Bridge Housing Association, with 35 occupied pitches in January 1998, are now recorded as privately

---

i Matthew Brown, Long road to Equality, *Connections* (Quarterly from the CRE), Autumn 1998.

j Pat Niner, Howard Davis and Bruce Walker, School of Public Policy, University of Birmingham, Local Authority Powers for Managing Unauthorised Camping, DETR, October 1998.

k Official Report, House of Lords, March 3, 1998 Column WA160.

l Gypsy and Traveller Community Housing Action Group, unpublished letter, March 9, 1998.

m Nick Raynsford MP, Parliamentary Under Secretary of State, DETR, unpublished letter, June 22, 1998.

owned sites. The statistics ought to separate the provision of new sites by the private sector, from those merely transferred to them by local authorities, if we are to get a feel for the ability of the private sector to satisfy the demand.

We should also monitor continuously the number of planning permissions being awarded by local authorities, or succeeding on appeal, to see whether Circular 1/94 is succeeding in its objective of increasing the contribution of the private sector. It was not surprising that the Tory government showed a lack of interest in comparing the number of pitches in planning applications submitted and granted before and after the Circular.[n] Now at least we shall have the study by ACERT, part funded by the DETR, into the success rate of Gypsy planning applications and appeals, which is due to report next month. In the meanwhile, according to a study by the Friends, Families and Travellers Support Group (FFT), the rate of success of appeals has actually declined since the Circular,[o] and Rachel Morris gives totals for 1991–93 and 1994–96, showing that the number of appeals had dropped by some 40%.[q] Toby Williams of ACERT finds that the number of appeals fell from a peak of 144 in 1992 to 86 in the year of the Circular, to a measly 32 in 1997,[p] though in 1998, the figures up to the end of November show some recovery in the number and a jump in the success rate, though from a very low base.[r] It would be a reasonable assumption that over this period there were also fewer applications.

It has been suggested that the Secretary of State should adopt a more generous attitude to appeals concerning the 'tolerated' sites, which at the time of the CJPO Bill, accounted for 283 out of the 1,250 caravans owned by Gypsies on land without planning permission,[s] and now stand at 317 in the July 1998 coun.[t] The then Minister in the Lords, Earl Ferrers, did say that while every case had to be considered on its merits, it would be relevant that the land in question had been used as a site for a substantial period and that the local authority had not previously objected to it.[u] The Secretary of State could also differentiate between local authorities which had made an effort in the past, as indicated by their designation under the 1968 Act, and those which had manifestly failed to provide enough accommodation for Gypsies. If he were more generous with appeals relating to land in the former category of authorities, it would help to ensure a more equitable sharing of responsibility.

The ACERT study is likely to show that there is little if any correlation between the adoption of criteria-based policies and the growth of private site provision. Mark Wilson's study has already shown that there is no relationship between the existence or nature of policies and the number of caravans in the area of a local authority, and

n See Official Report, House of Lords, June 7, 1994, 1175 (Criminal Justice and Public Order Bill, Committee Stage, Fifth Day).

o Planning Appeals and Gypsies and Travellers, Friends, Families and Travellers Support Group, January 1998.

p Rachel Morris, Gypsies and the Planning System, *Journal of Planning and Environment Law*, July 1998, 635.

q Toby Williams, Gypsy Sites Planning Project, unpublished communication, February 9, 1999.

r Official Report, House of Lords, February 15, 1999.

s Official Report, House of Lords, July 11, 1994, Col 1538 (Criminal Justice and Public Order Bill, Report Stage, Third Day).

t Official Report, House of Lords, February 15, 1999.

u Ibid., Col 1543.

that the existence of criteria may even be used to justify the refusal of planning permission.[v]

If there is enough evidence to show that Circular 1/94 is not working, then it needs to be replaced by a new Circular, and the work should be set in motion now. Some ideas on how this might be done have been suggested,[w] and a good many more are contained in the present draft report.

I was glad to see that the proposal to use Geographic Information Systems, discussed at the launch of the Birmingham report, is included. The Minister has now said that the Department does have sets of designated areas such as SSSIs and National Parks in digitised form that can be used in a GIS, but they are not making them available until they have ensured that the information is accurate and up to date. In any case, he says, the Department has to consider the practicalities of making the information available to anyone who wants it. They would not have the resources to deal with people calling in and wanting information about particular areas of land. However, local authorities may be better equipped to provide information on non-designated land in their own areas, and they are encouraged to offer practical help to Gypsies on planning matters by Circular 1/94.[x]

One authority has pointed out that Gypsies tend not to request advice from local authorities before they buy land with the intention of applying for permission, and it has been suggested that local authorities might take the initiative by offering advice to local Gypsy representative groups.[y] This would still not benefit a traveller from outside the area who bought land, but it might help to increase the level of understanding of the planning process throughout the whole traveller population if it was done systematically.

A factor in the equation which as far as I know has received little attention so far is that local authorities, no longer obliged to provide accommodation for Gypsies, will be tempted by the development potential of existing sites. One local authority site was closed in 1997 with a loss of 15 pitches, whether for development or other reasons, and there was a reduction of 79 pitches on 15 existing sites.[z] The 1999 count has not yet been collated, but in one county alone, on the incomplete statistics of 9 out of 14 districts, there has been a loss of 23 pitches over the last year. Thus repeal of the 1968 Act did not lead just to the abandonment of plans for new building after 100% funding dried up. It is causing a steady and potentially catastrophic loss of existing places, and surely it ought to be provided that at least if an owner closes a site, he provides facilities at least as good elsewhere.

There is no realistic prospect of the government restoring the 1968 Act obligations, in spite of the fact that the present Lord Chancellor argued effectively against repeal five years ago.[aa] We can only see how these matters ought to be handled by looking at

v Mark Wilson, *A Directory of Planning Poloicies for Gypsy Site Provision in England.* The Policy Press, University of Bristol, 1988.

w See for example Luke Clements and Penny Smith, *Proposals for Traveller Law Reform*, TLAST/Traveller Law Research Unit Conference and Consultation Report, Cardiff Law School, 1997.

z Nick Raynsford, unpublished letter, January 11, 1999.

y Terry Holland, Gypsy Services Manager, Buckinghamshire, Unpublished letter, January 27, 1999.

z RSL Social Research for the DETR, Gypsy Sites provided by local authorities in England 1st January 1998, DETR, March 1998.

aa Official Report, House of Lords, July 11, 1994, Col 1529 (Criminal Justice and Public Order Bill, Report Stage, Third Day).

Ireland, where their recent legislation not only places duties on local authorities, but obliges them to consult with travelling people. There is financial assistance, also, for voluntary bodies as well as local authorities providing accommodation.[bb] Here, it is an article of faith now shared by the Labour and Conservative Parties, that individuals and non-accountable agencies of various kinds are more capable of delivering the services local authorities used to provide, whether for Gypsies or anybody else – and that they ought to be able to do it without any money.

The doctrinal argument is not important. What is essential, and it is after all a trivial matter compared with many of the projects this country has undertaken since the war – Concorde, the Channel Tunnel, the Dome – is to ensure that travelling people have places to live that suit their needs. It does not matter whether the accommodation is provided by the people themselves, or by local authorities, or by Housing Associations providing as well as managing sites as the Bridge Housing Association has suggested,[cc] though it stands to reason that if all of them are encouraged and helped to play a part, they have a better chance of succeeding together. Of one thing we can be sure, however. If the travelling people are left to deal with this problem on their own, we shall be storing up trouble for the future, as their children grow up uneducated or semi-literate, unemployable, suffering bad health, and prey to appalling social problems. Even if we are not concerned with the human waste and suffering this implies, the cost of picking up the pieces will be far greater than the bill for completing the unfinished business of 1968 today.

Eric Avebury

LORD AVEBURY

---

bb Housing (Traveller Accommodation) Act, 1998.
cc Living on the Edge of Your Town, Bridge Housing Association, March 1998.

Contributors to Part II

Diana Allen is a partner at Lance Kent and Co. Solicitors in Hertfordshire.

Penny Ballinger is a Health Visitor for Travellers, working for the Herefordshire Community Health Trust.

Dr Malcolm Bell is a Planner at Ward Hadaway Solicitors in Newcastle upon Tyne.

Philip Brown is an Associate at the Bolton Emery Partnership, Chartered Town Planners and Development Consultants, in Macclesfield, Cheshire.

Sarah Cemlyn is a Lecturer and Researcher in the School for Policy Studies at the University of Bristol.

Colin Clark is a Lecturer in Social Policy in the Department of Social Policy at the University of Newcastle.

Michael Cox is the Principal of Michael Cox Associates, Chartered Town Planners and Development Consultants in Hurstpierpoint, West Sussex.

Sarah Cox is a Barrister at Holborn Chambers, Lincoln's Inn Fields, London.

Stephen Field is a Barrister at 10-11 Gray's Inn Square, Gray's Inn, London.

Bill Forrester is the Head of the Gypsy Unit for Kent County Council; Chair of the National Association of Gypsy and Traveller Officers (NAGTO); and Chair of the Advisory Council for the Education of Romany and other Travellers (ACERT).

Paul Goltz is the Traveller Community Worker for South Somerset District Council.

Debbie Harvey and **Liz Hughes** are Traveller Support Workers for the Children's Participation Project, the Children's Society, Midsomer Norton, Bath.

Chris Johnson is a solicitor with the Traveller Advice Team of the Community Law Partnership in Birmingham.

Dr Donald Kenrick is the author of Moving On: the Gypsies and Travellers of Britain (University of Hertfordshire Press, 1999) and an independent adviser on education and planning issues.

Michelle Lloyd and **Richard Morran** are Development Workers in the Traveller Section of Save the Children Fund (Scotland).

Alan Masters is a Barrister at 10-11 Gray's Inn Square, Gray's Inn, London.

Rachel Morris is the Research Associate of the Traveller Law Research Unit at Cardiff Law School.

Annie Murdoch is a Councillor on South Somerset District Council.

The National Association of Teachers of Travellers (NATT) is the professional association of teachers, working in local education authorities throughout the UK, who provide additional support for the education of travelling children (Gypsy and Traveller, Fairground, Circus and New Traveller).

Jim Spiller works, with Heather Spiller, on the Anglia Gypsy Traveller Health Information Project (AGTHIP) in Burnham Market, Norfolk.

Rodney Stableford is the Secretary of the Staffordshire & Shropshire Gypsy Liaison Group in Bridgnorth, Shropshire.

The Land is Ours (TLIO) campaigns peacefully for access to the land, its resources & the decision-making processes affecting them, for everyone. See their web site at http://www.oneworld.org/tlio for further information.

Tony Thomson is a researcher and worker for the Friends, Families and Travellers Support Group in Glastonbury, Somerset.

Richard Trahair is the Property Secretary for the Salisbury Diocesan Board of Finance.

Part 1 The need and momentum for reform

1

Introduction

The principles that have informed the law reform proposals are simple. Gypsies and other Travellers do not seek 'special' or 'preferential' treatment. All that is sought is equal treatment: an equality of opportunity, equal access to civic life and social welfare services; accepting the responsibilities that must accompany such a right. Gypsies and other Travellers seek to have their cultural traditions and life style respected. The essence of any pluralistic democratic society is 'respect for different-ness'. Clearly that brings with it the responsibility on Travellers to respect the life-styles of others. We however have a system which gives pre-eminence to owner-ship and the settled way of life, which upholds these rights over and above any other life-styles. This is simply unjust. Why should the law enable Travelling people to be evicted from land of uncertain ownership, when they are causing no harm or annoy-ance? Why should the law of trespass enable an absentee freeholder who owns several square miles of wasteland (or land 'set-aside') evict anyone who steps on that land, regardless of whether the 'trespasser' is causing damage or nuisance?

The right to respect is very much at the heart of the law reform agenda. Respect for a different culture requires grown up attitudes; the avoidance of stereotyping and the 'anecdotal'. It brings with it, for instance, the right to be believed; all too often this is a right that is simply not extended by the state to Travelling people. Clearly there are badly-behaved Travellers, just as there are badly-behaved people evenly distributed throughout all cultures and strata of society. Whilst the law reform agenda has not balked from this issue, it has nevertheless highlighted the inappropriateness of current 'non-toleration' policies; effectively these encourage all the worst aspects of human nature.

A consequence of making the principle of 'equal treatment', or non-discrimina-tion, central to the reform agenda, has been the development of strong links with many non-Traveller communities who are also badly treated by the present legal and administrative system. For example, the great need Gypsies and Travellers have for decent accommodation, i.e. in the form of safe stopping places, is a need shared by many other poor non-land-owning people. The loss of public funding for site construction has been mirrored by severe cutbacks in the grants available for the con-struction of public rented housing. The enormous difficulties Travellers face in obtaining planning permission for sites is mirrored by the equally hostile (and irrational) response of the planning system to other forms of sympathetic rural development, for instance low-impact environmentally sensitive development.[1] The draconian trespass laws in the UK create real injustices not only for Travelling people, but also ramblers and other people who merely seek access to the countryside.

The experience of poor and landless people of the criminal justice system has always been radically different to the experiences of the middle classes; the over-representation of young Travellers in the criminal justice system is mirrored in many other marginalised communities, for instance, young black Afro-Caribbean people. It is not only teenage Gypsy and Traveller children who feel alienated from the secondary education system, as increasingly large numbers of teenagers from all strata of society are having great difficulty in finding anything in the national curriculum of relevance to their lives or their aspirations.

What is perhaps unique about Travelling people is that they sadly have to face all these different forms of social exclusion. (Indeed, they do not even seem to have a place in the Governments' Social Exclusion Unit. The Unit has thus far declined invitations to examine the particular problems faced by Travelling people, and have examined 'rough sleeping' and homelessness only in the context of lack of accommodation for housed people). They have therefore been likened to the miners canary. Their health is a crucial indicator for the health and stability of the general community. The measure of the vibrancy of any society is not how it treats the ruling classes but how it treats its minorities. Vaclav Havel has called the treatment of Roma people "the litmus test of a civil society". A reform of the law which ensures that their rights are respected will immeasurably improve the lot of many more disenfranchised people who are similarly excluded.

Gypsies and other Travellers often refer to the fact that their difficulties are ignored. "When we speak we are not heard, when we complain we are not seen: it is as if we are invisible, all the Council can see are our vehicles". It is the duty of all non-Travellers involved in the reform process to ensure that we affirm to all Travelling people that we see them, that we hear them, that their uniqueness is visible to us; that we believe their account of their life experiences and that we see all the positive aspects of their unique way of life and their culture; that they have a right to be different and that it is their voice which directs the law reform process.

The next stage of this process is perhaps the most difficult. Gypsies and Travellers, having created a common platform and identified many key reform issues, must now transform these achievements into actual reform in the law and administrative procedures. This can only occur if Parliament is prepared to listen and the Government is prepared to take action similar to that taken by the Irish Government in convening its Task Force on the Travelling Community.[2]

There has already been some progress towards fairer, more equal treatment of Travelling people. Chapter 5 on planning outlines the guidance sent to all local planning authorities in 1998 urging equal and fair treatment of Gypsies in the planning

---

1 See Elson, Martin. *Green Belts and Affordable Housing,* Bristol, Joseph Rowntree Foundation / The Policy Press, 1996; and Fairlie, Simon. *Low Impact Development*, Charlbury, Oxfordshire, Jon Carpenter publishing, 1996

2 See *The Report of the Task Force on the Travelling Community, Ireland, July 1995*, and the Housing (Traveller Accommodation) Act 1998

system. More money is being put into Traveller education in England and Wales, and official education reports now acknowledge the difficulties faced by Travelling people due to the structure and nature of mainstream education. Home repairs assistance is now available to many Travelling people as it is to settled people.[3] This momentum must be sustained.

Non-discrimination and social exclusion

Equal rights thinking has become more sophisticated since the 1960s; it is no longer assumed that 'equal' means 'the same as'. Women's rights movements accept that not all women want to go to work when they have children and nor, necessarily, do men, but both genders should be treated equally when they are in the workplace. The idea is now that no-one should be discriminated against on the basis of irrelevant and immutable characteristics, and that those characteristics should be respected, even if they are seen as 'different' from the majoritarian 'norm'. The current Government recognises how inequality and discrimination over time can build up a range of inter-linking problems for some societal groups, resulting in 'social exclusion' and has set up the Social Exclusion Unit to tackle such 'joined up problems'.[4]

However, it is the view of Travelling people – arguably one of the UK's most excluded and marginalised groups – and those who work with them that the problem is more fundamental than this, and that the Government must take more radical steps to alleviate the difficulties imposed on Travelling people by the sedentary majority. An examination of the legislation, policy and practice relating to Gypsies and other Travellers since the sixteenth century shows that a powerful and negative message has consistently been, and continues to be, sent to the settled population:

- that it is acceptable to hold prejudicial attitudes and display discriminatory behaviour to Gypsies and Travellers;
- that they are invisible until they present a policing or a planning problem;
- that they are, in themselves, at best a 'problem' and at worst 'scum', 'parasites', and 'invaders' (as many newspapers persist in describing them);
- that non-Travellers need not respect the differences of Travelling people nor treat them equally.

"Such structural failure to recognise nomadism as a legitimate mode of existence 'has ramifications for almost every aspect of policy and practice in both government and non-government institutions.' This is clearly illustrated by the fact that accommodation for settled people is defined as a basic human right, while sites for nomadic people become an act of generosity by government."[5] The Government state that they recognise the legitimacy and legality of the travelling way of life, but their policies and laws send a more powerful and negative signal. Until that message is recognised and changed – by the Government, the Churches, the police and criminal justice and planning systems, and the media – no policy or law reform which attempts

---

3 Morris, Rachel. Repair grants and press regulation, *Legal Action*, February 1999. p.23
4 In Scotland, this body is called the *Social Inclusion Unit*.
5 Molloy, Siobhan. *Accommodating Nomadism: Summary*, Traveller Movement (Northern Ireland), 1997. p.3

to redress the problems for Travelling people, however well-intentioned, can or will succeed.

The very fact that nomadic matters are currently included in an Act of Parliament concerning issues of criminal justice and public order sends a powerfully negative message about Travelling people to local authorities and to other, more settled, citizens. As seen in Part I Chapter 4, the Association of Chief Police Officers and some of the local government officers charged with employing the powers given to them by the state recognise this. The form of the signal sent by the state makes their work more difficult as it exacerbates already extreme tensions between Travelling and settled peoples. Most settled people despise and fear Travelling people and feel that they have the reason and right to do so. Successive governments have allowed and encouraged them to think and feel this way, making a rod for their own back in the process.

Fundamental to the 1990s policy change with regard to accommodation and eviction was the notion that settled people owed Travelling people nothing, and that the latter could live how they wished but should and must provide for themselves. (Some of the ramifications of this 'privatisation' of site provision, one of the last Conservative privatisation projects, are further explored in Chapters 5 and 11 on planning). Circular 1/94 on Gypsy sites and planning replaced earlier guidance and removed a so-called 'privilege' from which Gypsies had 'benefited', whereby Gypsy sites were deemed appropriate development for Green Belt land.[6]

The 1994 Circular says that "People who wish to adopt a nomadic existence should be free to do so, provided they live within the law in the same way as their fellow-citizens. This choice should not, however, entail a privileged position under the law or an entitlement to a greater degree of support from the taxpayer than is made available to those who choose a more settled existence. Travellers, like other citizens, should seek to provide their own accommodation, seeking planning permission where necessary like anyone else".[7] The argument that Gypsies should be the same as everyone else simply means that they should fit in with the needs, wishes, and values of the settled majority, and never vice-versa. This policy gives no recognition to the fact that it is settled people who are privileged under the planning system, in that they rarely if ever have to endure any contact with it. There is a huge infrastructure of land and housing development, mortgage systems, tax subsidy and a liquid housing market to meet the needs of settled people, whether seeking long or short term, rented or purchased, or public or private accommodation.

The overwhelming view of the Traveller Working Group meetings is that no special treatment is requested for Gypsies and other Travellers. Not only would this be counter-productive – for arguably the perception of a 'privileged position' for them has contributed to the difficulty in providing sites in the face of settled opposition, before and after the Caravan Sites Act 1968 – but it is unnecessary. It is perfectly possible to accommodate, literally, the Travelling way of life, using existing financial and administrative mechanisms. All that is required is recognition that Travelling people are equal to but different from settled people, and that their right to be different must be

---

6   For arguments as to why this policy has not yet worked, see Morris, Rachel. Gypsies & the Planning System, *Journal of Planning and Environment Law,* July, 1998. pp.635-43

7   *Gypsy Site Policy, and Illegal Camping: Reform of the Caravan Sites Act 1968* Consultation Paper, Department of the Environment / Welsh Office, August 1992. para.23

respected. An equal but different approach ensures that Travelling people will be on the mainstream agenda and have equal access to mainstream goods and services without the danger of enforced or disguised assimilation. To recognise that the same needs may require delivery in a different way is not to create unfair 'privilege' but simply to recognise the validity and value of a legal and legitimate way of life. It has been done in Eire, it can be done here; all that is required is the political will.

Research by the Traveller Law Research Unit has established that, as stated above, the media – and in particular the press – have a powerful role to play in reflecting and creating attitudes about and behaviour towards Travelling people. In addition to convening those meetings listed above, the Unit has been looking at the wretched standards of journalism in some national and many local newspapers displayed when covering issues concerning Travelling people. In recent years, for instance, tabloids and broadsheets have carried many stories about the arrival of asylum seekers from Central and Eastern Europe. While it is distasteful to create hierarchies of discrimination, it is probably the case that Black and Asian citizens no longer endure such consistent and explicit xenophobia from the British mainstream press (with the possible exception of Islamic peoples).

In response, the Traveller Law Research Unit collaborated with the CRE in arranging a series of meetings attended by a number of media regulators such as the Press Complaints Commission (PCC), the Broadcasting Standards Commission and complaints and equality sections of the BBC, as well as other organisations campaigning to improve standards of journalism such as PressWise, some members of the press, and Gypsy and Traveller organisations. Frustrated by the PCC's seeming reluctance to tackle the problem, in December 1998 the CRE sent guidelines to all newspaper editors in Great Britain – developed with the aid of those at the meetings – which suggest good practice in approaching stories about Gypsies, Travellers and asylum seekers. The CRE says the guidelines are "a constructive intervention, to help the press face its responsibility to treat this ethnic group in a fair and factual way, and impact positively on race relations in the long-term". The guidelines appear in Appendix 3.

This aspect of the Unit's work in the past year is an illustration of the underlying cause of the profound legal and civic discrimination experienced by Travelling people. History shows us that the message sent to settled people by the state, and other powerful voices such as the media, has been a negative one;[8] and that relations only improve when the state is no longer prepared to allow such stereotyping. Although there has been some improvement in the relationship between Travelling people and the state since the current Government took office in May 1997,[9] it is their continuing failure to restrain such highly offensive press coverage (more than anything else) which is perpetuating the enormous socio-legal deprivation experienced by Travelling people.

"The state, by means of legislation, directives and actions, has succeeded in giving prominence and legitimacy to particular definitions, boundaries and images of the

8 For an interesting look at the relationship between Gypsies and state policies, see Mayall, David. *English Gypsies & State Policies,* Hatfield, Gypsy Research Centre, University of Hertfordshire Press, 1995

9 For instance, the Department of the Environment, Transport and the Regions (DETR) now insists that all of their staff capitalises 'Gypsies' in recognition of their ethnic minority status. The DETR has also consulted with Traveller organisations and other interested bodies in the formulation of their latest research on *Managing Unauthorised Camping.*

group. These in turn provide both the foundations on which the official response is built and justified, and also the framework within which the response of society in general takes place. Through its choice of characteristics, the state is able to advance or block the antipathetic treatment of minority groups ... sentiment in Britain being determined by the institutionalisation of racism within all levels of the state structures, from legislation and the actions of the judiciary to policing and education ... In effect then, the issue is whether or not the minority group is categorised, identified and defined as a 'problem' requiring an official, legislative solution. To offer such a definition and classification is to institutionalise and so legitimise discrimination." (Mayall, 1995: 88-9).

The law cannot in isolation solve social problems and achieve social justice, and changes are also needed in policy and practice, but nor can society function without the law. It is in recognition of this principle that the ideas, recommendations and background which follow in Parts I and II have been formulated by the members of the Traveller law reform platform.

Rights and international law

The present Government is committed to fundamental constitutional reform, the eradication of social exclusion and the 'bringing of rights back home' in the form of the incorporation of the European Convention on Human Rights. The Human Rights Act 1998 will require central and local Government to review all previous legislation and administrative policies so as to ensure that they comply with the requirements of the European Convention. This is clearly propitious in that it coincides with the final stages of the Traveller law reform proposals. The UK has ratified many other important international treaties concerned with the protection of human rights and the rights of minorities. Although these lack the effective enforcement machinery of the European Convention on Human Rights, they nevertheless establish bench-marks by which the Government measures minimum acceptable standards of behaviour.

Of considerable importance in this respect is the International Covenant on Civil and Political Rights, which has been ratified by the UK. Article 26 provides that "All persons are equal before the law and are entitled without any discrimination to the equal protection of the law. In this respect, the law shall prohibit any discrimination and guarantee to all persons equal and effective protection against discrimination on any ground, such as race, colour, sex, language, religion, political or other opinion, national or social origin, property, birth or other status". Article 26 is of importance in that it is significantly broader in its non-discrimination reach than Article 14 of the European Convention, albeit that there is no means of directly enforcing the Government's compliance with its strictures.[10] Nevertheless the adoption by the UK of Article 26 is of great importance in that it is now not able to suggest as acceptable any form of behaviour which contradicts this norm.

The same applies to Article 27 of the Covenant which entrenches the rights of

---

10 The 1990 Trust. Briefing on Incorporation of Article 26 from the ICCPR into the Human Rights Bill, 1997, p.2

minorities to (amongst other things) enjoy their own culture. The Human Rights Committee's General Comments to Article 27 have made it clear that "culture manifests itself in many forms, including a particular way of life associated with the use of land resources".

The existence of such international Treaties is of considerable assistance in the law reform debate, in that it obviates the need to argue from first principles the existence of certain rights; they can be taken as read. The Treaties also serve another important function, in that the reporting provisions provide a regular opportunity for the governments' performance to be assessed by the relevant international committee. Thus in 1997 the UN Committee on Economic, Social and Cultural Rights found it disturbing that the UK treats the Covenant as "principles and programmatic objectives rather than legal obligations, and that consequently the provisions of the Covenant cannot be given legislative effect".

A UN Treaty of particular relevance to the Traveller law reform process is the International Covenant on the Elimination of All Forms of Racial Discrimination. Under this Covenant (which has been ratified by the UK) states undertake to adopt practical measures to ensure within their jurisdictions that:

- there is no act or practice of racial discrimination against persons, groups of persons or institutions and to ensure that all public authorities and public institutions, national and local, act in conformity with this obligation;
- they do not sponsor, defend or support racial discrimination by any persons or organisations;
- they take effective measures to review governmental, national and local policies, and to amend, rescind or nullify any laws and regulations which have the effect of creating or perpetuating racial discrimination wherever it exists;
- they prohibit and bring to an end, by all appropriate means, including legislation as required by circumstances, racial discrimination by any persons, group or organisation;
- they encourage, where appropriate, integrationist multi-racial organisations and movements and other means of eliminating barriers between races, and discourage anything which tends to strengthen racial division.

The Committee overseeing the Covenant has taken a particular interest in the plight of Roma, for instance, in its March 1999 report on Italy it condemned (amongst other things):

- the lack of basic facilities for Roma;
- the fact that their accommodation not only led to a physical segregation of the Roma community from Italian society, but also political, economic and cultural isolation;
- the continuation of incidents of racial intolerance, including attacks against Roma, which it considered were not always recognised by the authorities as having a racial motivation or were not prosecuted;
- the omission of Roma from a proposed Italian law on minorities.

In view of these serious deficiencies, the Committee recommended that the Italian government undertake a number of measures, including:

- strengthening its efforts for preventing and prosecuting incidents of racial intolerance and discrimination against Roma people;
- giving more attention to the situation of Roma in Italy, in order to avoid any discrimination against them;
- intensifying education and training of law enforcement officials about racial tolerance and human rights.

A particularly rich seam of International Roma related resolutions is to be found in the archives of the Council of Europe and the Organisation on Security and Co-operation in Europe (OSCE). These resolutions have all been endorsed by the UK.[11] Other International documents relevant to Gypsies and Travellers can be found in Appendix 6.

The development by the present Government of a domestic rights-based agenda has entailed more than incorporation of the European Convention on Human Rights via the Human Rights Act 1998. Other initiatives, whilst less well publicised, are also of considerable potential relevance. For instance, in June 1998 the Home Secretary established a Race Relations Forum to focus on options for future action on race and discrimination; this might include reform of the Race Relations Act 1976, and the Commission for Racial Equality undertook their Third Review of the Act as part of this process. The Forum was also set up to provide ethnic minority communities with a new channel of communication to the Government. Travelling people are not represented on the twenty-eight member Forum.

The Race Relations Act, as the CRE has suggested to the Government in their Third Review, is in need of reform.[12] There are subtle forms of discrimination which do not fall within the definitions of discrimination contained in it. The Act does not apply to certain public bodies, including the police, the courts and probation services. It does not outlaw racial discrimination generally but only makes it unlawful in particular circumstances. The CRE proposals for reform were discussed at length by the law reform working groups who felt, on the whole, that the proposals were excellent. Comments were sent to the Forum by the Traveller Law Research Unit on behalf of the Groups (see Appendix 5).

Terminology and inclusion

Throughout this Report the term 'Travelling people' is generally used. This is intended to embrace all those who are, have been or will be associated with a potentially nomadic and/or alternative dwelling way of life, including:

- the minority ethnic group known as Gypsies, whether English, Scottish, Welsh, or Irish Travellers; whether mobile, of limited mobility, or no longer living a mobile way of life but settled in housing or in caravans on public or private sites;
- 'New' Travellers, some of whom are second, third, even fourth generation Travellers;

---

11 For a resume of the various international resolutions on Roma, see L.J. Clements, P.A. Thomas and R. Thomas, The rights of minorities, OSCE Bulletin (Warsaw) Fall 1996, Vol. 4 No. 4

12 A copy of their proposals for reform can be obtained from the CRE at Elliot House, 10-12 Allington Street, London, SW1E 5EH.

- Gypsies (Roma) from Europe who have obtained refugee status, including Kalderash, Romungri and Rudari communities;
- 'Bargees' and other individuals and families living on boats;
- fairground and circus families;
- those who live or wish to live in subsistence and low impact dwellings and settlements.

Where there are differences in experiences, or where other publications refer to such differences, these distinctions are noted in the text. Words such as 'Gypsy' or 'Traveller' are capitalised, except where they are quoted in their original lower-case form as cited by authors who do not realise or recognise the status of such groups.

Fairground families are not generally specifically included in the discussions and recommendations which follow, for the reason that the accommodation laws relating to them specifically are more favourable, and they comprise a strong union which is generally protective and more politically powerful than other Travelling group representatives.[13] Almost all Travelling showpeople are members of the Showmen's Guild of Great Britain, which holds a certificate exempting them from site licensing requirements. The Guild owns permanent sites throughout the country for the exclusive use of its members. Circus people are also not generally included. While these groups may have problems in accessing, for example, regular education, because of their peripatetic way of life, they do not ordinarily experience the discrimination and prejudice suffered by the groups listed above, and most local authorities have ensured provision of a winter base for them. It is hoped that those who do experience difficulties will find that the proposed reforms, if implemented, also of benefit to them.

Adopting a definition of 'Traveller' which relies on nomadism as an essential requirement excludes those Gypsies and Travellers, and potential Travellers, who currently live in houses. Relying on a definition which requires an economic purpose for travelling excludes those who travel only to christenings, funerals, weddings and to see family and friends, to attend traditional fairs and other social events, and those who are not employed, are receiving state benefits, or are retired. To accept as Travellers only those Travellers who have had travelling in their family for many generations is to put a gradual end to there being any Travelling people at all.

A paper by Dr Donald Kenrick entitled What is a Gypsy? is to be found in Part 2, Chapter 7. Gypsies are, at law and culturally, a distinct group with their own language, customs and identity. It is clearly important that this 'distinctiveness' is not imperilled by the search for inclusiveness. However, Dr Kenrick's paper highlights the tortuous intellectual wrangling to which the state and the courts have had to resort in their pursuit of pointless categorising.

Over-arching issues

Some issues discussed at the 1997 conference and subsequently by the working groups were too wide to permit inclusion in any of the chapters with fairly specific themes which follow. These issues are:

---

13 See, for instance, Acton, Thomas. *Gypsy Politics & Social Change*, London, Routledge and Kegan Paul, 1974. p.116 et seq.

UK task force

1.1 It was unanimously agreed, given that many of the issues raised below are inter-connected and deserve further exploration, that the Government should convene a national working party, on the 'Task Force' model used in the Republic of Ireland, to discuss such matters and make recommendations to the Government for future action. This Task Force should examine the situation in all parts of the UK, given that many Travelling people cross boundaries. Travelling people should be at the heart of any such consultative body, not a token add-on.

Advisory group

1.2 There was some debate as to whether an ongoing Advisory Group, improving on the models in Northern Ireland and Scotland, should be set up (with the partici-pation of Travelling people) to keep any reforms under review. While some fear that such a group would replicate the problems with such groups in other regions, there is no reason why lessons cannot be learned. In the 1997 conference report, Bill Forrester outlined the case for such a group for England and Wales and concluded that the principles in favour of setting up such a group outweigh the practical difficulties. One benefit would be that Government would no longer be advised only by civil servants but also by informed independent advisers.[14]

The need for such a body has long been recognised: "I have become convinced for the need for an official body appointed by the Secretaries of State to provide a national point of focus for those groups and persons in society who can be expected to give a lead, nationally and locally, in the promotion of under-standing and tolerance towards a minority group sharing common human needs, but having a right to a distinctive culture. They would advise the Secretaries of State, local authorities and others on all aspects of relations between house-dwellers and gypsies; and they would have the duty to promote, in every way open to them, improvements in those relations, especially in areas of current conflict. The Secretaries of State might also find it convenient to consult them about research required to fill the many gaps in knowledge of the gypsy way of life, and about residential, educational and other needs of gypsies."[15]

Media

1.3 The media in Britain, in particular the mainstream press, have a great deal of power in the dissemination and formation of ideas and beliefs. With this power comes a responsibility to report on issues such as relations between Traveller and settled communities, in a fair and accurate manner. Many newspapers, especially local newspapers, report on Travelling people in a pejorative and discriminatory fashion, further fuelling the prejudices of local people against them. It was widely

14 Clements, Luke and Smith, Penny, editors. *Traveller Law Reform: Conference and Consultation Report*, TLAST/The Traveller Law Research Unit of Cardiff Law School, 1997. Chapter 7

15 Cripps, John. *Accommodation for Gypsies: A Report on the Working of the Caravan Sites Act 1968*, DoE/Welsh Office, HMSO, London, 1976. para.7.10, p. 35

agreed that the Press Complaints Commission should take action against this form of reportage, either by amending their Code of Practice to allow third party complaints and a clause against collective racism, or by issuing a strong statement to all editors in Great Britain condemning such practice.

Discrimination

1.4 Many suggested that a review should be undertaken of government policy and practice to ensure that it contains no inherent discrimination or prejudice against Travelling people. This is in keeping with the Government's obligations under the International Convention on the Elimination of all Forms of Discrimination.

1.5 Those who provide or refuse to provide goods and services in a discriminatory manner on the basis of ethnicity should be subject to stronger sanctions than at present. The McPherson Report following from the Stephen Lawrence enquiry contains findings and recommendations which it would be useful for a Task Force or other body to examine in this context.

Gypsy counts

1.6 Current Gypsy counts as undertaken by the DETR need to be reviewed. Counting caravans does not take individual or collective needs into account, and studies in education[16] suggest that the current method of counting result in a significant underestimate of members of the travelling communities. The Welsh Assembly must reinstate counting procedures as formerly carried out by the Welsh Office. Some people have argued that no counts should be undertaken, but many agreed that without some form of count there could be no effective monitoring of the equality of service provision. Many people have suggested that Travelling people should be included in the next national census.[17]

Save the Children Fund (SCF) Scotland note that the situation in Scotland is different. Until very recently, there had only been two counts of Travellers over a twenty-three year period and the methodology and accuracy of figures collected were criticised by Travellers and agencies like SCF. The Scottish Office have just introduced biannual counts, in January and July. To date, only the results from the July 1998 count have been published – there is confusion between the numbers of families (counted on local authority sites) and number of caravans (counted on private and roadside camps). Inaccuracy is almost certainly aggrandised because enforcement officers are collecting the figures.

Both the current English and Scottish counts ignore Gypsies and Travellers living in housing and thus do not represent an accurate estimate of the population. Honouring the principle of self-definition and providing clear and inclusive categories in any future form of census should allay this problem substantially.

16 OFSTED (1996), the University of Wales Cardiff (1998)

17 It has recently been announced that homosexual people are to be counted in 2002. Gypsies and other Travellers are not included in the census if they are not in houses, even within the sub-category of 'other' under ethnic minorities. This reiterates the point that Travelling people are invisible unless seen as a 'problem'.

Social Security

1.7 Research has shown that many Travelling people have difficulty accessing Benefits Agency (BA) services, often because of difficulties with proving identity. The onus to prove or disprove identity should be shifted from the claimant to the BA. Discretionary powers given to staff in local offices can also lead to service and treatment inconsistencies; the BA should review its discretionary powers to assess ways of making the identity requirements more appropriate to different sections of the population, and should lift any 'blanket bans' it may have on specific forms of ID. The social security system generally, and the BA specifically, should ensure that the needs and experiences of Britain's ethnic minority groups are included in all non-discriminatory and racial equality initiatives. The BA should also consult with and listen to Gypsies and other Travellers in its annual National Customer surveys.[18]

---

18 See the section on Social Security in Britain by Colin Clark at Part 2 Chapter 12.

2

Education

"Within education there is still an enormous task facing us. There are too few Gypsy and Traveller children participating freely and fully ... [t]he level of literacy within the community is still significantly below that for the 'settled' populations. School attendance is generally unsatisfactory. In the OFSTED report[19] it is stated that as many as ten thousand Gypsy and Traveller children at the secondary stage are not even registered in any school in England. A further cause for concern is that Gypsy and Traveller pupils feature disproportionately in the statistics on exclusions from school ... too frequently the result of misunderstandings and a professional misjudgement about pupil behaviour ... the life of the school cannot be other than a reflection of the wider society. We know, of course, that many schools do attempt, and indeed achieve, an enlightened approach based on a positive vision and ethos. This is what schools ought to be about, but too frequently many fail to reach the standard and continue to be the mirror images of the prejudiced communities they serve."[20]

The education Traveller working group

The 1997 conference identified the principles on which the provision of education services to Travelling children and adults should be based, namely that:

- education is a two-way process – there should be intercultural respect in all aspects and at all levels of the system of education and training in the UK;
- people of all ages, abilities, and ways of life should have equal access to educational opportunities;
- diversity should be valued; individual difference should not just respected but celebrated;

19 Office for Standards in Education (OFSTED). *The Education of Travelling Children: A Report from the Office of Her Majesty's Chief Inspector of Schools, 1996,* HMR/12/96/NS

20 Ivatts, Arthur R., HMS Inspector of Schools. From his Afterword to Jean-Pierre Liégeois. *School Provision for Ethnic Minorities: The Gypsy Paradigm, 1998,* Centre de recherches tsiganes, Hatfield, University of Hertfordshire Press. pp.285–6

- the provision of 'outreach services' must be in response to the needs of Travellers and handled sensitively; as on the one hand they can be seen as 'special treatment' or impeding integration, whilst it is recognised that on the other hand mainstream education does not always meet Travellers' needs;
- appropriate service provision must be centrally enforced.

State education for Travellers in England and Wales is primarily provided in some 3,400 ordinary mainstream schools which are supported by peripatetic teaching staff working in local education authorities (LEAs). The attendance and achievement of Travelling children at primary school level has, as a result of such work, vastly improved in recent years. But there is still a long way to go to achieve equality with settled children, particularly with regard to the attendance of secondary-aged pupils.

The first meeting of the Traveller Working Group on Education and Health was hosted by Dr Derek Hawes of the School of Policy Studies at the University of Bristol and soon divided into four sub-groups,[21] each with a co-ordinator;[22] the recommendations subsequently formulated by these sub-groups are detailed below. While it was agreed that existing legislation with regard to education for Travelling children is largely satisfactory, much can be done to build on and improve existing policy and practice, and this ethos informs much of what follows.

In addition to the proposals formulated by the sub-groups, a submission was received from the National Association of Teachers of Travellers (NATT)[23] regarding school exclusions and truancy; it can be found in Part 2, Chapter 8. Their main recommendations are contained below (under the sub-heading *School exclusions and truancy*).

Although the Education Reform Act purports to provide education for all, this generally only applies to settled members of society and Gypsy and Traveller children are often disadvantaged, especially those who are highly mobile or are seasonal travellers. This is receiving recognition by the Government, and has been identified with respect to England in a number of OFSTED Reports. The most recent of these is *Raising the Attainment of Minority Ethnic Pupils*, published in March 1999. This report identifies that:

- Gypsy Traveller children are the group most as risk in the education system, low attainment at secondary level being a particularly serious matter for concern;
- 'hunches' rather than ethnic monitoring are used to gauge the performance of ethnic minority pupils;
- the impact of specialist staff and funding is patchy as it is dependent largely on the attitude and commitment of the senior management of the schools;

---

21 In addition to education, the groups considered interagency working, the provision of services to sites, and equity in healthcare provision; all of which can be found in Part 1 Chapter 6 on Health and Social Services.

22 The co-ordinator of the Education sub-group was Trish McDonald, Senior Advisory Teacher at the West Midlands Consortium Education Service for Travelling Children (WMESTC) who, with the help of Fran McGeown, collected and collated views from Traveller Working Group discussions and submissions from Patrice van Cleemput (Health Visitor for Travellers, Community Health Sheffield NHS Trust) and Liz Hughes (Traveller Support Worker, Children's Participation Project, The Children's Society, Bath).

23 A revised form of which was originally submitted to the Social Exclusion Unit in response to their consultation on Truancy and School Exclusion, 1998; the subsequent SEU Report does not reflect the issues raised by NATT.

- many schools have written policies for combating racial harassment and promoting good race relations, but few monitor their implementation or effectiveness;
- the schools which are most successful in raising attainment are those which recognise and counter the hostility faced by ethnic minority, and especially Gypsy Traveller, pupils.

Professor Thomas Acton criticises the methodology and therefore the conclusions of this report, in that OFSTED "selected in a wholly non-random way just 48 schools, mainly in poor deprived areas, with around double the national average getting free school meals. They then found that Bangladeshi, Gypsy and Black Caribbean (but not Pakistani) pupils in those of these schools that bothered to keep "fragmentary" records were doing less well than national averages. They did not target other ethnic groups whose achievement they presume to be satisfactory". He notes that "All this shows us is that children in economically deprived areas tend to do less well in school. It does not tell us about ethnicity, because like was not compared with like".[24] Nonetheless, given the usual invisibility of Gypsies and Travellers in official surveys, reports, research and policy documents, such findings are cautiously welcomed.

Education in Northern Ireland, Scotland and Wales

Most of those involved in the Education sub-Traveller Working Group live and work in England, and so the position in the other nations of the UK was less well explored. Nevertheless, research has been undertaken which suggests some common problems and, perhaps, some possible solutions.

Northern Ireland

In the 1997 Conference Report, Paul Noonan of the Belfast Travellers' Education and Development Group identified the weakness of government guidelines for ensuring equality of opportunity; this also applies to the rest of the UK. The Report noted that:

- most Traveller children attend mainstream schools with the exception of a Traveller-only school in Belfast (which is now, in 1999, under threat of closure);
- The policy of the Department for Education in Northern Ireland (as detailed in its 1993 guidance *Policy and Guidelines on the Education of children from Traveller Families*) is that Travellers are entitled to the same rights as other (settled) parents and children in Northern Ireland;
- there has been some voluntary sector criticism of the guidelines in that they are only permissive in nature and do not commit specific agencies to specific actions;

24 Professor of Romani Studies, School of Romani Studies, University of Greenwich. From an e-mail to the 'Traveller-acad' discussion group.

- but that the guidance had resulted in some positive developments, most notably the development of a Forum for Traveller Education in Northern Ireland.

The main problem particular to Northern Ireland and Scotland, clearly leading to other problems, is a lack of specific directed funding; and much less funding is entering Wales than England. An additional problem in Northern Ireland identified in the 1997 conference report is that there is no provision for or resources directed at Traveller-specific training centres, such as exist in the Republic of Ireland and some parts of England, despite low take-up by Travellers of mainstream training opportunities (Clements and Smith, 1997: 32).

Scotland

In 1996 the Scottish Traveller Education Project (STEP) identified that "All schools need to acknowledge the cultural diversity within the Scottish population and many local authorities have well established intercultural initiatives for schools"(Clements and Smith, 1997: 14). STEP stressed that "[it] is important that schools review their current intercultural practice and identify areas where Travellers' specific needs are not being met ... There is still a strong rejection of Travellers, particularly Gypsy Travellers, within society and this can include many staff and pupils at schools who are prejudiced or ignorant of them and the reality of their lifestyle".

In 1999 the Traveller Section of Save the Children in Scotland submitted information to the Traveller Law Research Unit regarding Traveller education in Scotland. They strongly condemn the Scottish Office Education Department for their failure to address the needs of Travellers. "There is a complete lack of 'supportive' legislation, policy, guidance, or, most importantly, funding in relation to the education of Traveller children in Scotland. The Scottish Office do fund a 0.5 post at Moray House College (STEP) but their work mainly focuses on teacher training and developing European contacts. Suffice to say, in our experience, there has been little direct benefit for Traveller families and teachers 'on the ground'.

"Chapter 4 of our report *The Right to Roam* specifically looked at educational issues and our impression is that little has changed since 1995-6. Our research indicated that attendance levels were extremely poor, only 41 per cent attending Primary with any degree of regularity and 29 per cent never or rarely attending. Not surprisingly, the situation at Secondary is even worse, with only 20 per cent attending regularly. Attendance is not just an issue on roadside camps but our experience indicates that there are also difficulties on local authority sites too (as schools and councils know the kids are there, but often just turn a blind eye).

"The situation in Scotland is not unique, but rather reflects a Europe-wide experience. However, some governments have tried to tackle some of the issues. We believe the lack of policy and funding from central government has seriously disadvantaged Traveller children in Scotland. There are of course a few authorities in Scotland who employ teachers to work with Travellers, but these are few in number, often part-time, and seem to depend more on the goodwill and interest of an individual rather than a strategic, co-ordinated approach."

SCF made some specific suggestions for reform to counter these problems, which appear below.

Wales

A report entitled *Traveller Children and Educational Need in Wales*[25] was published by the School of Education at the University of Wales Cardiff in 1998. Like the OFSTED Report in England of 1996, this report identifies far greater numbers of travelling children in Wales than official, governmental counts would suggest. This can be partly be explained by the fact that only those people deemed to be Gypsies in the Romany or 'traditional Traveller' sense were counted by the Welsh Office (WO); because the researchers requested information from departments other than the Planning or equivalent department approached by the WO; and because Traveller children may have been unrecorded in the WO counts if they were unseen.

The researchers interviewed Travellers in Wales and ascertained that there were two major obstacles to the provision of education for Traveller children: their nomadic life-style and culture, and the incompatibility between these and the conventional provision of education. "A general lack of appreciation of Traveller life-style and culture has culminated in misunderstandings and misconceptions on all sides."[26] Travellers seemed keen to at least provide education for their children at a primary level, but also felt that school provided only a part of their children's education. Some local authorities in Wales seem to refuse to acknowledge the presence of Travelling families in their areas, and thereby do not meet their statutory educational duties. There also, and despite the recommendations of Welsh Office Circular 52/90, appears to be little co-ordination between different departments within local authorities with regard to the provision of services to Travellers.

The Report concludes that "[w]ithout in some way increasing the relevance of the curriculum to the needs of Traveller children school will continue to be seen by them and their parents as playing only a small part in their education. Although the majority of Travellers interviewed in Wales have adopted a more settled life-style this has not always been from their own choice but as a result of the repeal of the Caravan Sites Act 1968 which removed the duty of local authorities to provide sites for Travellers, and the introduction of new legislation such as the Criminal Justice and Public Order Act 1994 which has made it more difficult for Travellers to find a legal place to put their caravans and, therefore, to pursue their traditional life-style."[27] Recommendations emanating from the report are detailed below.

In a Parliamentary debate on local government finance in Wales on 11 February 1999,[28] MP for Cardiff North Julie Morgan stated that, while she welcomed an increase in funding from the Welsh Office for 2000/01 from £150,000 to £300,000, the Report mentioned above "showed that the number of traveller children in Wales was twice the number estimated by the gipsy count which used to be carried out by the Department of the Environment. There are about 2,000 traveller children in Wales. Although the grant has been doubled, we are really keeping the status quo because the original grant was based on a lower number of children. The grant is only for one year, and I am sure that it's because the National Assembly will take over funding for

25 October 1998, for the Save the Children Fund Wales Programme. Thanks to Laura Morgan, Researcher, for providing TLRU with this Report.

26 Ibid., p.26

27 Ibid., paras.7.50-51, p.31

28 House of Commons Hansard Cols.508-10

traveller education. However, a one-year grant is not enough: it is causing havoc in planning and in recruiting pupils and teachers".

Reform proposals for education in England

DfEE

2.1   Every LEA should be required to establish a Traveller Education Policy, perhaps within their Education Development Plan. Many individual TESs have a policy but this is not always integrated into the whole LEA policy.

2.2   Training for teachers and governors should include specific modules on Gypsies and Travellers within minority training. Such modules should include a recognition that it is not only school-based skills and knowledge which are valuable and to be valued, and that valuing diversity is not always linked to ethnicity.

2.3   Quality Curriculum and Assessment (QCA) should support schools in providing training regarding the curriculum and non-academic qualifications at Key Stage 4.

2.4   There should be more stringent monitoring of achievement and levels of exclusion.

2.5   The 'Education Otherwise' (EO) monitoring provisions need to strengthened, and funding extended to help EO support services such as voluntary bodies.

2.6   The legislation regulating the attendance of travelling pupils should be reviewed.

2.7   Traveller Education Support Services (TESSs) should be inspected within the OFSTED framework in England, following the attainment of appropriate training and expertise by inspectors.

Records of children's educational achievement

2.8   The present system of reliance on parents to initiate the obtaining and forwarding of school records is unrealistic. A regional or wider system, which supports parents in taking on 'ownership', would be more appropriate and effective. Distance Learning (DL) packs

2.9   Where children are remaining on a school register, and the school is receiving capitation for them, that school should have primary responsibility for providing DL throughout the travelling season, with TESSs advising and supporting such work.

Funding

2.10   While valuing the 20% increase in spending by the Government on education for Travelling children this year in England and Wales, the present system of funding currently may not be based on needs but upon competitive bidding which leads to inequality of funding. This must be reviewed. Section 488 is now within the Standards Fund, is not therefore ring-fenced, and some LEAs may not want or be able to obtain it as they have to match it with 35%. Support for Traveller children's schooling should be consistent throughout the country.

2.11   3-year Project status should be removed in favour of much longer-term funding.

2.12 'Sure Start' funding would enable Traveller and other voluntary organisations to access funding if appropriate.

2.13 The focus of funding should be extended to include vocational training, and it should recognised that outreach services are invaluable as school attendance is not appropriate for all children.

2.14 The use of funding by all to whom it is given should be monitored.

Local Education Authorities

2.15 Every LEA should establish a Traveller Education Policy.

2.16 Although the value of the Literacy and the Numeracy Hour is recognised, the possibility of the differing ability of Travelling children to fit into such programmes – if they have been unable to attend school from statutory school age on a regular basis – should be a matter for recognition and assessment.

School exclusions and truancy

2.17 Regional and local targets, if implemented, should be based on monitoring of exclusions detailing the gender, ethnicity (including Gypsy and Traveller pupils), age, type of exclusion (as short term exclusions can be as damaging as permanent exclusions), type of school, pupils' previous history of exclusion, and any special educational needs identified.

2.18 Caution is needed in comparing schools. Regional targets can lead to the formation of a group of 'unattractive pupils' which schools resist taking on roll. More emphasis needs to be given to researching in detail the processes which lead to school exclusion, though current evidence suggests that school ethos and organisation, provision for special educational needs and curriculum relevance are likely to be important factors.

2.19 Multi-agency initiatives, which take a whole-school approach to teaching about the issues often involved in exclusions, such as racism and bullying, should be developed.

2.20 Additional flexibility in the secondary curriculum would benefit many pupils, with possible availability of structured basic literacy tuition at secondary school level and the introduction of exciting and worthwhile input (with status) for the 12-14 age group, such as awards schemes, life skills, interpersonal skills and parenting skills.

2.21 Where Education Otherwise is being monitored, officers may be sanctioning inadequate, narrow teaching programmes of one or two hours a week. LEAs should be required to evidence achievement and progression for young people receiving EO.

2.22 The more extensive introduction of mentors from within the travelling communities as positive role models, which have status within the school, would be a longer term aim, which could be supported by the extension of funding to cover Adult Basic Literacy, combined with suitable training opportunities.

2.23 The Social Exclusion Unit, with its inter-departmental focus, should consider a review of the workings of the Criminal Justice and Public Order Act 1994, as it affects the quality of, and attendance and achievement in, education for Gypsy and Traveller children.

Reform proposals for education in Scotland[29]

2.24 Funding from central government, along the lines of the funding structure in England, should be used to specifically address the educational needs of Traveller families.

2.25 All local authorities should adopt policies in relation to the education of Traveller children which should be published and monitored.

2.26 Peripatetic teachers should be provided to work with families.

2.27 There should be provision of school transport for primary aged children from all sites to encourage attendance.

2.28 There must be a clear routing out of racist and/or bullying behaviour, with a clear message to parents about how this will be dealt with if it arises.

2.29 Research has indicated that many families would welcome the provision of mobile classrooms, preferably which could work across local authority boundaries.

2.30 New and experimental measures, i.e. a network of tutors for additional support and tailored learning, or promotion – where appropriate – of family learning, should be explored.

2.31 There should be improved provision of information and support for those parents who wish to provide 'education otherwise' to their children.

2.32 There should be development of appropriate skills training initiatives for young Travellers.

2.33 The relevance of the curriculum to the needs of Traveller children and their parents should be examined.

Reform proposals for education in Wales

2.34 LEAs should have close co-operation with other departments and with the travelling communities themselves, in order to assure that the LEAs have good sources of information.

2.35 In-service Traveller Awareness training for all those local authority employees coming into contact with Travellers is desirable.

2.36 All local authorities in Wales should publish and adopt policies and procedures relating to the education of Traveller children. These might also be translated into policies and procedures for each school including strategies for equal opportunities and to counteract bullying.

2.37 There must be effective monitoring and analysis of the attendance and progress of Traveller children; including the establishment of a national database for monitoring this.

2.38 There should be regular review and target-setting meetings between schools, children and parents, to include monitoring of individual education plans.

2.39 Flexible approaches might be taken by schools to attendance policies, school uniforms, timetables and punctuality.

2.40 The relevance of the curriculum to the needs of Traveller children should be improved; otherwise Travelling children and their parents may rightly feel that school plays only a small part in their education.

29   Proposals by Michelle Lloyd and Richard Morran, Development Workers, Save the Children Fund Scotland (Traveller Section), Dunfermline.

3

Accomodation and Site Provision

"With a view to ensuring the effective exercise of the right to protection against poverty and social exclusion, the Parties undertake ... to take measures within the framework of an overall and co-ordinated approach to promote the effective access of persons who live or risk living in a situation of social exclusion or poverty, as well as their families, to, in particular, employment, housing, training, education, culture and social and medical assistance ..."[30]

The Accommodation and Site Provision Traveller Working Group

All people need access to appropriate accommodation. "Equality of treatment, in relation to accommodation, requires that people should be able to choose the type of accommodation that most suits their needs. This requires diversity via a range of accommodation options. Equality of treatment also requires that where possible Travellers should enjoy equivalent rights to those enjoyed by non-Travellers in similar situations" (Clements and Smith, 1997:p.358). Travelling people do not have the same choices available to them as settled people; if they live on a secure public site, they do not have the 'right to buy' and their security of tenure rights are materially weaker than those enjoyed by non-Travellers. The enormous planning law obstacles they face means that the choice of private site ownership is generally not available to them. The site conditions and locations of many of the 350 public Gypsy sites in England and Wales are appalling. Frequently they are in locations deemed unsuitable for any other development; on old waste tips, beside (or even underneath) motorways, far removed from shops and other amenities, often with one or two taps serving perhaps twenty families and with no foul drainage; muddy quagmires in the winter and dust bowls in the summer. It is the case however that this disgraceful neglect is also experienced by many tenants on run-down council estates; a concerted effort to improve the minimum standards of acceptable public accommodation would benefit Travellers and non-Travellers alike.

The UK has failed, in its domestic law, to honour its international Treaty

---

30 European Social Charter, Article 30

obligations. Poor and landless people do not have any right to accommodation which meets their reasonable needs, let alone any 'choice' of accommodation. This situation can be contrasted with that in Ireland which has emerged as a direct consequence of the Traveller Law Reform initiative. In chapter 5 of the 1997 Conference Report John Murphy, Principal Officer in the Irish Department of the Environment's Traveller Accommodation Unit, explained that the basic aim of housing policy in Ireland was "To enable every household to have available an affordable dwelling of good quality, suited to its needs, in a good environment, and as far as possible, at the tenure of its choice".

"It is the fact that people are living in unauthorised camps which matters, not their particular origin, style or categorisation. The passion for unnecessary labelling is highly suspect and leads to unresolved problems of subjective definition. It is more-over an invitation to discriminatory, emotive and often pejorative attitudinising. There is a perfectly adequate and wholly objective identifier in the official homeless legislation literature, namely, occupants of moveable structures who have no autho-rised site. By definition such people are 'homeless'."[31] In the UK however, whilst a person is defined as homeless if s/he lives in a mobile dwelling and has nowhere legal on which to station it, there is no requirement that the local authority respond in an 'appropriate' way.

Thus, if the local authority accepts that there is a priority need for accommoda-tion, Government guidance merely draws attention to the fact that for some Gypsies the provision of a hard-standing for a caravan would be the appropriate response.[33] In such cases Councils invariably refer to the lack of available sites and offer homeless Travellers a house; this is as culturally inappropriate a response as offering a homeless ex-house-dweller a pitch on Gypsy caravan site. The reforms in the Republic of Ireland show recognition that suitability should not be a discretion but a right. Platform members felt that this should also be the case in the UK.

A number of underlying principles and issues emerged from the working group meet-ings and underlie the reform proposals detailed below, namely:

- The need for legal stopping places for Travelling people is a matter of some urgency, in order that their quality of life and the relationship between Travelling people and settled communities does not deteriorate any further.
- A vacancy rate, i.e. extra sites, would be needed for the market to remain fluid, just as for housing.
- Settled society seem to feel that Travelling people should just start living in houses, although it expects that there should be a range of accommodation options for settled people.
- Traditional stopping places are vanishing, usually through being made inacces-sible, at an incredible rate. Tony Thomson of the Friends, Families and Travellers Support Group[34] made a submission on Traditional Stopping Places.

31 Letter from M.J. Treble CBE, Vice President, Somerset Association of Local Councils, to the Traveller Law Research Unit, Cardiff Law School, October 1998

32 Housing Act 1996 s.175

33 Such discretion can be challenged only by judicial review; R v Brent LBC ex parte Omar (1991) 23 HLR 446

34 Now at Community Base, 113 Queens Road, Brighton BN1 3XG tel. 01273 234777.

His paper is included in this report in Part 2 Chapter 9. The main recommendations emanating from that paper are however noted below under the sub-heading *Traditional stopping places and customary use*.

- Of those authorised sites that do exist, site standards can be appalling, rents too high, and license agreements insufficient to protect people's rights; these being conditions which would not be considered acceptable in the context of housing, there is clearly discrimination in the provision of sites for mobile dwellings.
- Travelling people and Gypsy and Traveller organisations have insufficient input into the need for, and provision, location and design of sites for their use.
- There is too little data collected at present by governmental or other bodies to enable empirical analysis of these issues. More research needs to be done to quantify the problem.

It is recognised by all platform members that lack of legal stopping places leads to an endless cycle of instability and expense for Travellers and settled people alike; a fact that has been known for a long time. "It is worse than useless and unavailing to harass them from place to place when no retreat or shelter is provided."[35]

Liz Hughes made a submission for Part 2 (at Chapter 7) following observations from research by the Children's Participation Project.[36] Her main recommendations are noted below under the sub-heading The needs of children. A written submission to the working group was also made by Paul Goltz, Traveller Development Worker for South Somerset District Council,[37] in which he highlights the importance and value of a community development approach in dealing with issues around relations between settled and Travelling communities; his paper is included in Part 2 Chapter 9. The principle recommendation in that paper is noted below under the sub-heading Community development. Finally, a submission was made by Richard Trahair, Property Secretary of the Salisbury Diocesan Board of Finance, emphasising the important and positive role that religious organisations can play, both as landowners and as influential community members; his paper is also included in Chapter 9. The principle recommendation following from that paper is included below under the sub-heading A role for the church.

Finance and funding

The Traveller Law Research Unit carried out a study in 1997 in which some local authorities gave details of how much evictions of Travelling people had cost in terms of officer time, building works and legal costs.[38] The final estimation of the annual national cost of evictions was £3.5 million, not including costs borne by district councils and the police, corporate private landowners such as the National Trust,

---

35 Hoyland, J. *A Historical Survey of the Customs, Habits and Present State of the Gypsies: designed to develope the Origin of this Singular People, and to Promote the Amelioration of their Condition*, London, 1816. p.161

36 The research examined the issues of site provision and accommodation, and how these affect Travelling children in South West England. The Children's Participation Project (Wessex), the Children's Society. *My Dream Site*, 92B High Street, Midsomer Norton, Bath, BA3 2DE, 1998

37 With an introduction by South Somerset District Councillor Annie Murdoch.

38 Campbell, Sue. *Eviction is a Waste of Money, Housing*, April 1998. p.13

RailTrack and other rail operators, water authorities, local planning authorities, central government departments such as the Ministry of Defence and the Forestry Commission, and individual private landowners. Thus the total figure could, at least, be doubled. In the 1992 consultation paper on reform of the Caravan Sites Act 1968 it was said that the cost to the exchequer of providing sites for Travelling people between 1970 and 1992 was £56 million, or £4 per annum.

> "In considering the cost of provision for travellers, it is important that a local authority should attempt to add up all its previously hidden costs of coping with travellers in order to estimate the true cost of setting up a properly controlled site. Simply deducting the annual rent from the annual out-goings on the site itself disguises the saving in time of a variety of officers and other employees of the authority, as well as of the police. Over and above the these kinds of benefits, there will be the less tangible, but nonetheless real, effects on the community at large stemming from an improvement in amenity and reduced social friction, and on the travellers themselves as they begin to play a fuller part in community life."[39]

The gross social housing investment in Great Britain for 1997–8 was £4,096 billion. Mortgage interest tax relief was £2,700 million. Total assistance with housing costs for home owners, council and private tenants for that period was £11,876 million. £1.3 billion was budgeted for 1996–7, and the same amount again in 1997–8, to improve a quarter of a million homes in the UK. The transfer in recent years of 36 local authorities to housing associations has raised £1.6 billion in investment from the private sector. The Government has now released the capital receipts (£800 million) from the sale of council housing for use as expenditure on remaining public housing, and councils continue to set aside over £500 million of new housing receipts each year.[40]

These figures show that the £56 million spent on Gypsy sites over not one but 22 years under the Caravan Sites Act 1968 was very little indeed. Most of the subsidy and assistance listed above went to settled people; the only Travelling people who will have seen any of it were those in public housing, and those on public sites and on housing benefit (though the latter provide their own 'house' in most cases). During the 1999 Conference on Traveller Law Reform, Sylvia Dunn of the National Association of Gypsy Women pointed out that Essex County Council is currently expending time and money seeking plots of its land that can be used to impound the vehicles of evicted Travelling people: "if they can find land for pounds, they can find land for sites".

Housing ministers say that central government will not fund sites for Travelling people because they can't find the 'pot of gold' necessary. There is money, and there is political will where housing is concerned. (The Chairman of the new Countryside Agency has recently suggested that tax incentives should be offered to encourage an increase in affordable homes in rural communities).[42] The platform agrees that there should be recognition of the validity of forms of accommodation other than housing, planned for and funded in the same way in which housing is planned and paid for. It is right that central and regional government should have no more a role in ensuring provision of sufficient and suitable accommodation for Travelling people as they do

---

39 Ministry of Housing and Local Government. *Gypsies and Other Travellers*, London, 1967. p.68
40 Wilcox, Steve. *Housing Finance Review 1998/99*, Joseph Rowntree Foundation, York, 1998
42 Elliott, Valerie. *The Times*, 30 March 1999

for housed people, but nor should they play a lesser part. This is particularly important with respect to transit sites or temporary stopping places, where only a network co-ordinated at a higher level will be effective in ensuring that Travelling people are not continually pushed through area after area in search of respite.

The DETR administers section 180 grants to the voluntary sector for the prevention of single homelessness worth some £8 million a year; the DSS runs a separate administered resettlement programme funding 4300 hostel beds and move-on accommodation; this costs some £18 million per year. Central government seems then to accept responsibility for people who need to be housed, but continue to demand that 'homeless' Travelling people should provide for themselves. In addition to Housing Corporation money, 'right to buy' schemes, and a system of loans as similar as possible to the mortgages available for permanent housing, it is suggested that central government should give money to enable site provision for a limited period; in part to make up for the accumulated shortfall in sites and to encourage swift provision but also, once again, to send a message to settled society that Travelling people are equal and as entitled to assistance as any other member of society.

This needs no extra money after an initial push to compensate for the existing shortfall in provision which has resulted from unequal treatment in the past, to create a more level playing field. The management structure already exists. This would not be a special privilege for Travelling people, on the contrary, it would, for the first time be treating them as equal with settled people. Same needs, different delivery of services to meet them: an already established and accepted principle in respect of housing and other services for other minority groups. It needs no new, special, ghettoising legislation, although housing legislation might need some small amendments.

Reform proposals for accommodation and site provision

Fundamental issues

3.1   The Government should set up a Task Force or other form of working party, with Gypsy and Traveller representation as a central principle, as a matter of urgency.

3.2   Local government is necessarily given broad discretion in the way it operates, and is subject to severe local political pressure. Therefore, clear and strong guidance from regional and central government regarding Traveller-related service provision is essential and might produce an important change of culture within local authority working practices, and their approaches to educating the settled population. Whilst the new DETR guidance is welcome it – at best – only treats symptoms and is unlikely to tackle systematic problems in achieving acceptable provision for and treatment of Travellers.

3.3   The views of Travelling people, including children, must be sought and incorporated at all stages of the reform process, from platform level, to the ensuing Task Force or other form of Government review, to subsequent action, i.e. location and design of publicly-provided sites. The further ahead the reform process moves, the stronger the danger that Travelling people will be disenfranchised and compromises made that will eventually disadvantage them.

3.4   If the right to travel and, more importantly, to stop, were to be legally protected, this would need to be stated in a 'Travellers Charter' or some other, new,

legislation. Such a Charter might commence with 'This Act recognises the freedom to choose to exercise the right to a nomadic way of life, including the rights
to travel and to stop, whether temporarily or permanently, for economic and
other purposes, enshrining the principles of equality of treatment, rights and
responsibilities, and freedom of movement, as recognised in European and
International documents to which the UK is a signatory'.

3.5   If a Right to Stop cannot be directly enshrined in legislation, at the very least
the principle should be recognised by the adjustment and/or adoption of
appropriate policies and practices.

Choice of accommodation options

3.6   A choice of a range of accommodation should be available to Travelling people
as it is to the rest of the population; e.g. private provision by individuals for
themselves and for others, supported and unsupported and self-build; public
provision, supervised and unsupervised; sites including work areas; rental and
other short-term forms of provision. There is a general consensus that smaller
sites work better.

3.7   The definition of 'accommodation' as used by authorities should be widened so
that there can be greater involvement in provision by housing authorities;
'suitable' should be altered to 'appropriate'. 'Control' of unauthorised encampments should be altered to 'management', and the use of the racist word
'toleration' discontinued; perhaps to be replaced by 'non-harassment'.

Funding and finance

3.8   A public funding strategy for Traveller accommodation is necessary to underpin
initiatives outlined in other recommendations. Sites should be treated on an
equal basis to housing, in that Housing Corporation funds, Housing Capital
Receipts, Single Regeneration Budgets and other finance mechanisms should be
available for all accommodation, not just housing. Mortgages should also be
available for private Travellers' sites.

Equality and parity with housing

3.9   The duty of local authorities to provide sites and the exchequer grant to assist in
doing so should be restored (or, in the case of Scotland, introduced); but only
until existing housing policies, procedures, bodies and finance have been broad-
ened. In the longer term, and similar to the new situation in Eire, public site
provision should be attained in the same way and through the same mechanisms
as apply to housed people, i.e. through Housing Association, co-operatives,
etc.[43]

---

43 Further information on possible funding arrangements can be seen in Chapter 7 of the TLAST and
Traveller Law Research Unit Conference and Consultation Report *Traveller Law Reform*, Cardiff Law
School, 1997

3.10 Proper tenancy agreements and rights and security thereunder should be available to Travellers as they are to most others; model agreements could be developed.

3.11 The right to buy pitches could be developed with appropriate safeguards, to ensure that public stock does not dwindle below the level of need and poorer families lose access to much-needed accommodation, as with public housing.

3.12 The fairness of site rents should be amenable to review and investigation, with rents on public sites possibly being standardised. This would encompass an examination of the role of housing benefit in keeping rents high and the role of high rents in keeping some Travellers dependent on housing benefit.

3.13 The safety of site locations and conditions must be amenable to review and investigation as are those in public housing, including risk assessments. For example, health workers have expressed concern at the proximity of many sites to landfill sites and electricity cables.[44] Grants for improvement and regeneration of accommodation should be equally available to Travellers as to sedentary people.

3.14 There is no real reason why sites cannot be located amongst conventional housing. Studies have shown that this can work,[45] and that well-designed, well-run sites settle in well and the objections of settled people quickly prove unfounded.[46]

3.15 The mechanisms governing the right to vote, and other forms of democratic participation, should be altered to be more inclusive of all who are landless and/or without a permanent address.

Allocation of accommodation

3.16 Allocation policies and procedures on publicly-funded sites should be reviewed and brought into line with those in mainstream housing as a matter of urgency, and best practice developed and formalised. For example, the London Borough of Hackney allows Travellers to be on the waiting list for pitches even while they are housed, thus recognising that housing may not be a choice for some Travelling people but an undesirable necessity. This practice should be mandatory.

3.17 Young Travellers and/or Traveller couples may, when they leave home, be unable to obtain a pitch on the same site as their families, have difficulty proving sufficient disadvantage to obtain public housing, and may confront racism and other obstacles to private housing. These young people have an 'invisible' homelessness problem and can be very isolated from their communities. Their problem, and the population growth of all Travelling communities, should be acknowledged and provided for.

---

44 SCF (Scotland) draw attention to recent research which indicates a raised risk of congenital anomaly in babies whose mothers live close to landfill tips, and ongoing international debate about the connection between power cables and childhood cancers.

45 McKeown, Kieran and McGrath, Brid. Accommodating Travelling People: a Report prepared for Crosscare (the Catholic Social Service Conference of the Archdiocese of Dublin), 1996. pp.v-vi

46 Duncan, Tom. Neighbours' views of official sites for travelling people: A survey based on three case studies in Scotland, The Planning Exchange, Glasgow / The Joseph Rowntree Foundation, York, 1996

3.18 Local authorities should have a Code of Practice for interviewing Travelling people prior to allocation of accommodation.

Addressing discrimination

3.19 Existing anti-racism legislation and policy should be reinforced in order that anti-Traveller bias can be addressed in all areas of accommodation and service provision. The definition of 'Gypsy' in this respect should be widened in some way in order to encompass all Travelling People, or abandoned.

3.20 The role of racism and/or lack of awareness within race equality organisations themselves should be addressed.

3.21 Other means should be explored to fight discrimination against non-ethnic Travelling people.

3.22 Some means of educating the settled population as to the culture and needs of Travellers must be found; or local opposition might make reforms, no matter how practicable on paper, unworkable in practice.

Monitoring

3.23 Mechanisms for relevant and sensitive collation of data regarding service provision to Travellers, or lack thereof, should be formulated, in order that such provision can be monitored and assessed. This should encompass the inclusion of Traveller children within Children's Services Plans.

3.24 The use of local authority and police powers of eviction should be monitored, as are stop and search powers, to ensure that such uses are lawful and to highlight areas using 'zero-toleration' policies in contravention of public and common law principles.

Planning

3.25 There should be a duty on all local authorities to include fairness in planning for Gypsy and Traveller sites to ensure that provision is made rather than *to provide*, demand-led and subject to continuous assessment.

Traditional stopping places

3.26 The potential role of traditional sites and stopping places, many of which have been made inaccessible, should be examined. Established use of traditional stopping places should be recognised. A process of registration should be undertaken to ensure that these stopping places are not lost to other forms of development. This would be similar to the legal position of Rights of Way in that it acknowledges and protects the long-standing but occasional usage of a location by different individuals.

3.27 Green lanes should be recognised as an accommodation resource for nomadic peoples within the context of a network of sites and an inclusive management regime. The duration of stay should relate to the intensity of usage. Green lanes should be identified and protected where there is a clear case of illegal closure or encroachment.

3.28 Local authorities can use their compulsory purchase powers under section 24 of the Caravan Sites and Control of Development Act 1960 to protect traditional stopping places.

3.29 Facilitation should be sought of private or Highway Authority acquisition of an 18m strip of land leading to existing green lane.

3.30 There should be identification and, if necessary, upgrading of existing green lanes of appropriate width for use.

3.31 De-enclosing agriculturally over-exploited land as a matter of public interest, would create green lanes as a necessary initial step to retard soil erosion and enhance bio-diversity.

3.32 Agenda 21 principles of sustainability should be applied to the provision and enabling of sites.

The needs of children

3.33 Children should be consulted when decisions are being taken that affect them, particularly in relation to sites and eviction.

3.34 Site provision needs to represent the diversity of life-style that is found within communities of Travelling people.

3.35 Planning procedures should take into account the needs and wishes of children.

3.36 Play space needs to be given greater priority when considering site suitability.

Community development

3.37 Community development approaches, including a partnership and mediation role, have been proved to work and should be incorporated into local authority best practice.

A role for the church

3.38 Government and religious organisations, including the Church of England and the Quakers, could and should meet with interested Gypsy and Traveller organisations, to explore means of co-operating in the provision and enabling of sites for Travelling people.

4

Eviction and Criminal Justice

The criminal justice system impacts disproportionately on the lives of poor people, both as the victims of crime and as residents in communities who have less access to political power capable of redressing these inequalities. The concerns of Travelling people in relation to the criminal justice system envelop all the usual problems of poor and disenfranchised communities; for instance the lack of reliable data and the disproportionate number of young Travellers in custody or on parole or probation. The concern, however, extends further as it includes the role of the police in evictions. At best this role is peripherally concerned with their criminal law functions and at worst it is not radically dissimilar to the role of bailiffs in the Highland clearances or under the Enclosure Acts.

As at the first conference on Traveller Law Reform in 1997, a major area of concern has been the lack of data about the use of eviction powers under the Criminal Justice and Public Order Act 1994. The report of that Conference noted a comment by a member of the West Mercia Constabulary, that it was impossible to estimate the scale of the problem unless accurate "records of the operation of statutory powers existed" (Clements and Smith, 1997: p.17). Another area of discussion has been the existence of police powers of eviction under section 61 of the 1994 Act. It is felt by many, including senior police officers, that the power puts the police in the position of being 'bailiffs for private landowners', and that they would wish to be involved in the eviction of Travelling people only where a mass trespass or other public order issue was concerned. However, while many people would prefer to see the section repealed and a return to the powers under the Public Order 1986,[47] it is largely accepted that such an expectation is not politically realistic.

New guidance for police officers on the use of section 61 was drafted by the Association of Chief Police Officers (ACPO) in spring 1999; it has not yet been made publicly available. It is an improvement on their previous guidance in that it is more proportionate, advises a multi-agency approach where appropriate and reminds officers that section 61 confers a power and not a duty to evict. It is to be hoped that the

---

47 The 1994 Act extended the previous provision under the Public Order Act 1986 s.39 which was concerned with the consequences of mass trespass and created an offence almost of 'individual trespass'. See also Clements and Smith, 1997. p. 17

police themselves, through such guidance, will begin to use their powers only in situations where public order is at issue, without the necessity for new legislation to compel them to do so.

There is general agreement that these matters would not be so problematic if the accommodation shortage for Travelling people were satisfactorily resolved; the question of accommodation lies at the heart of the need for reform. Nonetheless, it has been noted by many that on most occasions when settled people are discussing Travelling people, the topic of accommodation very quickly elides into assumptions and accusations of criminality. While it is acknowledged that the Travelling communities have their criminal elements as any other population, ACPO continues to assert that they have no disproportionate problems with criminality in the Travelling populations, and the continuing presumptions stem largely from stereotyping. It is important that issues around accommodation and criminal justice be discussed separately as they are usually entirely different matters.

The impact of crime upon the lives of Travelling people has been little appreciated or acknowledged. Those camping alone are, for instance, subject to significant violence from vigilantes and late night drunks. Stopping places can never be left unoccupied for fear of criminal damage being done to the vehicles and theft from the dwellings. This major criminal justice issue was considered in the 1997 Conference Report and stressed by the Institute for Jewish Policy Research, which called for "Immediate action [to] be taken to respond effectively to anti-Gypsy violence and harassment. The status of Gypsies as an ethnic group should be explicitly acknowledged by criminal justice provisions, affording protection to Gypsy communities."[48] It is regrettable therefore that whilst so little attention is paid to this question, so much ill-informed anecdotal comment identifies Gypsies and Travellers as being criminals. A number of contributors to the law reform debate consider that this issue had to be addressed in order to properly address the far more pressing issue of violence and criminal activity perpetrated against Travellers.

It does appear that those Travellers who are least well-behaved and most aggressive are given the widest berth by the statutory agencies (and indeed vigilantes). We have a system where there is a terrible lack of accommodation for one group of people, who have therefore little option but to sometimes camp in less than ideal situations. The system then provides neither rewards for good behaviour nor sanctions for bad behaviour; it is a system that encourages some of the worst aspects of human nature.

Many delegates agreed that it was essential that public bodies exercise fair, consistent and transparent 'toleration' policies, so that Travellers had an opportunity to camp in appropriate areas and were secure in the knowledge that they could remain unless certain forms of anti-behaviour occurred, i.e. be treated on a par with any other council tenant. This would require public landowners to provide refuse disposal and other basic services (on the same basis that they are supplied to council tenants).

By failing to take firm action against the small minority of badly behaved encampments (on the basis that these frequently move on after a short while) local authorities are creating a major problem for the vast majority of law abiding and socially responsible Travelling people. Recognising and changing this combination of response would, it was felt, go a long way to improving the relations between travelling and set-

[48] *The Roma /Gypsies of Europe: a persecuted people*, Policy Paper 3, December 1996. p.40.

tled communities. There would always of course be problems, as was noted, "there has been, and still is some friction between the settled and the travelling populations due to various factors including little or no security for the Travellers and different codes of behaviour leading to misunderstandings. A little effort on everyone's part is now required to redress the balance and encourage people to live in harmony. It has already been acknowledged that everyone has rights. With rights, however, come responsibilities and customary practice necessitates the observation of certain codes of conduct upon which reasonable people can agree as being 'common sense'."[49]

Many platform members have agreed that much of the discussion which has recently taken place in the media around racism in the police forces, stemming from the McPherson Inquiry into the death of Black teenager Stephen Lawrence, is to be greatly welcomed. Nonetheless, it has almost always focused on Black and Asian communities and Gypsies continue to seem an invisible ethnic minority. Some aspects of the findings and possible reforms stemming form the Lawrence Inquiry which may have a bearing on Gypsies and Travellers are related in Part 2 Chapter 7, in a piece by the Traveller Section of the Save the Children Fund (Scotland).

The eviction and criminal justice traveller working group

After its first meeting the Planning and Criminal Justice Traveller Working Group split into two sub-groups.[50] The Eviction and Criminal Justice sub-group agreed key principles while awaiting the introduction of the DETR Good Practice Guide.[51] The Guide offers local authorities and the police further details on 'Managing Unauthorised Encampments' in addition to DoE Circular 18/94, and does recommend that eviction should only be one of many options available to public bodies. Some of the more useful sections of the Guide are highlighted by Chris Johnson in Part 2 Chapter 10. Discussion and research on other criminal justice matters, the history and role of legislation , the role of the police and other justice agencies, resulted in the following conclusions.

The role of the police

In 1998 the Home Office published research investigating the role of the police during the first two years of operation of the Criminal Justice and Public Order Act 1994.[52] The findings included:

- Police willingness to direct trespassers from land, especially if they have self-identified as and/or are deemed to be Gypsies, varies from force to force. Some forces appear to feel more strongly that trespass is a matter for individual land

---

49 Goltz, P. and South Somerset District Council . *Travelling People: Moving On – an information booklet for the travelling and settled communities*, 1998. p.2

50 The first meeting and the subsequent Eviction and Criminal Justice sub-group meetings were hosted by the Traveller Advice Team, formerly of McGrath and Co. Solicitors in Birmingham.

51 Managing Unauthorised Camping: A Good Practice Guide, and the associated Research Report were issued by the DETR in late October 1998.

52 Bucke, Tom and James, Zoë. *Trespass and Protest: policing under the Criminal Justice and Public Order Act 1994*, Home Office Research Study 190, London, 1998

owners and local authorities except in exceptional circumstances.

- Full enforcement was rarely resorted to from the outset; usually matters of trespass were dealt with via a number of steps and consultations with all parties concerned. Directions to trespassers to leave a site usually required further measures (towing of vehicles, a token arrest or threat of it, or 'a large number of officers having to attend the site'.[53]

- Arrests were rarely if ever made with regard to trespassers returning to a site within three months, as it was difficult to prove that the same persons were involved.

- Officers were not keen to seize vehicles in pursuit of their powers under the Act; not, seemingly, because they were concerned that this would literally mean impounding peoples' homes but because of the storage and other organisational and financial difficulties involved.

- Eviction of Gypsies and Travellers from one unauthorised encampment only leads to another illegal site elsewhere, displacing but not eradicating problems.

It was recorded that police officers directed trespassers from land 67 times in 1995; the numbers of people and vehicles evicted in each incident varied greatly. Prosecutions were very rare, with a total of 8 in the years 1995-6.

The Home Office research found that the police were more likely to resolve situations by informal discussion and negotiation. The only change which the 1994 legislation appears to have brought about from the policing position under the Public Order Act 1986 is that police officers may be in a stronger legal position to take action when dealing with cases of public disorder than previously. Of course, the consequent effect on Travelling people is that they are less able to challenge action taken against them, whether on traditional stopping places or unobtrusive unofficial encampments. This finding suggests a further shift in the balance of power between nomads and the state, to the disadvantage of Travelling people.

The Association of Chief Police Officers (ACPO) guidance to police forces (until Spring 1999) on the use of section 61 states that "The police, as officers of the law, are responsible for public order, and the prevention and detection of crime. It is therefore only in such circumstances that the use of section 61 should be considered as a primary response". Many senior police officers have expressed the view that they do not wish to be used as bailiffs for private landowners.

However, attitudes by lower-grade operational officers to Gypsies and Travellers seem to vary widely. The Home Office Research Study states that a "problem police officers associated with encampments of trespassers was a rise in property offences in the local area."[54] It goes on to say that "[s]ome officers believed the issue of trespass could be solved by the provision of more legal sites for travellers and gypsies. Others suggested that a change on social security regulations to exclude these groups from eligibility from benefit would drive them from their way of life."[55] It is arguable that officers holding the latter belief might be less likely to apply section 61 and other powers with respect to Travelling people in a fair and equal fashion.

During 1998 the Traveller Law Research Unit of the Cardiff Law School contacted

53 Ibid., p. viii
54 Ibid., p. 8
55 Ibid., p. 16

a number of police organisations to ascertain their views on the 1994 legislation generally, and whether those views had changed since they wrote to the Government in response to the 1992 consultation paper on reform of the Caravan Sites Act 1968. The response of the Police Superintendents Association of England and Wales in 1992 was that "[i]deally, the adequate provision of properly designated sites may go some way to provide solutions and we would strongly support that option. At this stage we have reservations as to how effective the revised proposals would prove to be, given the complex nature of this subject. The practical effects of any enforcement can be far more complicated than is often realised by those that draft such legislation. As mentioned at the outset of this response, ideally it is a matter for the appropriate agencies with minimal police involvement."

Six years on, the Association feels that time and experience have proved them right: "The practicalities of applying the legislation have negated many of the benefits it was intended to bring to both landowners and Travellers alike. We are still of the opinion that such legislation is primarily for Local Authorities to implement and enforce. Yet four years into the Act many have still to provide suitable designated sites. This situation has in our opinion contributed significantly to the problems associated with the current legislation. It is essential that adequate provision be provided for Travellers, together with their vehicles to camp in circumstances that are satisfactory to everyone." The Association posits that there is a place on the statute books for the 1994 Act as a workable piece of legislation, but only in cases in which it is appropriate to apply the criminal law such as mass trespass or deliberate disruption.

The ACPO view, in 1994, was that local authorities should have a responsibility to accommodate Gypsies and Travellers; that they were resistant to proposals to criminalise the act of living in a caravan as it was a "unique situation to proscribe a way of life, formerly accepted as being within the law and then to introduce penalties"; and that the police do not have any great difficulty policing the Travelling communities. They were also concerned that the new legislation had heavy resourcing implications for both the police and the courts. In July 1997 the ACPO Public Order Sub-Committee wrote to Chief Constables, "with the intention of reviewing our collective experience of the Criminal Justice and Public Order Act 1994."[56] Forty two forces replied to their enquiry and the results were summarised as follows:

- "Forces have experienced difficulties with the overlap between Sections 61-2 and 77 of the Act. The decided case of R v Wealden Council exposed the anomaly and exacerbated operational problems. It follows that the service would welcome authoritative guidance as to which agency should take the lead in removing trespasses from land.
- The majority of forces are opposed to the routine use of Sections 62 of the Act. Officers are reluctant to cause unnecessary disruption for travellers' family life; at the same time they are keen to protect the rights and privileges of landowners. Consequently, police officers prefer to negotiate and reason their way through any conflict.
- A number of forces have produced guidelines, in respect of Sections 61, 62 and 77, in partnership with District and Borough Councils.

56 Letter to Mr Terry Christie, Chairman, the National Romani Rights Association, from the Honorary Secretary of the ACPO General Purposes Committee, 21st March 1994.

- Forces acknowledge that the enforcement of Sections 62 to 65 can be labour-intensive and occasionally impractical."[57]

Traveller Working Group members all suggested that police involvement with unofficial encampments can confirm the prejudicial assumption by many of the settled population that Travelling people are criminal by nature. Many suggested, in line with the Police Federation view, that the police should only be involved where mass trespass is concerned, and/or where the size and nature of the encampment is sufficiently disruptive to become an appropriate matter for public attention. This is also similar in approach to the DETR guidance mentioned above and the views of ACPO, who believe that although there is a place on the statute books for the 1994 Act, the powers are only appropriate in cases involving mass trespass or deliberate disruption. ACPO believes that negotiation is generally far more productive than employing section 61 powers.

The criminal justice system

There is some evidence to suggest that young Travelling people are over-represented in the criminal justice system and that bail conditions are set for them disproportionately. A short study undertaken by probation officers in Newark found that amongst the travelling communities were a range of indicators of deprivation, including unemployment, under-achievement in education, shorter life expectancy and incidence of mental health problems, as well as over-representation in the criminal justice system. Most of the offences related to the condition and use of vehicles. The staff found that Travellers tended to be held overnight and presented before magistrates because the police wanted bail conditions on road traffic matters, which is not common practice. They found that a Traveller had a much harder task to establish a case for unconditional bail and was therefore more likely to be remanded in custody.

In 1993 the Association of Chief Officers of Probation and the National Association for the Care and Resettlement of Offenders published a twelve month survey of juveniles remanded into custody whilst awaiting trial in criminal proceedings.[59] The survey found that young people recorded as Travellers featured highly in remands to Feltham Young Offenders Institution, but that information about admissions to prisons elsewhere in England and Wales was anecdotal and was not recorded. The report revealed that a significant number of young people who were remanded to custody from courts in the London region were identified as Travellers. This group of young people accounted for 38% of admissions of all young people classified as white from these courts.

This abnormally high figure may well reflect a prejudicial assumption by courts about the mobility of Gypsies and other Travellers and therefore a belief that they are likely to abscond. The Association recommended a review which might explore a corporate approach to providing a co-ordinated service for particular groups of young people such as Travellers, across metropolitan areas or regions. There is as yet

---

58 Letter to the Traveller Law Research Unit of the Cardiff Law School from the ACPO Public Order Sub-Committee, 15 June 1998.

59 Stanton, A.K. An Impressionistic Account of the Discrimination Suffered By White Ethnic Minorities in Newark, London, 1994

no evidence that this recommendation has resulted in any such review. A parliamentary answer has revealed that information about Irish Travellers at Feltham is still not recorded.[60]

There has been very little research into this area by any official academic or governmental agencies. For example, Research Studies issued by the Home Office on *Ethnicity and Contacts with the Police, Offending on Bail and The Prison Population 1997*[61] contain no reference, either directly or indirectly, to Gypsy and Traveller offenders. The only recommendation that can be made in this area at this time is that, as ever, more research must be done so that Travelling people are no longer invisible and the difficulties they face can be acknowledged and quantified.

The potential dangers to Travelling people resulting from the implementation of the Crime and Disorder Act 1998 were identified by Bill Forrester in a submission to the working group (which is reproduced in Part 2 Chapter 10). He noted however that the legislation could also produce significant benefits for Travellers, particularly if the Act's 'Partnership Initiatives' were to result in improved police and local authority inter-agency working.

A member of the Health and Education Traveller Working Group, Officer Jack Hawkins of HM Prison Cardiff, is the only known Prison Officer in England and Wales to be appointed as a Traveller Liaison Officer. His role was created after a young Traveller man, remanded on a minor charge, committed suicide in custody. It is not known what proportion of the prison population are Travelling people, and whether they have needs while in custody which are different from those of settled prisoners. As result of Officer Hawkin's participation in the Working Group, a recommendation was made which can be found under the subheading *The criminal justice system and Travelling people* below.

Much academic work has been published on the history of legislation pertaining to Travelling people. In addition to the piece by Bill Forrester, a number of other pieces of legislation have been discussed at various Traveller Working Group meetings, and recommendations stemming from the conclusions reached can be found under the sub-heading *Legislation* below.

Reform proposals for eviction and criminal justice

Task Force and other bodies

4.1   Minister Hilary Armstrong has been heard to express the view that the DETR is not opposed to the idea of a National Working Party of some form, and the notion seems to be supported, if quietly, in the Birmingham research which informs the DETR Good Practice Guide. Any movement towards such a government review needs to be sparked by clear and realisable ideas and be led by Travelling people.

4.2   The Social Exclusion Unit should be encouraged to play a role in the process of reform.

---

60 Hansard, 13.06.96. Information in this section was provided by the Action Group for Irish Youth.
The Irish Community: Discrimination and the Criminal Justice System, The Bourne Trust, London, 1996. p.7
61 Nos. 59, 72 and 76 respectively

Equity for Travelling people

4.3   It must be ensured that the views of Travellers and their families are sought and incorporated at all stages of this reform process. The question of how Travellers' views are to be sought should be tackled throughout the process. Community development work may be a way forward in this regard.

4.4   The right to travel and to stop should be available to all Gypsies and Travellers, regardless of ethnic origin, time spent travelling and related issues.

4.5   The Race Relations Act is currently under its 3rd Review by the CRE and by a 28-member panel set up by the Home Office Minister in 1998 (none of whom are Travelling people).[62] It is recommended that, in future, any such initiative involving ethnicity must have Gypsy and Traveller participation.

The need for data

4.6   Those authorities who experience 'no' unofficial encampments may do so due to police harassment and media coverage; this aspect should be the subject of further research.

4.7   There should be a statutory duty to record and report all evictions by local authorities and the police, although clearly this proposal raises issues of enforcement, and concerns that Travellers would thereby be made to feel different from settled people (however, stop and search powers are recorded and monitored, and highlight discriminatory practice). Records should be carefully drafted in order that personal information regarding Travelling people cannot be used for purpose other than such monitoring.

4.8   Proper analysis of the true costs of eviction versus public site and other provision (possibly following the models used by the Audit Commission) should be undertaken.[63]

4.9   Local authority eviction policies should be collated by the DETR and examples of best practice highlighted.

4.10   It is generally accepted that the biannual counts in England are inaccurate; the Welsh Office no longer collates the Welsh counts and Scottish practice is inadequate. A good system of statistics or assessment regarding Traveller numbers (including birth rate, household formation and needs) must be created, in order that ten-year projections regarding affordable accommodation requirements can be undertaken for Travellers as it is for the housed population.

Informing opinions

4.11   Local authorities should consider involving and educating the local media, i.e. by taking them to proposed sites, to work towards an improvement in the tone of media coverage of provision for Travellers, and therefore in managing local

---

62 A submission has been made to the panel by the Traveller Law Research Unit of the Cardiff Law School on behalf and at the request of the traveller working groups, which can be found at Appendix 5.

63 See the Travellers' Times newsletter of the Traveller Law Research Unit issue 4 pp. 4 and 5 regarding the TLRU preliminary research into eviction costs.

opposition. Speaking personally to those in opposition locally and going over issues with them can also contribute to best practice.

4.12 A dialogue with police is essential if eviction is to be the last resort. More contacts within the force are needed if they are to be included in this movement toward reform, and if reforms are to be effective. Concrete data on the policing of Travellers, including eviction, is desirable.

4.13 Community development approaches, including a partnership and mediation role, have been proven to work and should be incorporated into local authority best practice.

4.14 Some means of educating the settled population as to the culture and needs of Travellers must be found, or local opposition might make reforms, no matter how practicable on paper, unworkable in practice.

4.15 Proper language should be encouraged at all times, i.e. the capitalisation of Gypsies and Travellers, and disallowing the use of words like 'itinerants' and 'tinkers'.

Fair evictions

4.16 A minimum period of 72 hours could be created before which eviction of an unofficial encampment is not permitted, to allow for needs audits and inter-agency co-operation. However, this limit should not be treated as a maximum.

4.17 Temporary stopping places on public land should be provided with a skip or other method of refuse disposal, not as an incentive to stay but as a helpful step to both Travellers and landowners.

The criminal justice system and Travelling people

4.18 The Prison Service should consider expanding the development of Traveller Liaison Officers such as the post created in Cardiff to other areas, and conduct research into the effects of imprisonment in bricks-and-mortar structures on prisoners who are Travelling people.

Legislation

4.19 A review should be undertaken of obsolete legislation which is still directed and inappropriately against Travelling people from time to time, for example the Fraudulent Mediums Act, the Pedlars Act, the Vagrancy Act, and bylaws relating specifically to Gypsies which are no longer legal but which are still used in some local authority areas[64] This would be in keeping with the state's obligation under the UN Convention on the Elimination of All Forms of Discrimination (see Appendix 6).

---

64 See Clements, Luke and Morris, Rachel. Fraudulent and Incompetent Mediums, *New Law Journal*, Vol. 146 No. 6766, Friday 1 November 1996. pp.1574-6 and *Travellers' Times* issue 4, the Traveller Law Research Unit of Cardiff Law School, November 1997. p.6. The Trespass (Scotland) Act 1865 is often used to prosecute Travellers there.

4.20 Part V of the Criminal Justice and Public Order Act 1994 is discriminatory, in that it removes the duty to ensure accommodation for Travelling people, thereby implying that Travelling people are not equal to settled people. It also associates Travelling people with criminal justice and public order, which is offensive in its confirmation of a negative, prejudicial, offensive and widespread stereotype about Travelling people, and only serves to exacerbate poor community relations. It is not expected that the legislation will be repealed, but some recognition by the Government about the divisive message sent to the settled population about Travelling people is essential if progress is to be made towards equality and improved community relations.

5

Planning

The planning law reform working group

The Report of the 1997 Conference on Traveller Law Reform recorded the unanimous view of delegates that the planning system, as it presently operates in England and Wales, discriminates unfairly against Travellers (Clements and Smith, 1997:5). It also noted however that this inequality of treatment is not unique to Travellers; low-impact housing development also appears to be the subject of unreasonable control (when, for instance, contrasted with the way in which the planning regime is applied to farmers).[65]

The principle of 'valuing diversity' requires that Development Plans cater for a range of accommodation; from 'high tech' sites with full facilities to low impact temporary sites. Policies would therefore need to be site appropriate; thus, for instance, in some cases, policies would permit sites with working areas, i.e. industrial, reclamation, horticultural, etc., whereas in some cases they would not.

It is recognised that many Travelling people would like to purchase their own sites as the Government recommends, but that many of those who can afford it find the planning and other obstacles insurmountable. "This is much better than being on the site. We feel independent and there are no restrictions. Most Gypsies would like to do this but they do not have the money and cannot get a mortgage. Even if they had the money, it's impossible to get anyone to sell land to a Gypsy. A non-Gypsy ought to pretend to be a Gypsy to see what a hopeless task it is."[66]

The legal starting point for any development of land in England and Wales is the Town and Country Planning Act 1990 section 54A; this requires that all development should be in accordance with the relevant Development Plan except in special situations relating to agriculture and forestry. As has been noted on many occasions, this requirement operates at a fundamental level against Travellers.[67] Very few rural

---

65 See for general discussion on this issue Elson, Martin. *Green Belts and Affordable Housing*, Joseph Rowntree Foundation and The Policy Press, 1996; and see Fairlie, Simon. *Low Impact Development*, Jon Carpenter publishing, Charlbury, Oxfordshire, 1996

66 A Gypsy, quoted in Thomas, P.A. and Campbell, S. Housing Gypsies, Cardiff Law School, 1995. p.v

67 See for instance the comments of Planning Consultant Michael Cox noted at page 8 of the 1997

restraint policies include Gypsy sites as an exception to the presumption against development. It is only when Gypsies have exceptional circumstances sufficient to warrant a material consideration for the purposes of an application for planning permission that they may succeed in obtaining a residential permission.

Research has ascertained[68] that nearly two-thirds of authorities do not have a Gypsy policy in their Local Plans. Those that have such a policy may be employing criteria-based policies in a restrictive way, and/or probably have not cross-referenced them to the countryside policies of the plan which are likely to prove impossibly restrictive. The Government has accepted that Circular 1/94 has not, as yet and in itself, been sufficient in encouraging local planning authorities to fulfil the stated central aim of achieving adequate sites by dint of private provision. In May 1998 the DETR sent a letter to all Chief Planning Officers, local planning authorities and the Local Government Association in England. In this, they drew attention to the research carried out on their behalf by ACERT (see footnote 68) which suggested that many authorities had not paid sufficient attention to Circular 1/94. This is evidenced by the fact that they have not included a site policy in their development plans, or have done so but are using criteria-based policies in a restrictive manner to justify refusals of planning permission for new sites.

The DETR made some helpful suggestions to planning authorities including:

*   a reminder that local authorities have statutory duties to Travelling people under homelessness and other legislation;
*   therefore, at an early stage in the preparation of structure, local and unitary development plans, local planning authorities 'should discuss Gypsies'[69] accommodation needs with the Gypsies themselves, their representative bodies and local support groups;
*   Structure plans and Part I of unitary development plans should set out broad strategic policies, and provide a general framework for site provision;
*   Local plans and Part II of unitary development plans should provide detailed policies;
*   compliance with the guidance in Circular 1/94 is essential to fulfilling the Government's objective that Gypsies should seek to provide their own accommodation, 'applying for planning permission like everyone else';
*   planning authorities should be aware that the absence of adequate site provision might prejudice successful enforcement action against unofficial encampments or give grounds for appeal against refusal of planning permission for a new site.

The 1997 Conference report recorded the 'overwhelming view' of the delegates that Circular 1/94 be significantly strengthened to incorporate the pre-1994 guidance (Clements and Smith, 1997:p.7). Developing this basic premise and with the (above quoted) recent governmental statements in mind, members of the Planning Working Group produced papers which identified the necessary ingredients of a reformed planning guidance system.

Michael Cox, Sarah Cox and Alan Masters prepared a background document setting out the contextual framework for reform in this area and Philip Brown and Diana

---

69 The DETR also issued an internal memo at around that time suggesting that all departmental staff should spell 'Gypsy' using the appropriate capitalisation.

Allen prepared an alternative Circular which was then the subject of discussion by the Working Group. A submission by Rodney Stableford focuses upon the strategic importance of the development planning process and how it can be modified to resolve the chronic shortage of Gypsy sites with planning approval. Stephen Field provided a paper highlighting the importance of strengthening the non-discrimination provisions of the Race Relations legislation as it relates to planning. Malcolm Bell outlines how recommendations 5.12 and 5.14 below regarding amendment of the General Permitted Development Order might be drafted. The organisation The Land Is Ours (TLIO) have produced a document for general publication entitled *Defining Rural Sustainability*,[70] which includes fifteen criteria for sustainable developments in the countryside, along with three model policies for Local Plans. The criteria and the other papers listed above can be found in Part 2 Chapter 11.

Reform proposals for planning in England and Wales

An overseeing body

5.1   Consideration should be given to the establishment of an independent body, with a remit to oversee and advise on planning applications; the body to comprise a representative of the DETR, Travelling people and their organisations, and independent planners.

Criteria-based policies

5.2   The abuse of criteria-based policies to procure predetermined refusal of permission must be tackled. Current guidance allows much room for subjectivity; Inspectors who are disinclined to allow Traveller-related developments can read whatever they wish into Circular 1/94 and their local policy.[71] Model criteria and guidance on how they should be interpreted fairly should be imposed on local authorities in addition to much clearer guidance in general.

5.3   It would take at least three years to revise many of the flawed policies, so interim measures may be required of local authorities.

5.4   Where criteria requirements are measurable, i.e. 'reasonable proximity' to services, the standards already used in other areas of regulation should be employed where appropriate. For example, Local Education Authorities expect children to travel up to five miles to attend school, so being five miles from services might therefore also be considered reasonable.

5.5   Locational based policies combined with criteria based policies are needed to enable target site provision to be reached within the planned period. Criteria based policies on their own would relate to the development of relatively small Gypsy sites for one or more families which may not have been included within the target provision set at national, regional or local level. This situation also occurs in the development of smaller housing sites that do not feature as site

---

70 The full TLIO document can be ordered from TLIO's new planning campaign group, Chapter 7, at 20 St Michael's Road, Yeovil, Somerset, BA21 cost £5 waged, £3 unwaged; or download it from the internet at http:///www.oneworld.org/tlio/research/defining.html

71 Subject to Rexworthy, see *Travellers' Times* Issue 5.

specific locations in the Local Plan and are seen as windfall sites where they are judged only on criteria based policies.

5.6   Model criteria based policies need to be drafted to cover urban, rural and Green Belt areas.

Appeals

5.7   Appeal decisions often fail to take into account personal circumstances. Human rights and personal circumstances need to be firmly established as important ingredients within the criteria used by the Inspectorate and where applicable weigh heavily in favour of allowing appeals. Government must reinforce this in circulars and planning policy guidance notes as well as a brief to the Inspectorate on the importance of the need to take into account personal circumstances.

Policy relationships

5.8   The relationship/hierarchy between conflicting policies, i.e. Local Plans, Countryside Policies, Circular guidance and Planning Policy Guidance notes (PPGs), needs to be made explicit. This might encompass the Circular 1/57 approach whereby it would be recognised that Gypsy and Traveller sites are an appropriate countryside development. An amended Circular must take precedence over inconsistent PPGs and Plans.

Green Belt

5.9   It is recognised that there may need to be a distinction between Green Belt and non-Green Belt land, the former needing a balancing approach. At the same time, there needs to be a move away from Travellers having to present themselves as vulnerable cases in order for their needs to be taken seriously, in circumstances in which non-Travellers would not have to make such representations.

Parity with housing

5.10   Gypsy and Traveller site provision needs to be incorporated, in the same way as housing, within the same planning framework with overall site provision targets in terms of double pitches at national and regional level and the provision levels reflected in the Unitary, Structure and Local Plans. New or expanding Gypsy sites would be identified in site specific terms in Local Plans in the same way that sites for new housing are also identified to allow for monitoring and review. Vacancy rates need to be incorporated into the calculation of need in order to prevent clogging-up of sites and the inevitable loss of mobility between sites.

5.11   Derelict land should not be considered as acceptable as a Gypsy site unless it is uncontaminated, free from pollution and would be acceptable as a housing site for dwellings. Derelict land is often unfortunately seen as a site of Gypsy caravans, but can prove uneconomic to develop because of the cost of decontaminating the site. Derelict sites should be seen as hazardous to the health of those who have to live there.

Land and legislation

5.12 Amending the Commons Registration Act and General Permitted Development Order (GPDO) might allow the use of some traditional stopping places and transit sites. These places could be available to all who need them, i.e. Caravan Clubbers, as 'holiday' type sites should be. Clearly site licensing legislation would have to be amended so that private agreements with farmers could be facilitated.

5.13 Set-aside farmland might be considered as possible temporary stopping places and developed as transit sites where strategically appropriate.

5.14 GPDOs should allow Gypsy sites to accommodate visiting Gypsy families and relatives to stop for a limited period as guests of residents.

Addressing discrimination

5.15 Some mechanism is needed that acknowledges and somehow deals with the way that opposition and prejudice on the part of the general public can subvert all other influences on the planning system, including central government guidance.[72]

5.16 Local authorities also need to assess local need in drafting plans, as they must for housing. The approach might then become, not "How can we prevent this development?" but "How do we meet these needs?", which approach would be more in keeping with the Governmental direction to Gypsies to meet their own accommodation needs.

5.17 Section 19A of the Race Relations Act 1976 regarding non-discrimination in planning is insufficient on its own without other reform of the Act.

The need for data

5.18 Statistical analysis by government of planning applications, permissions and appeals by Travelling people is essential if it is to assert that private provision should take the place of public in the longer term. Links and patterns could be found between such data and certain criteria. It would also highlight how small the 'problem' actually is, thereby defusing the 'floodgates' arguments used to counter broad definitions of 'Traveller'.

5.19 Geographical Information Systems should be used to identify what parts of the country are Green Belt. Some areas are nothing but, which assures no-go areas and is surely discriminatory in light of the Circular 1/94 presumption against Green Belt development.

---

72 See Rachel Morris, Gypsies and the Planning System, *Journal of Planning and Environmental Law*, July 1998. pp.635–43

6

Health and Social Services

The health and social services traveller working groups

The Law Reform Working Group which considered Health and Social Services (together with education) issues, commenced with a review of the proposals formulated in the 1997 conference Report and then convened several specialised sub-groups, which reviewed specialist areas. The co-ordinators of each sub-group (or a representative) collected and collated information on these particular themes:

1. The provision of services to temporary sites.
2. Equity in healthcare provision.
3. The role of social services and interagency working.[73]

The 1997 Conference Report concluded that Travelling people have significantly impaired access to health and social care. It noted that the centralisation of NHS provision over the last decades has reduced the health choices available for many people, not only Travellers, and that the principle of valuing cultural diversity required that services should be adapted to meet individual need where possible; rather than individual need being adapted to meet the convenience of the service providers. The National Association of Health Workers with Travellers (NAHWT) advised the Conference that in its opinion Gypsies and Travellers continued to experience difficulties in gaining and maintaining access to primary healthcare services,[74] and obtaining referral to secondary healthcare.

The 1997 Report referred to the research which has clearly demonstrated that the health of Travelling people is amongst the poorest among ethnic minority groups, with higher incidence of stillbirth and neonatal death, and higher incidence of accidents from the appalling conditions in which many are forced to live. Research by Pahl and Vale[75] has found that almost twice as many low birth-weight babies (less

---

73 The co-ordinators of the sub-groups being: (1) Debbie Harvey, the Children's Society; (2) Jim Spiller, Researcher, with Heather Spiller, Anglia Gypsy Traveller Health Information Project, Norfolk and (3) Sarah Cemlyn, Bristol University and Ian Holding, Bristol City Council.

74 NAHWT considered that access to GP and other primary care services was seen as a particular difficulty, with the majority of GPs being reluctant or refusing to take on Gypsies and Travellers as patients.

75 Pahl, J. and Vaile, M. *Health and Health Care among Travellers*, University of Kent, 1986

than 2500gms) were born to Traveller mothers (12.8%) than the national average (6.9%).

The 1997 Conference specifically recommended that the Government should:

* require Health Authorities to enforce GPs to register Gypsies and Travellers residing within their practice boundaries either as permanent or temporary residents;
* ensure that Travelling people were offered an equitable and appropriate primary healthcare service, with referral to secondary services where necessary;
* oblige Health Authorities to consider how the needs of Travellers are met and ensure that appropriate funding is available for the appointment of specialist outreach health visitors with responsibility to assess the healthcare needs of Travellers, working on a non-GP attached basis. The aims and objectives of such outreach work should be interagency and working directly with the Traveller Community to improve and maintain access to mainstream healthcare services;
* (as part of Agenda 21 and Healthy Alliance) advocate at central and local government level, the need for improvement of health and the social conditions in which people live. For Travelling people this should be a continuing programme of site provision, both temporary and permanent, with access to clean water supplies and rubbish and sewage disposal; and
* that Health Authority Care Plans and Social Services Community Care Plans should contain a detailed statement of the provision of services for Gypsies and Travellers, and other ethnic minority groups, and this should be the basis of enforcement.

The 1997 report drew attention to the discrimination that also existed against Gypsies and Travellers in relation to the delivery of community care services, and instanced the effective unavailability of home repairs grants for Gypsy and Traveller (but not non-Traveller) mobile homes.[77] As a direct result of the conference report and further research by the Traveller Law Reform Unit at Cardiff[78] this discriminatory provision has now been removed.[79]

A cause of major concern in this area has been the condition (and location) of Traveller sites, both official and unofficial, and in particular the issue of access to water. All too often the environmental health department has alleged that provision of water was the responsibility of the social services department; who in turn suggested that it was the responsibility of the other.[80] The working group expressed continuing and serious concern about this problem. Debbie Harvey, Traveller Support Worker with the Children's Society, has provided a detailed paper on the inadequate provision of services to sites (including fresh water). Jim Spiller of the Anglia Gypsy Traveller Health Information Project produced a scoping paper covering the major issues

76 See Chapter 2, *Community Care in the Next Decade and Beyond, policy guidance*, HMSO, London, 1990

77 See Morris, Rachel. Repair grants: caravans and houseboats, Legal Action, August 1997. p.22

78 See Morris, Rachel. Travellers: Repair grants and press regulation, *Legal Action*, February 1999. p.23

79 The Home Repair Assistance (Extension) Regulations 1998 SI No. 2998 came into force 1 January 1999.

80 The Chartered Institute of Environmental Health (CIEH). *Travellers and Gypsies: An Alternative Strategy*, London, 1995. CIEH believe that environmental conditions resulting from the existing legal regime result in health risks to Travellers and other members of the public.

which emerged in the discussions; in producing this paper he drew upon material and case examples submitted by members of the group, including a case example provided by Penny Ballinger, a specialist Health Visitor for Travellers in Herefordshire. All of these submissions can be found in Part 2 Chapter 12.

There was unanimous agreement that the Criminal Justice and Public Order Act 1994 has had a deleterious effect the health of Travelling people, damaging access to healthcare, safe and sanitary environmental health, and causing stress resulting from the infringement of the rights of families and children. The major recommendations arising out of the scoping paper are those at 6.1–14 below. Recommendations 6.15–27 were proposed by Patrice van Cleemput, Specialist Health Visitor for Travellers in Sheffield.

Sarah Cemlyn of the School for Policy Studies at the University of Bristol, who co-ordinated the working group that specifically considered the role of social services, drew on her expertise as a researcher in this field. In 1998, funded by the Nuffield Foundation, she undertook research into *Policy and Provision by Social Services for Traveller Children and Families*. The study aimed to "investigate the policies and services of social services departments towards Traveller children and families, given that this was an under-researched and under-developed area, and to explore the impact of the Criminal Justice and Public Order Act 1994, the management of competing powers and duties, inter-departmental co-ordination, and consultation with Travellers."[81]

In brief, the study's main conclusions were that "Travellers do not necessarily need greater provision of social services and, in fact, other research suggests that Travellers may have less need of such services than the settled population. They are more likely to come into contact, regardless of need, due to the combined effects of the Criminal Justice and Public Order Act 1994 and ensuing case law requiring increasing intera-gency participation in eviction processes. With this in mind it is especially pertinent to note how few Social Services Departments (SSDs) have developed specific policies and practices for working with Travellers. SSDs have an important role to play in vali-dating the culture and ethnic status of Gypsies and Travellers and in ensuring that such services as are needed and provided are culturally appropriate. The relationship between Travellers and SSDs is not improved by the fact that encounters will often only occur when a situation – either within a family or due to external difficulties such as the lack of a legal stopping place – reaches crisis point. Without an awareness and understanding of Gypsy and Traveller culture, social services interaction with such families runs a grave risk of further isolating and pathologising them, rather than assisting them to strengthen their community connections."[82]

Some of the recommendations arising from the study highlight examples of best policy and practice which have been developed and achieved in working practices in relation to and with other user groups, and which can usefully be adopted with regard to Gypsies and Travellers.[83] The recommendations emerging from Sarah Cemlyn's research were put to the 1999 conference and a further meeting was arranged to

---

81 Summary of Research Report, p.1
82 Report on Research Study, p.89
83 From pp.16-20 of Summary of Report and pp.99-103 of Report on Research Study.

discuss them; the resulting proposals on which consensus was reached appear at 6.28-6.44 below.[84]

An essential element of work with Travelling people for social services and other agencies is multi-agency or inter-agency working (IA). Without it, staff can become isolated, lacking support or access to new knowledge; can inadvertently plug holes left by lack of other provision when already under-resourced and over-stretched; any work with other bodies can be informal, passive and reactionary; and, most importantly, Travelling people can find services fragmented, inaccessible, and unresponsive. Sarah Cemlyn and Rachel Morris have submitted a piece on IA which can be found in Part 2 Chapter 12.

The health of travellers in Scotland [85]

In Scotland information about the health status of Travellers and their views on access to, and the provision of, health services is severely limited. Save the Children's views are based on regular contact with Traveller families across Scotland, a range of health professionals – in particular, Health Visitors – and a cross-section of young Travellers who have participated in our health education programmes in rural and urban areas. We also draw on our own research *The Right to Roam*[86] which goes beyond the anecdotal experience to quantify Travellers' experiences of family health services and details how the external environment impinges on the Traveller way of life. In Save the Children's view, it is essential to include the wider physical and social environment in any consideration of overall health.

This overview concurs with the Scottish Office definition of the Government's approach at 3 levels: Life Circumstances, Lifestyle topics and Health topics, recognising that the circumstances in which people live bear heavily on people's health and contribute much to health inequalities.[87] The Secretary of State's Advisory Committee on Scotland's Travelling People (hereinafter the Advisory Committee) is in the process of reviewing health issues in relation to personal and family matters and access to the N.H.S.

The Right to Roam study in 1995–6 included a percentage of the Traveller population who were, at that time, residing in houses. For an accurate profile of Traveller health to be achieved we consider this sub-group must be included in any survey and assessment of needs. This perspective is shared in other major health studies referred to elsewhere in this chapter and in Part 2 Chapter 12. In Scotland there has been little attempt to research the health needs of Travellers, despite the Advisory Committee's suggestion that such work was needed in their Third Term Report (1982). In 1998 the Committee's Eighth Term Report also identified 'health' as an area to be addressed and a sub-group was been set up. It is disappointing to note that no attempt has been

---

84 Thanks to Margaret Thompson, Assistant Programme Director (Midlands), Save the Children, for helping to arrange this meeting.

85 The information in this section has been provided by the Traveller Section of the Save the Children Fund (Scotland).

86 Save the Children Fund. Dunfermline, 1996. Chapters 5 and 6 detail survey data on a range of environmental and health issues and concerns; seventy women (aged under thirty five) and twenty eight 'under 18s' were interviewed and their views recorded.

87 The Scottish Office. *Working Together for a Healthier Scotland*, 1996

made to bring together Travellers and Health staff, from different areas of Scotland, who have knowledge and expertise to share.[88]

Reform proposals for health

Role of specialist health visitors

6.1 Designated health visitors have an important linking role but need more resources.

Recording and monitoring

6.2 Nation-wide patient-held medical records are potentially very useful and their introduction should be explored.

6.3 Ethnic monitoring (including principles of self-classification), must be implemented.

Inter-agency work

6.4 Inter-agency service planning should be improved and inter-agency service meetings must have Traveller input.

6.5 Traveller-service providers need to involve themselves in non-Traveller-specific forums where the issues are nonetheless relevant.

6.6 There must be a duty to inform service providers of new sites in order that they can meet their statutory duties.

Policy and promotion

6.7 Many problems can be created by inappropriate health promotions and policies; their impact from the Traveller perspective should be explored before implementation.

6.8 There is a need for health impact statements in all Traveller policies.

6.9 Provision for Traveller needs must be built in to the system as their geographic dispersal and other issues mean that they have no political or other clout with which to ensure provision (in common with some other societal groups).

Equity in healthcare provision

6.10 Traveller awareness training should be introduced for practitioners.

6.11 Recent Government research and guidance on health,[89] while offering improved recognition of Black and Asian health needs and access problems, does not include Travelling people either directly or indirectly. The first reform must be a

---

88 Meeting between SCF and the Advisory Committee, 3 March 1999.

89 For example, Health Service Circular 1998/129: *Assessing health needs of people from minority ethnic groups*, and the eponymous book to which it refers edited by Rawaf, Salman and Bahl, Veena. Royal College of Physicians and Faculty of Public Health Medicine, London, 1998. Similar examples can be found issuing from the Welsh Office.

raising of awareness of the needs, problems, strengths and situation of Travelling people among healthcare professionals. The provision of good and appropriate services to a social group cannot be facilitated so long as that group remains invisible except when it presents a 'problem'.

6.12 It must be formally recognised that poor site sanitation creates health issues.

6.13 Ways must be found to encourage and ensure provision by recalcitrant GPs.[90]

6.14 There must be more consultation with Travellers regarding sites, play areas, etc., including on health and safety issues.

Proposals by Patrice van Cleemput, Specialist Health Visitor for Travellers, Sheffield

6.15 Introduce ethnic monitoring of Travellers, allowing self-classification, following consultation with Travellers and agencies working with Travellers.

6.16 Set up a Task Force to address the complex interwoven factors leading to poor health and welfare of Travellers, and within this remit fund national research into health status.

6.17 Direct each Health Authority Provider to include objectives for reducing inequalities of health of Travellers in their annual business plans.

6.18 Have a named Health worker responsible for Travellers who works on a geographical basis rather than by GP attachment.

6.19 Place an obligation on local and health authorities to hold regular inter agency meetings of all service providers to address the needs of Travellers.

6.20 Centrally fund production and launch of Traveller hand-held health record and oblige each Health Authority to ensure these are both distributed and used by service providers.

6.21 Place responsibility on each Health Authority to create structures and policies to encourage GPs to accept Travellers for temporary or permanent registration.

6.22 Consider separate means of including Travellers in targets for immunisations, smears, etc. and give responsibility for these targets to the Health Authority via the named health worker.

6.23 Establish a means for centrally recording smear results and immunisations and ensure that Travellers can access this information themselves.

6.24 Ensure that cultural awareness training with specific reference to Gypsies and Travellers is mandatory for all Health Service and Local Authority personnel involved in policy making and in service provision at all levels and grades.

6.25 Ensure that policy makers in central and local government produce health impact statements regarding any policies concerning Travellers (including site provision).

6.26 Produce a minimum standard and an obligation upon local authorities to formally consult Travellers regarding design of local authority-provided sites.

6.27 Provision of water, refuse disposal and sanitation to unofficial sites should be a statutory responsibility.

90 Especially important as Primary Care Groups will generally be GP-dominated.

Reform proposals for social services

6.28 Social services should recognise the right to secure accommodation as a fundamental basis to family life, well-being and welfare. Links need to be made with the forthcoming human rights legislation.

6.29 Gypsies and Travellers must be included in the development of all policies, both corporate and departmental.[91]

6.30 Gypsies and Travellers must be included in all departmental, local authority and inter-agency plans (e.g. Children's Services Plans, Early Years Development Plans, Community Care Plans) to promote their right to secure accommodation and equal access to services.

6.31 Gypsies and Travellers must have a voice in policy development, and this requires supportive facilitation through various means including liaison with democratic Gypsy and Traveller organisations, representation in committees, working parties and other fora, outreach and community development approaches, and inter-agency partnerships.

6.32 All social services departments should ensure that training on anti-racist practice and cultural awareness includes issues affecting Gypsies and Travellers, and this should underpin all work with Gypsies and Travellers. Where possible Gypsies and Travellers should themselves be involved in delivering this training. Inter-agency partnerships are a crucial mechanism for developing and delivering such training.

6.33 Departments should ensure that information about their services is available and accessible to Gypsies and Travellers. This may require alternative forms of communication than the written word such as tapes and videos, as well as inter-agency liaison and outreach.

6.34 Outreach and community development models, especially those which involve partnerships, have proved to be effective approaches to work with Gypsies and Travellers.

6.35 Mentor and mediation roles from within Gypsy and Traveller communities are extremely effective and should be promoted and supported.

6.36 There should be a duty on the environmental health department of local authorities to provide basic services – including water, w.c. and refuse disposal – to unauthorised sites.[92] Until this is implemented, section 17 of the Children Act 1989 should be used to provide such services. In addition, social services support should be offered to Gypsies and Travellers in dealing with the practical problems they encounter, including lack of sites and dangerous conditions and inadequate facilities on unofficial sites.

6.37 Social services departments with Gypsy and Traveller communities in their area should establish a specialist post or posts, both to provide an improved service, and to assist the development of departmental policy and practice (following best practice in specialist and health services). This is likely to be particularly

91 See the McPherson Report paras.6.34 and 6.54

92 Some members of the platform were not sure that this role should be given to environmental health, due to its connection in the public mind with pest and waste control.

applicable where Travelling people experience enforced mobility, do not have a settled history in the area, or are particularly isolated from the general population.

6.38 Social services referral systems should be adapted to meet the needs, traditions and culture of Gypsies and Travellers. In practical terms such adaptations would include appropriate prioritisation, speed of response and continuity of service.

6.39 Inter-agency work relating to Gypsies and Travellers should be accorded a high priority by social services departments, to include active participation in inter-agency fora, flexibility about hierarchical, administrative and geographical boundaries, and clear links with strategic decision-making. This would build on the Government's own aims as outlined in the White Paper Modernising Social Services, in particular the section on Improving Partnerships.

6.40 Where social services become involved in assessments in relation to unauthorised encampments or planning enforcement, they should take full account of Gypsy and Traveller families' rights to security and equal access to services. Past, current and future needs should be fully considered. The impact of trauma, loss and stress resulting from harassment, evictions, violence, racism and accidents on Traveller children and families should be given full consideration in any assessment of and services for Traveller families. The Home Office/DETR Good Practice Guide on Managing Unauthorised Camping also states that "Local authorities should consider taking positive steps to improve the health and well-being of families with young children".[93]

6.41 Social services should actively facilitate the access of Travelling people to other rights and services, including welfare benefits, from which mobile families in particular are often effectively excluded.

6.42 The vital work of voluntary agencies with Gypsy and Traveller communities, and in supporting the work of social services, should be given greatly increased recognition, and wherever possible enhanced financial support, by social services departments and committees.

6.43 Specific areas where social services should develop their policy and provision for Travelling people, in partnership with other agencies, include early years services, family support, juvenile justice, foster care services, support for women and children experiencing domestic violence, community care services for elders and disabled Travellers, and support for carers.

6.44 Practice principles to be considered in direct work with Traveller children and families include the following:

- engage with Gypsy and Traveller cultures;
- build trust and familiarity in informal situations;
- accord appropriate priority to the problems of Gypsies and Travellers;
- provide clear, accessible information about services;
- understand the significance and facilitate the involvement as appropriate of wider family and community relationships.

93 Para. 3.20

"For young, single homeless people travelling is a chance to obtain viable accommodation without a great deal of capital, given that they receive so little assistance in obtaining housing. Furthermore, acceptance of, and care for, those new to travelling was evident on many sites. This care included teaching practical skills like, for example, how to make a shelter, how to make a fire and the importance of burying human waste. The level of care, particularly for young homeless people and other vulnerable people, led one established new age traveller to describe some sites as constituting an 'alternative social services'."[94]

94 Davis, Jim, Grant, Rachel and Locke, Alison. Out of Site, Out of Mind, The Children's Society, London, 1994. p.4

Part II Voices for reform

7

Over-arching issues

The case for change? *Michelle Lloyd and Richard Morran*

Introduction

A ny process of legal reform is slow, but the momentum for changes to the law affecting Gypsies and Travellers grew from the introduction of the Criminal Justice and Public Order Act 1994. Many agencies collaborated during the Parliamentary progress of this Bill to press for removal of certain clauses which would directly affect Gypsies and Travellers. Unfortunately, the government chose to ignore the lobbying.

Since 1994, there have been significant developments in relation to Travellers and ethnic minorities which have reoriented the basis for reform. These were the enactment of the Race Relations (N.I.) Order 1997, the Commission for Racial Equality's proposals for reform of the Race Relations Act 1976, the introduction of racially aggravated offences in the Crime and Disorder Act 1998, and, most recently, the publication of the Lawrence Inquiry Report.

These developments signal a growing understanding that racism, particularly institutional racism, is endemic in British society and further legislation or the reform of present statutes is required. Despite this realisation it is our view that Gypsies and Travellers are not perceived as the subjects of racial harassment and discrimination because racism is only considered in terms of colour. Our research in *Failing the Test* (1997) clearly illustrated the extensive levels of overt discrimination faced by Travellers in trying to access accommodation.

Criminal Justice and Public Order Act 1994

The draconian nature of the legislation united a broad church of interested bodies in lobbying against the particular sections affecting Travellers. The government, however, chose to ignore the representations and ensured that the clauses directed at assembly; the lowering of the number of caravans and other vehicles needed to trigger an eviction; the removal of duty on local authority to provide sites (in England and Wales); the associated 100 per cent central government capital grant for such provision; and the power to impound vehicles and caravans and charge owners for their storage, were all passed.

The concerted opposition resulted in monitoring of the Act's usage and, where appropriate, challenge in the Courts. The controversy engendered during the Bill's Parliamentary stages made the Police and Prosecuting authorities wary of using the appropriate sections. The judgement of Sedley J. in R v Lincolnshire County Council in 1995 partly resulted in the publication of the DETR Good Practice Guide which makes it clear that "Local authorities must consider welfare issues when deciding whether to proceed with eviction whatever the powers being used..."[96]

Non-statutory agencies have closely monitored the Circulars and Government Codes of Guidance introduced at the commencement of the Act. In the four years since the enactment of the legislation various agencies have continued to observe the authorities' use of the particular sections of the Act, including TLRU, Friends and Families of Travellers, the Children's Society, Save the Children (Scotland), and Gypsy and Traveller organisations. A number of agencies have also researched the effects of the Act – in Scotland, SCF are currently carrying out research with Dundee University which looks at the social and legal effects of being 'moved on', in particular examining use of the CJPOA. In England and Wales the Traveller Law Research Unit (TLRU) have conducted research into the after-effects of the Act.

Context

The conference in Cardiff in March 1997 organised by TLRU 'formalised' the lobby and the sub-groups have met to discuss and clarify proposals which could be incorporated in an agenda for change and possibly presented in the form of a Private Members Bill. In the intervening period four developments, in relation to ethnic minorities and Travellers, have helped to progress the debate.

The first of these changes was the passing of the Race Relations (Northern Ireland) Order 1997 which named Irish Travellers as a racial group[97] and provided a significantly more accurate definition – "the community of people commonly so called who are identified, both by themselves and others, as people with a shared history, culture and traditions including historically a nomadic way of life, on the island of Ireland" (section 5(2)a) – than the definition in the Caravan Sites Act 1968 (section 16), which uses the term "gipsies", or the interpretation used in the case of CRE v Dutton (1989).

The second development in April 1998 was the submission to the Home Office by the Commission for Racial Equality of proposals for reform of the Race Relations Act 1976. The proposals include:

* extending the obligations on public bodies not to discriminate;
* allowing the CRE to bring proceedings if a public body has failed in its racial equality duties;
* clarifying the definition of indirect discrimination with the proposal that

96 Department of the Environment, Transport and Regions and the Home Office. *Good Practice Guide to Managing Unauthorised Camping, 1998*. para.4.11

97 In the parliamentary debates the terms racial and ethnic were used interchangeably. See Molloy, S. *Accommodating Nomadism*, 1998

"Indirect discrimination occurs where an apparently neutral provision, criterion, practice or policy which is applied to persons of all racial groups cannot be as easily satisfied or complied with by persons of a particular group, or where there is a risk that the provision, criterion, practice or policy may operate to the disadvantage of a particular racial group, unless the provision, criterion, practice or policy can be justified by objective factors unrelated to race";[98]

• and introducing the possibility of a 'class action' whereby courts and tribunals would be required to consider group complaints where discrimination affects a number of people.

The third development was the introduction of the racially aggravated offences in the Crime and Disorder Act 1998. Section 33, which only applies in Scotland, introduces a new specific offence of racial harassment, and section 96 provides that where it is proved that any offence was racially aggravated, that aggravation should be taken into account when sentencing. In the Scottish Office Introductory Guide to racially aggravated offences the definition of "racial group" includes a number of sub-groups including "Ethnic origin - such as Indian or Gypsy".[99]

In Britain there is still considerable ignorance and confusion about the 'ethnic status' of Gypsies and Travellers amongst local authorities, the police and government departments. This was illustrated in Scotland by the unwillingness of the Scottish Office or the Secretary of State's Advisory Committee on Scotland's Travelling People to confront or investigate the prevalence of discrimination towards Travellers.[100] This reluctance to take action, until there is a watertight legal precedent clarifying that Gypsies and Travellers come within the definition of an ethnic group as described in the Race Relations Act 1976, highlights the institutional complacency referred to in the Lawrence Inquiry Report.[101]

With regard to racial hostility, the new provisions in the Crime and Disorder Act refer to 'presumed membership of a racial group', making it clear that "regardless of which racial group the offender believes the victim to belong to, an offence will be racially aggravated if racial hostility is proved".[102] In this way hostility directed at a person because he was a Gypsy would meet the test even if the victim defined himself as a Traveller. Therefore, in this context, the legal definition of Gypsies and Travellers is largely irrelevant since it is the perception of the offender which matters.

The fourth development in March 1999 was the publication of Sir William McPherson's *Report on the Stephen Lawrence Inquiry* which makes seventy recommendations, a number of which are particularly relevant to the Gypsy and Traveller communities in England, Wales, Scotland and Northern Ireland. At least seven are important to note:

Recommendation 1, that a Ministerial Priority be established for all Police Services; "To increase trust and confidence in policing amongst minority ethnic communities".

---

98 Commission for Racial Equality. *Summary – Reform of the Race Relations Act 1976*, London, 1998. p.3

99 The Scottish Office Circular 12/1998, *Crime and Disorder Act 1998 Introductory Guide: Racially Aggravated Offences*. para.2.2

100 Meeting between SCF, Advisory Committee and Scottish Office, 3 March 1999, Edinburgh.

101 Sir William McPherson. *The Stephen Lawrence Inquiry Report*, 1999. p.321, para. 46.27

102 The Scottish Office, Circular 12/1998, op cit, para.3.9

Recommendation 11, that the full force of the Race Relations legislation should apply to all Police officers and that Chief Officers of Police should be made vicariously liable for the acts and omissions of their officers relevant to that legislation.

Recommendation 12, definition of a racist incident: "A racist incident is any incident which is perceived to be racist by the victim or any other person".

Recommendation 13, that the term "racist incident" must be understood to include crimes and non-crimes in policing terms. Both must be reported, recorded and investigated with equal commitment.

Recommendation 61, that the Home Secretary, in consultation with Police Services, should ensure that a record is made by Police officers of all "stops" and "stops and searches" made under any legislative provision (not just the Police and Criminal Evidence Act). Non-statutory or so called 'voluntary' stops must also be recorded. The record to include the reason for the stop, the outcome, and the self defined ethnic identity of the person stopped. A copy of the record shall be given to the person stopped.

Recommendation 62, that these records should be monitored and analysed by Police Services and Police Authorities, and reviewed by HMIC on inspections. The information and analysis should be published.

Recommendation 70, that in creating strategies under the provision of the Crime and Disorder Act or otherwise Police Services, local government and relevant agencies should specifically consider implementing community and local initiatives aimed at promoting cultural diversity and addressing racism and the need for focussed, consistent support for such initiatives.

These four developments signal a growing realisation that many organisations within British and Irish society are discriminatory and their actions can be institutionally racist. The difficulty is that many individuals and agencies view racism and discrimination in terms of colour and consequently place Gypsies and Travellers outside that frame of reference. The CRE, in its evidence to Part 2 of the Lawrence Inquiry, maintained that racist crimes and incidents also affect white minorities such as Gypsies and the Irish.[103] Our experience shows that a wide range of police forces, central and local government officials, health authorities, the Crown Office, etc. view Travellers as a minority group to be 'suffered / tolerated / designated'.

In Northern Ireland and Scotland the government introduced and maintained policies of 'toleration' and 'designation' from the mid 1980s for specific numbers of Travellers in each area. The mere existence of 'toleration Policies' in the 1990s enshrines and legitimises the harassment of Travellers once the 'government quota' has been reached in a local Council area. Such government practices clearly fall within accepted definitions of 'institutional racism'; for the purpose of this article we will use the McPherson definition:

"Institutional racism has been defined as those established laws, customs, and practices which systematically reflect and produce racial inequalities in society. If racist consequences accrue to institutional laws, customs or practices, the institution is racist whether or not the individuals maintaining those practices have racial intentions".[104]

This State attitude towards Gypsies and Travellers is not unique to Britain and

103 Commission for Racial Equality. Submission to Part 2 of the Lawrence Inquiry, 1998. p.2, para.1.8
104 Sir William McPherson, op. cit. p.28, para. 6.34

Ireland but rather reflects a pattern across European countries. In her booklet *The Roma/Gypsies of Europe: a persecuted people* Brearley maintains that "[t]he problem of racist violence, racial discrimination and disadvantage experienced by minority ethnic groups across Europe has been subject to considerable attention in recent years, by policy makers and academics. But the contemporary experience of historically persecuted groups such as Roma and other Gypsy communities, has been relatively neglected."[105]

Our experience shows that despite legal judgements[106] and the policy of the CRE, the majority of central and local government officials refuse to acknowledge the position of Gypsies and Travellers as coming within the definition of an ethnic group as described in the Race Relations Act 1976. For the debate to move forward we consider there must be commitment, at a senior political level, to Gypsies and Travellers being expressly included in any amendments to Race Relations legislation to remove further avoidance of the issue.

Failing the Test

In 1997 Save the Children (SCF) instituted fieldwork in twelve local authority areas of Scotland – from the Highlands to Dumfries and Galloway. This involved visiting caravan parks to test whether they would provide space to Travellers when the park was not full. We found a consistent pattern of rejection and discrimination with 63 per cent of requests for accommodation refused – this dropped to 50 per cent where the caravan park was owned by the local authority. The reason for our research was to clarify whether the experience of our staff, Scottish Gypsy and Traveller Association members and Travellers was typical, and to 'test' whether the motivation for refusal was the ethnic origins of the applicant.

The exercise involved three field trips, all outside the peak holiday period, and our results were presented to the Scottish Office in March 1998. A number of meetings and correspondence with the Scottish Office and the Secretary of State's Advisory Committee resulted in the official view that "discrimination is deplored"[107] but, until there is a relevant court action, the case remains 'unproven'. Such official inertia, in the light of clearly researched evidence, highlights the need for legislative reform.

Recommendations

Our experience is not particular to Scotland, despite Northern Ireland and Scotland having had a government 'quango' for many years exclusively concerned with the welfare of Travellers; we perceive little difference in the level of discrimination between England and Wales and Scotland. We support Brearley's argument that "[a]ll European countries should ensure that they explicitly outlaw discrimination against Gypsies within the broader framework of 'race' discrimination legislation – according to the definitions and guiding principles of the International Convention on the

---

105 *Jewish Policy Research Paper No 3.* p.39
106 For example, Lord Fraser Mandla v Lee and others (1983) IRLR 209
107 Letter from the Secretary of State's Advisory Committee to Save the Children, dated 15 October 1998.

Elimination of All Forms of Racial Discrimination. In each country, Gypsies should be explicitly acknowledged as an ethnic group to be protected by legislative provision".[108]

In addition we would propose:

- commitment at Home Office/Scottish Office level to investigate discrimination towards Gypsies and Travellers;
- amendment to the Race Relations Act 1976 to include Gypsies and Travellers utilising the form of words in the Northern Ireland Statutory Instrument;
- the replacement of 'toleration Policies' with less discriminatory policies;
- the adoption and monitoring of the McPherson recommendations as noted above;
- adoption of the EC Burden of Proof directive, which provides for a partial shifting of the burden of proof to the respondent in sex discrimination cases, should be applied to race discrimination complaints;
- the legal aid scheme should be expanded to cover those seeking to take action in discrimination cases.

What is a Gypsy? *Dr Donald Kenrick*

Why do we need to define 'Gypsy'?

Even after Department of the Environment Circular 1/94 the fact that an applicant for planning permission is a Gypsy is a material factor and therefore it is important to define who is and who is not a 'Gypsy' in British law.

Historical introduction

I will deal only with the definition of 'Gypsy' in planning law and criminal law and will not consider the definition for the purposes of the Race Relations Act, nor that of 'Traveller' for the Education Acts.

Etymologically the word 'Gypsy' comes from 'Egyptian' and logically should therefore be spelled with a capital letter. It was the name given to the Romanies when they came to Western Europe as it was thought that they came from Egypt. In fact they came from India.

Until 1967 it was considered that the word Egyptian or Gypsy applied to a race, and indeed a foreign race. The first Act which was passed and applied in this sense was 22 Henry VIII c. 10 of 1530: Imposed a ban on the immigration of Egipcions and notice given to all Egipcions in England to leave the country. Similarly 1 and 2 Philip and Mary c. 4 of 1554: Egyptians forbidden to enter the country. Made provisions for the capital punishment of Egyptians if they remained in the country for more than one month.[109] In 1783 all existing laws concerning Gypsies were repealed. However, in 1822 the Turnpike Roads Act and, in 1835, the Highways Act, reintroduced the term 'Gypsy' into legislation.

The Highways Act 1835 penalised Gypsies who camped on the highway with a fine

---

108 Brearley, M. op.cit. p.41
109 Summaries from Mayall, David. *Gypsy Travellers in 19th Century Society*. p.189

of 40 shillings. The later Highways Act of 1959 section 127 said "If ... a Gypsy pitches a booth, stall or stand, or encamps on a highway he shall be guilty of an offence ...". For over a hundred years Gypsies who camped on the highway regularly paid up their 40 shillings until 1967, when a Mr Cooper contested a case and pleaded not guilty, saying that he was not a Gypsy, as it could not be proved that he was descended from Indian immigrants and of Romany race.[110] At this point it became necessary for the courts to decide on a definition of the term.

The Divisional Court in 1967 finally laid down that – as British law at that time could no longer be seen to be discriminating against a race – the definition of 'Gypsy' for the purposes of the Highways Act must refer to a way of life. Lord Parker said, "I think that in this context 'gipsy' means no more than a person leading a nomadic life with no, or no fixed, employment and with no fixed abode." Lord Diplock indicated that in his view 'gipsy' bore "its popular meaning, which I would define as a person without a fixed abode who leads a nomadic life dwelling in tents or other shelters or in caravans or other vehicles."

The Caravan Sites Act 1968 did not adopt this definition of 'Gypsy' but gave a wider definition, and also refers to "Gypsies residing in or resorting to an area". It seems clear that the drafter of the Caravan Sites Bill was aware that s/he was not following the earlier 1967 definition, as Lord Diplock stated in Greenwich v Powell. This case defined a council-run 'Gypsy' caravan site in reference to the position of those sites as opposed to other caravan sites. The 1968 Act and the Mobile Homes Act 1983 made a distinction between these types of sites. (In particular, residents of pitches on Gypsy sites are not tenants but licensees and so lack all of the rights of tenants). The question before the Court was whether the Greenwich Gypsy Site was a Gypsy site for the purposes of the Mobile Homes Act. Their Lordships decided that if the Council had set up a Gypsy site it did not matter whether the people residing on it were Gypsies or not, the site remained a Gypsy site for legal purposes. Contained in their judgement was an obiter (as an aside) definition of 'Gypsy'. Lord Bridge said, "I am inclined to conclude ... that a person may be within the definition if he leads a nomadic life only seasonally and notwithstanding that he regularly returns for part of the year to the same place where he may be said to have a fixed abode or residence." This means that a person can be settled for part of the year, but as long as they travel at times they are still Gypsies at law.

This was important at the time because the Caravan Sites Act 1968 made a distinction between Gypsies and non-Gypsies stopping in areas designated under the Act and also because of Circular advice from the Ministry of Housing and the Department of the Environment in which councils were encouraged to give planning permission to Gypsies.

With the emergence from 1965–70 onwards of 'New' Travellers – non-Romany house-dwellers who left their houses to travel, in caravans and buses – the question arose as to whether non-Romanies could be classed as Gypsies if they were nomadic. The key cases are *Rexworthy and Capstick*. In the case of *Rexworthy* the Council accepted that for the purpose of that case Mr Rexworthy was a Gypsy. However, the *Capstick* case was more important as it had a more general significance.

In the case of Mrs Capstick, Mr Justice Herrod heard that the "defendants had

110 Mills v Cooper [1967] 2 All ER 100, [1967] 2 QB

adopted, and intended to continue with, a travelling life-style and [travelled] basically from Yorkshire to the West Country and back during the year. None of the defendants, with one possible exception, came from families with a tradition of travelling but they had adopted such a life for various reasons e.g. force of circumstances, the absence of settled accommodation and attraction to the way of life." It was held that the applicants were Gypsies within the meaning of the Caravan Sites Act 1968 as they were, on the evidence, 'persons of nomadic habit of life'.

The definition of 'nomadic habit of life' was later refined in the case of *R v South Hams ex parte Gibb*. It was established in this case that be to be a Gypsy one had to travel for an economic purpose. The definition of 'Gypsies' in section 16 of the 1968 Act imported the requirement that there should be some recognisable connection between the wandering or travelling and the means whereby the persons concerned made or sought their livelihood.

This judgement was clouded by the statements of two of the judges that to be a Gypsy one had to travel in a group. However, Lord Justice Leggatt said that the term 'Gypsy' "was not expressly confined to those who travelled in groups and the Act did not stipulate that persons could not be Gypsies unless they did so.[111] Travelling in groups is now difficult as the Criminal Justice and Public Order Act 1994 for practical purposes dissuades Gypsies from travelling in groups; if more than six vehicles stop in one place, the police powers to evict under the Act may be triggered. Taken together, Lords Neil and Milletts' opinions that to be a Gypsy one must travel in a group, and the difficulty of doing do so following the 1994 Act, could mean that there are no longer such persons as 'Gypsies'.

Finally, the cases of *Dunn v Maidstone* and *Secretary of State v Dunn* have established the principle that the amount of money earned while travelling does not have to be more than the amount earned while not travelling. Maidstone contested the Inspectors' opinion that Mr Dunn was a Gypsy. However, the court found that Mr Dunn's "main occupation and source of income is from landscape gardening around the Maidstone area which does not normally entail other than daily travel to work. However, I note that he also breeds horses of which he currently owns eight and travels to horse fairs including Appleby, Stow-on-the-Wold and the New Forest where he buys and sells horses ... He could be away for up to two months of the year at least partly in connection with a traditional Gypsy activity which I consider ... also has an economic justification. I do not therefore conclude that taking into account the relatively short time during which he has adopted a generally more settled life-style, that the appellant has so abandoned travelling as to lose his status as a Gypsy under s. 16 of the 1968 Act."

The importance of these cases is that they mean a Gypsy family can settle during the winter and let their children go to school while travelling mainly in the Easter and summer holidays for an economic purpose and retaining Gypsy status and identity.

Questions pertaining to and arising from these cases

Do you have to be born a Gypsy to be a Gypsy?
No. It is possible for a house-dweller to obtain Gypsy status if they start nomadising.

111 *The Times* law report 8 June 1994

If you are not traditionally a Gypsy how long do you have to travel to become a Gypsy in the legal sense?

A case brought by Avon Council established the principle that 'New Travellers' had to travel for at least two years before the Council would class them as Gypsies.

If you are brought up as a Gypsy how long can you be non-nomadic without losing Gypsy status?

I would suggest five years. The first case known to me where it was ruled that an ethnic Gypsy was not a statutory Gypsy is *Horsham District Council v Secretary of State and Giles*,[112] where Mr Justice McCullough said that "Clearly there can, and indeed must, come a time when as a matter of fact the nomadic habit of life has been lost. When it is lost the Gypsy is no longer a Gypsy for the purposes of the Act." Mr Giles had lived at Billingshurst on the same site continuously since 1969 and before then in another settled place in Worthing since 1957 – a total of thirty two years, by far the majority of his life. It was argued on Mr Giles' behalf that he was a Gypsy because part of a family group, some members of which had travelled a great deal, but this was not accepted by the judge.

The judgement was reaffirmed in Cuss v Secretary of State and Wychavon District Council,[113] in which Mr Justice Vandermeer said it was "clear that the element of the nomadic habit of life had to present albeit that it might be seasonal. The Inspector had found that the predominant picture was of a relatively settled life-style and that Mr Cuss did not appear to have undertaken any regular seasonal migration or other travelling apart from occasional moves in search of a permanent pitch." However, the case note said that, although Gypsy status can be lost, "[t]he Converse is that the status can be regained again and so if the Cuss family were to take up again even just seasonal travelling the status could be regained."

Periods from two to five years have been suggested. It is also suggested that 'New' Travellers will lose their status more quickly than an ethnic Gypsy. In the 1990 case of a Mr Stacey it was ruled that he was not a Gypsy because he had a mobile home (not a touring caravan), and lived not on a Gypsy site but on a private site.

Is it possible to stop travelling but retain Gypsy status?

Yes, in certain circumstances. In the case of illness of the person or a relative, Gypsy status is retained while not travelling as long as there is an intention to resume travel at some time.[114] If a Gypsy stops travelling because of old age s/he retains the status. This was agreed by the Inspector in a planning case,[115] although permission was refused on other grounds. The question of whether a Gypsy still has that status at law when prevented from travelling due a prison sentence was discussed informally in the case of a Mr P. The Council felt that he should not benefit from being allowed to keep his Gypsy status because he had committed a crime. However, the punishment for committing the crime was a prison sentence. It would be unfair if, in addition to the sentence, the Gypsy also lost his status and the right to live on his own land. In the

---

112 QB 1989, cited in Dunn at p.586
113 1991 JPL 1033
114 *R v Shropshire County Council ex parte Bungay* (1990)
115 Re Mr Latimer

event the planning appeal was refused on another ground and no decision was taken as to whether Mr P had retained or lost his status.

If you have lost Gypsy status, how long do you have to travel to regain it?
As the note in Cuss states, if a Gypsy were "to take up again even just seasonal travelling the status could be regained." It is generally considered that a non-Gypsy needs longer to establish or re-establish Gypsy status than a Romany or other ethnic nomad.

Does applying for permission at all mean loss of Gypsy status?
Logically, applying for permission to reside on land implies the intention to give up nomadising and therefore ceasing to be a Gypsy. However, this would lead to a catch-22 situation in which an applicant could be refused permission on ground of not being a Gypsy; would be forced back onto the road; and would again become a Gypsy.[116]

Does applying for permission for a bungalow (as opposed to a caravan) mean that a person has given up Gypsy status?
No. As long as there is travelling for part of the year there seems to be no reason why living in a bungalow for the rest of the year is different from living on a fixed pitch on a caravan site.

In a study by Barbara Adams and others, they included in their study families which they found travelling in the summer although they had a house in the winter. There is an unreported case from Kensington Magistrates Court where a group of Irish Travellers stopping on unoccupied land were taken to court under the designation provisions of the Caravan Sites Act. It was claimed in their defence that they had houses in Ireland and were therefore not Gypsies to whom the Act applied. The court rejected this argument.[117] It should also be noted that the term 'caravan' includes a twin-unit mobile home which is – in spite of the name – not particularly mobile at all. It is brought onto a site in two parts on a lorry and put together on-site. It cannot be towed by a lorry and for practical purposes (as opposed to legal niceties) is the same as a chalet or bungalow. That is, it is a form of accommodation which falls between moveable (a trailer, tent, or other home which can be transported without being structurally dismantled) and unmoveable (a bricks and mortar dwelling, which must not only be dismantled but demolished in order to be moved).

The reason why Gypsies prefer a mobile home to a bungalow is partly financial (as cheaper), and partly because a mobile home is close in style to a caravan, which they are used to living in.

What happens if only one member of a family is a Gypsy?
In the case of a man who was brought up as a Gypsy and who marries a house-dweller, we may arrive at the situation whereby the husband has Gypsy status but the

116 The circular nature of such reasoning has not prevented some planning authorities from using it to justify refusal of planning permission.

117 It was later pointed out to the Department of the Environment that the Council had at one and the same time claimed to the court that these families were Gypsies but had not recorded them on their return for the Gypsy census. Irish Travellers are not protected as a distinct group under the Race Relations Act 1976 as Gypsies are, unless they experience discrimination by 'virtue' of their Irishness.

wife has not yet gained this status. If planning permission is sought for Mr X and his immediate family, then theoretically the wife would not be allowed to live on the site. Any children born during a period of settlement would not have Gypsy status and also would be unable to live on the site. This may be an argument for Inspectors to make permissions personal prior to some resolution of this apparent paradox.

How long each year does a person have to travel in order to retain Gypsy status?
The Comment in the case note for Dunn says: "This sporadic nomadic life ... does not have to be very substantial." Mr Dunn travelled for up to two months each year. In the case of the Greenwich site the occupants (at the time of the case) were allowed to leave the site for twenty weeks, paying half rent, without losing their pitch.

Does it matter what sort of economic activity is carried on?
I say no. References have been made by Inspectors and judges to 'traditional occupations'. (See Dunn, previously). However, Gypsies' occupations have changed over the years.

When Gypsies first came to Europe many were snake charmers and acrobats. In the early part of this century common occupations were door to door selling of clothes pegs and crochet work, fortune telling and, for the men, casual farm work. Times have changed and tarmaccing, roofing and garden landscaping are important new ways of earning a living. In the case of New Travellers with Gypsy status, occupations have included running a vegetarian canteen at fairs and festivals.

There seems no reason for the economic activity practised to be a traditional Gypsy trade.

Listening to children *Liz Hughes*

"We can't even get a library ticket. We can go and look at the books but we can't take them home."[118]

In the current debate around site provision the voices of children are often missed out. Yet it has been shown that issues of site provision and accommodation often affect Traveller children greatly. Research (Webster, 1995) has found that out of a group of Travellers who experienced multiple eviction from a number of sites in a short space of time only 15 per cent of the children were able to access school places. A lack of stable and secure sites led to other essential services such as healthcare being difficult to attain.

The United Nations Convention on the Rights of the Child, which has been ratified by the UK, affirms in Article 8 that "State Parties undertake to respect the right of the child to preserve his or her identity, including nationality, name and family relations as recognised by law without unlawful interference" and, in Article 30, that "in those States, in which ethnic, religious or linguistic minorities of persons of indigenous origin exist, a child belong-

---

118 Bob, Travelling child. The Children's Society. *Out of Site, Out of Mind*, 1995. p.15

ing to such a minority shall not be denied the right, in community with other members of his or her group, to enjoy his or her own culture, to profess and practice his or her own religion, or to use his or her own language."

In examining the issues of site provision and accommodation, and how these affect Travelling children. I will be drawing from the results of the recent research carried out by the Children's Society with thirty travelling children in south-western England. The research examined what services and facilities children wanted on or near to their site, and came about as a result of the renewed interest by some local authorities into the issue of site provision. We felt that within this debate it was important that the views of Traveller children were represented. "Including children in any decision-making processes leads to a greater involvement and ownership over decisions and a feeling of inclusion and support for any outcome or changes that might happen. As well as all of the above it is worth remembering that one of the best reasons for consulting with children is that they often have some very good ideas. Children also have a right to be consulted. The United Nations Convention on the Rights of the Child, particularly Article 12 ... gives children the right to be consulted over matters which affect them...".[119]

The children who participated in the research were aged between three and thirteen years. They lived on a variety of sites, some with planning permission, but most unofficial.[120] Their life-styles varied between highly mobile and living in vehicles to children who had lived all their lives on one site and lived in benders. "Over half the children were born on the road and although they often had some experience of living on a house, most of their life had been spent living on sites".[121] All the children involved were 'new' Travellers but the main findings of the research and the recommendations that came from it could apply to all Travelling children.

The research asked the children about their ideal size of site, the location, what facilities they would want near to their site, and how long a time they would want on a site. The responses from the children were both reasoned and articulate. They talked about the experiences that they had on different sites, with different facilities, and why this affected the choices that they made. The research never set out to provide a blueprint of a Traveller site from a child's perspective but it did set out to raise awareness of the importance of incorporating a child's perspective on issues which affect children.

When looking at site provision there needs to be a recognition of the nomadic nature of the Travelling life-style. When talking to children about their ideal site it became clear that they did not want to stop permanently on one site. The issue of sites and accommodation was not about having a pitch on one site, it was about being able to move from place to place. The services, locations and facilities might need to change depending on the circumstances of the different Travellers. There needed to be a diversity of sites and stopping places to enable people to move around. It is important that this is recognised when looking at the issue of site provision.

119 The Children's Participation Project (Wessex), the Children's Society. *My Dream Site*, 92B High Street, Midsomer Norton, Bath, BA3 2DE, 1998. p.2

120 For the purpose of this article, and in line with the research carried out, a broad definition of 'site' which includes both legal and unofficial stopping places is used.

121 *My Dream Site*. p.3

One of the main findings of the research was the consensus around play space. Children, when asked about play space on-site, saw it as important for them to have a safe area on-site in which to play. All of the additional suggestions that they made about site provision related to play tools such as swings and slides, places to ride bikes, and tree houses. A safe place to play on a site can be a luxury for many Traveller children. The inadequate number of sites provided for Travellers and the preventative measures taken to stop access to traditional stopping places has forced families to stop in places where the external environment is not conducive to safe play. The other main findings were the needs for trees, grass and grazing on-site. Almost all of the children asked wanted to have these things on their site.

The recommendations which result from the research, then, are that:

- Children should be consulted over decisions that affect them, particularly in relation to sites and eviction.
- Site provision needs to represent the diversity of life-style that is found within the Traveller communities.
- Planning procedures should take into account the needs and wishes of children.
- Play space needs to be given greater priority when considering site suitability.

8

Social and school exclusion and truancy
NATT

Background

The National Association of Teachers of Travellers (NATT) is the professional association of teachers, working in local education authorities throughout the UK, who provide additional support for the education of travelling children (Gypsy and Traveller, Fairground, Circus and New Traveller). From April 1999 projects are in the main funded through a competitive bid by LEAs to the Standards Fund. Funding is for three years, subject to a satisfactory Annual Report to the DfEE, and is paid at 65 per cent by central government, with a 35 per cent contribution by the local authority.

NATT provides professional development opportunities and guidance for teachers of Travellers and associate members involved with the education of travelling children. It responds on behalf of the membership to consultation documents, and has a positive relationship with the DfEE. NATT has strong links with Europe through its membership of EFECOT,[122] and takes part in innovative Europe-wide projects through the benefit of European funding under the Socrates programme. The need for additional support for the education of travelling children was first made clear in the Report of the Committee of Enquiry into the Education of Children from Ethnic Minority Groups (DES 1985) and the comment made in that Report still rings true today: "In many ways the situation of Traveller's children in Britain today throws into stark relief many of the factors which influence the education of children from other ethnic minority groups – racism and discrimination, myths, stereotyping and misinformation, the inappropriateness and inflexibility of the education system and the need for better links between homes and schools, teachers and parents."

Approximately one-third of Traveller families currently have no secure stopping place. Though progress in the provision of accommodation was made under the 1968 Caravan Sites Act, the duty on local authorities to provide caravan sites was repealed under the Criminal Justice and Public Order Act 1994. This has meant that these families are subject to a continuous round of frequent forced eviction from public or

---

122 European Federation for the Education of the Children of the Occupational Travellers, Brussels.

private property, sometimes by the police, with as little as one hours notice, and no likelihood of any alternative for the future.

Preliminary evidence collected by NATT about school access for such children through 'Mobile Months', a data collection exercise due to last until later in 1999, is showing that:

- more children of school age are being reported;
- families' length of stay is getting shorter;
- less children are getting access to school.

Only a fundamental review of the workings of the Criminal Justice and Public Order Act 1994 in relation to Gypsy and Traveller families, across all relevant departments, can begin to address the plight of these families, who are not seen as the responsibility of any particular local authority and who see themselves condemned to a life of continual social exclusion. The provision of reasonably secure accommodation and humanitarian treatment at the hands of public authorities cannot be separated from the entitlement of the children to a quality experience of education in school.

Traveller families, whose children's education is supported by Traveller Education Support Services (TESSs), may reside on unofficial encampments, local authority and private caravan sites and in housing, if settled for not more than two years. Most Traveller families have a distinctive culture and life-style, which retains mobility as a significant reference point.

Despite the excellent work undertaken by TESSs as recognised in the OFSTED Report (1996), which has shown that improvements have taken place in access to school at primary level, the situation regarding secondary pupils is very serious. "Access to the curriculum for secondary aged children remains a matter of grave concern. There are possibly as many as 10,000 children at this phase who are not even registered with a school. The attendance at school of Travelling children is slowly improving, but the average figures are still unacceptably low."[123] The continued funding of additional support for the education of travelling children on a stable basis, without competitive bidding, is therefore vital to continuing the improvements in access and attendance, which have been achieved at primary level, into the secondary and further education sectors.[124] The Report of the European Commission into School Provision for Gypsy and Traveller Children[125] makes this point: "negative stereotypes and prejudice colour the attitudes and behaviour of political leaders, administrators, teachers, parents, and other pupils; rejection thus continues to be an important component of the situation hindering Gypsy and Traveller children's access to school."[126]

Prejudice against the travelling communities remains unacceptably high in all areas of public life. It is against this background of social exclusion, racism and discrimination that we address the specific questions of school exclusion and truancy.

123 The OFSTED Report. p.8
124 See NATT document *Traveller Education: The funding of additional support for the education of travelling children*
125 1996; reports on the implementation of measures in the Resolution of the Council and of the Ministers of Education meeting with the Council, 22nd May 1989 (89/C 153/02).
126 Ibid., p.76

School and local authority performance targets

- National and local targets, if implemented, should be based on monitoring of exclusions detailing the gender, ethnicity (including Gypsy and Traveller pupils), age, type of exclusion (as short term exclusions can be as damaging as permanent exclusions), type of school, pupils' previous history of exclusion, and any special educational needs identified.

- School targets could involve improvement on previous profile of exclusions, including a reporting responsibility on strategies used to reduce the rate. This could lead to a transfer of best practice between successful schools.

- Schools with low or improving exclusion rates should be praised publicly for their inclusive and pro-active approach.

- We support the Government's drive to raise standards. However, when success is measured across a narrow academic band, this can devalue investment in pastoral care and special educational needs provision in schools. It is important to acknowledge that for some pupils effective pastoral strategies and a well-resourced special needs department are crucial to raising achievement. Exclusions have risen dramatically since schools have been operating in a competitive environment. The effect of the Government giving status to efforts to reduce exclusions and truancy cannot be underestimated.

- Caution is needed in comparing schools. National targets can lead to the formation of a group of 'unattractive pupils' which schools resist taking on roll.

- More emphasis needs to be given to researching in detail the processes which lead to school exclusion, though current evidence suggests that school ethos and organisation, provision for special educational needs and curriculum relevance are likely to be important factors, which disproportionately affect particular groups of young people.

- Targets would need to be supported by funding a supportive infrastructure, referred to later in this section, if success is to be achieved.

Preventing exclusions and truancy

Exclusions

Early intervention strategies

- Early identification of vulnerable pupils and early intervention characterised by a co-ordinated approach involving pupils, parents and other relevant agencies. This should be seen as a problem-solving approach, which aims to define the best education provision for a pupil. Adequate resources are needed to support this intervention at an early stage with a preventative emphasis, rather than resorting to crisis management.

- A welcoming ethos which values the child's contribution and culture has been noted to improve behaviour. Some Traveller Education Support teachers have the unusual experience of seeing the same child in a number of different schools due to mobility. They can therefore observe the same child's responses to the differing ethos and environment of different schools.

- Multi-agency initiatives, which take a whole-school approach to teaching about the issues often involved in exclusions, such as racism and bullying.
- Good home-school links, including an outreach component can promote positive relationships before any problems arise. Schools often value highly the support provided for home-school liaison by TESSs.
- Structured early warning systems in schools, which ensure all staff are well informed and have clear reporting procedures. Staff should be certain of a response from senior management.
- Senior staff giving a strong lead in attitudes towards bullying and racism. Pupils should be clear about the structures in place which actively deal with issues of bullying and racism. Key identified staff for vulnerable groups of pupils, such as Traveller pupils, often increases confidence and raises the awareness of other school staff to cultural issues.
- More explicit attention should be paid in OFSTED inspections to the effectiveness of a school's policies on equal opportunities, bullying and racism.

Surrey Traveller Education Service: Social Skills Days for Junior Schools

A whole school approach to issues of bullying, prejudice, behaviour and friendships, which aims to prevent social and school exclusion.

Agencies involved:

Police – on bullying;

Traveller parent, Traveller Education Service: differences, prejudice and lifestyle; **Traveller Education Service, class teachers:** Circle time on friendships and how we treat each other.

Curriculum strategies

- Additional flexibility in the secondary curriculum would benefit many pupils. Returning some responsibility to schools for the provision of a relevant and inclusive curriculum would help in preventing exclusion and disaffection.
- The availability of structured basic literacy tuition at secondary school level if needed, with a special time-table for a set time-scale.
- The introduction of exciting and worthwhile input, with status, for the twelve to fourteen age group, such as Awards Schemes, life skills, interpersonal skills and parenting skills.
- Positive profiling of school and college partnerships for the 14 and up age group, not just as a tool for maintaining disaffected pupils in the system, but as a positive, flexible alternative for all pupils, to prevent disaffection.
- The promotion of classroom practice which takes account of different learning styles.
- Senior management should spot check the work of vulnerable pupils to ensure that there is progression and appropriate matching, taking action at the curriculum level if not.
- The encouragement and financial resourcing of mentoring and buddying schemes.

- The use of trained classroom assistants to support the building up of a repertoire of social skills, as in some Traveller Education Services.
- The existence of well-resourced and structured special educational needs departments, which respond quickly to staff concerns.
- The use of all available support services, flexibly, to maintain engagement with the educational process.
- Support services should be adequately staffed to ensure a speedy response to need.

Additional measures for the prevention of truancy

- First day follow-up of non-attendance by telephone, then subsequently by visits. Schools should be resourced at a level which allows them to take responsibility for this. This sends the message to the child that they are valued and missed.
- Spot checking of registers in lessons throughout the day, providing early alerts to pupil's absence patterns.
- Use of education social workers to offer a variety of methods such as family work, counselling and mediation, where patterns are becoming established and unresponsive to other school strategies.

Examples of Good Practice in the West Midlands

West Midlands consortium Education Service for Travelling Children (WMESTC)

- Initiatives in 14+ schools/college partnership, where in some instances parents are working alongside their children.
- Amending the Compact 2000 framework to include Traveller youngsters and enabling them to achieve a nationally recognised accreditation.
- Inter-agency partnerships established in each of the LEAs participating in the consortium – an active network of professionals with ongoing development of expertise.
- Introductory packages to school for new pupils / dropped-out secondary youngsters' taster sessions at school / college post 14. Group sessions in schools focussed on Reading and Writing in the Community.
- Good practice (and DfEE-sponsored video of practices) in some Wolverhampton schools to deal with bullying and safety e.g. pupils being given a map/plan of the school and being asked to mark areas where they feel threatened and unsafe and to say what times of day etc. Senior management teams then take action to address the problem.

The practice of exclusion

Structures should be put in place with the aim of preventing exclusion. This should be seen as a concerted effort to make the best educational provision for the pupil. The process should be structured so that pupils, parents and schools are required to show what efforts have been made to avoid exclusion. A more radical approach would involve completely changing the negative language surrounding this area and take an approach which involves 'special measures' for targeted pupils, aiming at a positive overall end-point of engagement in the process by all parties, with praise for successful schools.

A staged process could involve:

1. Pupil informed and pastoral meeting arranged to plan next steps in response to difficulty, implemented and reviewed to a pre-arranged time-scale.
2. Parents involved in planning with a pastoral team and other appropriate agencies implemented and reviewed to an agreed timetable. A multi-agency specialist team should be available to respond to requests for involvement, which could include representatives from support services, educational psychology services, educational welfare service, social services, health services and the youth service.
3. Procedures followed for exclusion from classes or the school site. The school should be responsible for providing a distance learning programme for the pupil; TESs have considerable expertise in supporting provision of school-based distance learning. Pupils should not be taken off a school roll until alternative full-time provision is secured. It is unacceptable that pupils should be seen as becoming 'someone else's problem'. It is behaviour that is rejected, not the child.

The expectation should be that permanent exclusion is a very extreme solution, which is in both the pupil's and school's interests. Expectations, work and a structure needs to be automatically put in place on exclusion, if parents and child are to take seriously that school and education matter. Leaving parents without guidance, and children without expectations of them, confirms to them that no-one cares and nothing will be done. Interruptions to the patterns of regular full-time working opportunities may exacerbate the difficulties of re-integration and increase feelings of hopelessness.

Effective solutions for excluded pupils

Where pupils have been excluded, Pupil Referral Units can maintain a pattern of education, which is difficult to re-establish once broken. Re-integration should be supported by a specialist multi-agency team, and monitored and reviewed regularly. Within the school a re-entry package should be co-ordinated and overseen by a key worker and supported by documentation with which all staff are familiar and required to support. The clear expectation should be of a fresh start, with a welcoming ethos. Gradual introduction could involve support for teaching staff and a short-term, part-time timetable with phased introduction to subjects and lessons where interest and success is likely. Flexibility in the curriculum and in the provision of school and college partnerships and quality work experience would allow schools to offer a relevant curriculum to more young people at fourteen and up.

An Essex secondary Head Teacher's inclusive approach to Traveller education

"We have worked consistently and successfully to counter and eradicate the racism, prejudice and hostility which is sometimes directed at Travellers. We acknowledge their needs as a minority group and are sensitive to their educational needs. We never knowingly compromise our policies, but we can and do adopt a flexible approach to school rules and procedures; this is the key to our sensitive provision for Travellers. It is not unusual for us to create a temporary individual timetable designed to meet a new Traveller pupil's expressed needs, before progressing to a full timetable once we have the child's confidence and commitment; it is not unusual for us to enter a Traveller for GCSE using coursework amassed before the Travelling season; it is not unknown for me to visit the wholesalers in Whitechapel on a Sunday morning so that a Traveller can join us the next day in school uniform. If I had insisted upon punctuality when nobody worked to a clock in the Traveller household, or the removal of earrings to conform to our school rules, or a written note to explain absence when nobody in the Traveller home could write, then I would have lost the trust of Travellers ... they have been integrated into the school without compromise to their identity; and as a result the school has gained."

Reward systems may succeed with some pupils, as can mentoring and buddying schemes. Whatever the supportive approach, it is important that all staff are positive and that a strong lead is taken by senior management. Staff training in the use of interpersonal skills, group work, conflict resolution, positive behaviour management and cultural differences could be helpful.

Where parents opt to educate their children 'otherwise than at school', as increasing numbers of Gypsy and Traveller parents are doing, children can become invisible in the system. Schools are currently allowed to take children off the roll when they have been notified of parent's intentions. This should not be allowed until an Education Officer has approved that arrangements for Education Otherwise are in place according to the legislation (including full-time provision). This would mean that there would be an incentive to schools and LEAs to ensure Education Otherwise is managed effectively and that parents, including Traveller parents, are not using it as a route of condoned absence because they know nothing will happen to them.

Where Education Otherwise is being monitored, and it is slow or not effective at all in some areas, officers are sanctioning inadequate, narrow teaching programmes of one or two hours a week. Government needs to require LEAs to evidence achievement and progression for these young people.

Helping multi-agency working[127]

The Report of the European Commission (1997) makes this point at paragraph 290:

---

127 See also the section by Sarah Cemlyn and Rachel Morris in Part 2 Chapter 12 on *Inter-agency working*.

"The analyses and demands of Gypsy and Traveller organisations, families' personal experience, studies carried out over the last few years and the publications arising from them, the experience of teams working in the field, and many other facts and testimonies are in total convergence in emphasising that it is unrealistic to consider any aspect of the situation of Gypsy and Traveller communities (be it school provision, health, economics, accommodation …) in isolation. In attempting to ameliorate this situation, it is essential to take account of all the factors and parameters determining it, and to tackle all of these fronts."

Multi-agency working is essential to a proper consideration of the factors involved in social exclusion and in school exclusion and truancy. However, to be successful it needs to be given status and credibility within the system. To be effective multi-agency working involves using a number of high-level skills; accreditation of these through higher education or APEL modules, or the creation of new course modules, would help with increasing the status of professionals involved. If the Government feels that it should give status to the resolution of truancy and exclusion issues, then multi-agency working needs to become integral to practice in schools, and not simply an 'extra' tool. Otherwise there is a danger that schools will see it merely as a distraction from the 'main' tasks of education.

One possibility would be the creation of a 'Children's Ombudsman', who would be responsible for multi-agency working and have the power to direct agencies to co-operate for children's welfare. Certainly there is a need for all appropriate agencies to designate personnel whose priority it is to work within this remit, otherwise any initiatives become immediately undermined by lack of priority, when agencies are already under stress. The role of the education welfare officer is very variable across authorities, with some authorities moving towards a split between using Education Welfare Officers (EWOs) for routine follow-up of absence, with education social workers taking up more difficult case work. Others are training their EWOs to manage case loads of, for example, pupils with serious negative or difficult family experiences which exacerbate truancy or lead to exclusion, and minimising routine work.

Therefore a clear understanding of the respective roles of personnel from other agencies is essential. Where status is given to this form of working, from the Government level, through budgeting and accredited training, then skilled leadership will mean that teams can agree and work to mutually reinforcing objectives. The quality of the leadership is essential to securing well-organised good practice. Similarly, proper accountability and good communication networks are essential. Where good practice already exists, it should be given appropriate status in the education system.

Witchford Village College, Cambridgeshire

A Traveller Youth Club has been formed at the school, with positive outcomes. This is the result of joint working between the Traveller Education Service, the school and the Youth and Community Service. As such joint working is expensive, it will only continue due to a grant from the National Lottery.

Groups particularly affected

Evidence is beginning to accumulate that Gypsy and Traveller pupils as a minority group are excluded from school in disproportionate numbers.[128] Since 1997, TESSs have been required to report on the exclusions of Traveller pupils in their annual report to the DfEE. However, not all LEAs currently monitor exclusions by ethnic categories which include Traveller children, nor do TESSs support all Traveller pupils in a locality. Therefore, it is essential that ethnic monitoring of exclusions at an LEA level is strengthened to include Gypsy and Traveller pupils.

Though the overall level of attendance of Traveller pupils has improved significantly over the years, it is still unsatisfactory and much work remains to be done in order to build on this success. It is important that LEAs treat travelling families in the same way as all other families with regard to the non-attendance of their children at school. Education Welfare Services need to implement the same policies based on the same legal requirements, but with due regard to the need for sensitivity. The intensity of some Traveller pupil casework is often more than can be facilitated within the constraints of available resources and, in these circumstances, the specialist appointments under Section 488 can be a helpful catalyst to both the development of good practice, and the extent to which main LEA welfare services respond – or are encouraged to respond – to their legal responsibilities for travelling children.[129]

An amendment to the Education (Pupil Registration) Regulations 1997 (SI 1997 No. 2624) under the new registration category 'approved educational activity', which added properly arranged and monitored school-based distance learning to the types of approved activity, would strengthen the responsibility of base schools towards Traveller pupils in the travelling season, and emphasise the responsibilities of parents towards their children's education whilst travelling. Such an amendment would be very helpful to TESSs, who support the efficient use of properly organised and quality distance learning as a continuity measure.

TESSs have placed great priority on the formation of good communication and trusting relationships with parents, and achieved considerable success in encouraging and maintaining regular school attendance. This is time-consuming and resources are needed to support this work, which has important benefits for current and next-generation Traveller children. The positive involvement of schools and other statutory agencies in outreach work to families is essential to continuing success.

As previously stated, there is a fundamental problem of any access at all to the school system for a considerable number of families. Parents often have very little experience of formal schooling themselves and are fearful for their children's safety and well-being. Accumulated experience in society generally leads them to expect hostility, disrespect, racism and discrimination, which is expressed openly as well as covertly. The Criminal Justice and Public Order Act 1994 has helped to create a climate in which families are moved on frequently, though no secure alternative stopping places are available, and has placed families in a situation where they are concerned with economic and social survival and cannot be blamed if education is not their first priority.

128 See OFSTED Report 1996. paras.40-1
129 bid., paras.61-6

In collecting information for the Annual Report to the DfEE, one TES examined comparative data for the past three years. Effective liaison with other agencies has meant that a speedy educational response to children on unofficial encampments has been possible. However, the accumulated data for those children who were unable to obtain a school place (even with a quick response and the existence of a 'toleration' policy for small groups of Travellers within the county and district councils), shows that the principle barrier to access to schooling is frequent and fast eviction by the police and private landowners, combined with the inability to provide discretionary school transport in the short time available.

"Throughout the whole of Europe, rejection in a variety of forms remains the dominant characteristic in relations between Gypsies and their immediate environment: accommodation difficulties, health hazards, denial of access to public places …Any analysis of school-related issues is thus simultaneously an analysis of overall policy…

"In such a context, and given the fact that the school as an institution is often part of an environment perceived by Gypsies as aggressive, it may be experienced as yet another imposition, and one whose quality leaves much to be desired. Parents may feel that the school's proposed 'moulding' of their children may deform, that is, culturally estrange them … In consequence, we must not take the effects of the overall situation (disinterest, absenteeism, outright refusal …) as the causes of scholastic failure. As long as relations between Gypsy and Traveller communities and surrounding society remain conflicted, parents' and childrens' relations with the school will remain largely determined by the negative profile of these broader relations."[130] This profound feeling of rejection of their culture and life-style, combined with the erosion of traditional work patterns and lack of formal education skills, can lead teenagers – who are viewed as adults within their own community – into a situation of cultural and economic limbo, which places them at risk of criminal activity (e.g. drugs and car related crime) and rejection of parental authority. Both parents and young people can find it difficult to be sure of the opportunities that school can offer them.

Initiatives by NATT/EFECOT which promote parental involvement

- Supporting the establishment of an Education Liaison Officer in each of ten sections of the Showmen's Guild of Great Britain. On-going training and support for them in operating as mediators in the community and self-representation at school and on public platforms, bringing schools and parents closer.
- The A6 project: designing and piloting parent-held educational records for Gypsy and Traveller children whose stay in any one school is likely to be under four weeks. Involving parents in the transfer of information about their child's progress at school.
- Education Contacts Booklet for Travelling Families, part-funded by the DfEE, lists names, addresses and contact numbers for Traveller Education Services and other personnel who will provide advice and support for access to school or for distance learning.
- National Circus Parents Group: support with the establishment and continua-

139 Report of the European Commission (1997). paras.08–9

tion of this group which aims to bring circus parents together to consider educational issues.

- Establishing a winter base schools network. Building a database of all schools registering fairground and circus children to engage them in a partnership of sharing information and practice; keeping the families' profile raised so that children are not forgotten, 'written off' or a 'nuisance factor' on their return from travelling.

- The more extensive introduction of mentors from within the Travelling community as positive role models, which have status within the school, would be a longer term aim, which could be supported by the extension of funding to cover Adult Basic Literacy, combined with suitable training opportunities.

Pupils from vulnerable groups, such as African-Caribbean boys and Gypsy and Traveller young people, need to see their experiences and aspirations reflected positively in the school, both in social terms and within the curriculum. It is essential that quality professional development opportunities are available to staff, and that senior management takes a strong lead in promoting high expectations and clear policies. A Code of Practice, along the lines of that for Special Education Needs, would focus attention on what needs to be done.

In summary, the characteristics of a school which is likely to become successful with such groups are:

- an open, welcoming ethos with a carefully planned induction programme, which gives clear guidance to pupils on who is the key person to approach in particular circumstances;
- whole staff professional development, and good induction of new staff;
- outreach practices, which narrow the gap between home/community and school;
- rigorous application and monitoring of policies on equal opportunities, bullying and racism; early warning systems, leading to early intervention;
- priority and status being given to strategies for dealing with truancy and exclusion;
- investment in monitoring systems, which have high status within the school;
- effective communication networks and speedy follow-up; and
- structures and strategies in place which have an efficient 'plan, implement, review' cycle.

"The right to schooling applies to all children, unconditionally, and must be put into practice with an eye to ensuring equal opportunity and in a context guaranteeing respect for the child's culture."[131] The Government's past and continuing additional support, under Section 488 Specific Grant, for the education of travelling children, is to be welcomed. TESSs have achieved a great deal in a short time and demonstrated positive and creative thinking and action. Clearly much work remains to be done, however. NATT would strongly request that the Social Exclusion Unit, with its inter-departmental focus, considers a review of the workings of the Criminal Justice and Public Order Act 1994, as it affects the quality of education, attendance and achievement of Gypsy and Traveller children.

131 The Report of the European Commission (1997). para.325

9

Accomodation and site provision

Traditional stopping places and customary use by Tony Thomson

Migration is present throughout nature; manifest in man, it is called nomadism, and has shaped the evolution of our species for over two million years. Nomadism has been indigenous to the British Isles since the first hunter-gatherers crossed the European land bridge over 500,000 years ago. The long transition to agriculture can be best understood as a continuum without a distinct boundary between hunter-gathering on the one hand and agriculture on another. Nomadism is a culture of subsistence and not of accumulation; shelter is portable and occupation transitory. Possession extends only to that which can be carried, therefore nomadism in its truest form makes no possessory claim to land.

Agriculture brought new attitudes to food ownership and the ability to create surplus enabled elite groups to seek to control territories. Common rights enabled older, more co-operative forms of culture to continue beneath feudalism, which depended on indigenous agriculture to sustain itself. Thirsk, the agricultural historian, has suggested that the rights of grazing over pasture and waste were perhaps the oldest element in the common fields system descended from "more extensive rights ... enjoyed from time immemorial, which Anglo Saxon and Norman monarchs did not graciously institute but rather regulated and curtailed."[131]

The expansion of mono-culture into the commons environment has led to violent assaults on customary practices on a global scale. Crises in agriculture and in urban culture are not unrelated. The system of land tenure and organisation underpinning it is contrived to concentrate and maximise the flow of resources in ways which we are now beginning to realise are unsustainable. "Where pollution and physical degradation have been identified as the exploitation of the worlds material resources it is, perhaps, not too much to suggest that poverty – from the absolutes of starvation and landlessness through to the relativities of unemployment and disadvantage in the midst of prosperity – can also be seen as a harmful product of the inequitable exploitation of the worlds human resources ...powerful people and institutions

131 Thirsk, Joan. The Common Fields, *Past and Present*, No. 29, December 1964

provide the framework within which all these things occur."[132] Nomadic dwelling brings into high relief these antagonisms, the conflict between market forces and customary practice, the continuing enclosure of the commons environment, the quasi-feudal hegemonies that operate behind our democracy, and the movement of refugees generated by poverty-related conflicts. Expansion in the formal economic sphere has precipitated global environmental crisis.

In 1992 the UK government, along with 146 other countries, signed the Rio Earth Summit Agreement (including Agenda 21). The overall objective was to improve and/or restructure the decision-making process so that the consideration of social, economic and environmental issues could become fully integrated. Agenda 21 calls for a re-evaluation of our relationship with the environment through the resources we consume and the life-style we lead, and asks governments to recognise "traditional knowledge and resource management practices as contributions to environmentally sound and sustainable development."[133] Characteristic of indigenous peoples[134] are relationships with land which predate concepts of private and exclusive ownership and which are socially inclusive strategies for resource management. Oriented towards sufficiency rather than surplus, they are sensitive to the topography and ecology of place.

Customary use of the fringe benefits of common and greensward are most significant to the livelihood of the poor and the marginalised. Registration processes and definitive mapping have never provided an exhaustive account of the use of commons because of the systematic exclusion of those without property rights or feudal title to the land they inhabit. The emphasis on exclusion and eviction as a sanction of first resort to 'protect' the environment has led to the under-development of integrated and socially inclusive systems of resource management and environmental law. Statute has not been impartial in this process, in that the establishment or private and exclusive ownership of land has been one of its core functions.

The Law Commission's consultative document *Land Registration for the 21st Century* offers an opportunity for principles of human and cultural rights and the Rio Summit Agreement to inform and develop the regulation of land in the UK. The incorporation into British Law of the European Convention on Human Rights, particularly those Articles relating to family life, home, and freedom of movement – especially when read together with UN Conventions and Declarations on Human and Cultural Rights, the Rights of Minorities and the Rights of the Child – provides an opportunity to acknowledge the nomads' customary right to make camp on common and verge as an 'overriding interest'.

Eviction and site closure are indiscriminate in their effect. The nomad who lives within the law and pursues his way of life in accordance with his ethnic and cultural traditions suffers arbitrary punishments; moreover, it renders customary practices of

132 Report of UNED, UK Poverty Round Table, February 1997

133 *Recognising and strengthening the role of indigenous groups and their communities*, Section 3 Chapter 26

134 Indigenous and tribal peoples may be descendants of the original inhabitants of lands which were conquered or settled by other peoples, or may be groups who are not descended from such peoples but live in similar situations. They are generally self-identified, distinct communities with their own languages, laws, institutions and ways of life which differ from the dominant communities in which they now live (UNCED proceedings, Rio Summit).

rotational conservation increasingly difficult to follow. Traditionally used camping places, which evolved alongside the highway network as it developed, contain remnants of a landscape typical of pre-enclosure days. They are habitat to a diversity of life, including human, and have witnessed nomadic dwelling for millennia.

Until the eighteenth century roads were mainly indistinct tracks, drove roads, salt roads, and a few roads which were resurfaced during the Roman military occupation. Over the years, some were surfaced in response to increased use, while others retained their green surface. The 1949 National Parks and Access to the Countryside Act enabled counties to reclassify most of the public roads used mainly as public paths, through the 'definitive map' process. While not the express intention of the Act, it provided an opportunity for highway authorities to diminish their responsibility for road maintenance and give these roads an apparently lower classification, when they arguably should have remained on the county surveyor's public carriageway records; some were omitted altogether from the survey. The British Horse Federation estimate that sixteen thousand miles of bridleway has been 'lost' since the inception of the definitive mapping process. Many roads used as public footpaths (RUPPs) were 'downgraded' to bridleway under the 1968 Countryside Act, and permitted counties to reclassify RUPPs as footpaths without consultation. In Staffordshire 500 RUPPs were lost in this way.

In ignoring the record of highways collated in 1929 on the transfer of responsibilities of maintenance from rural district to county councils, the 'definitive map' process remakes the country road network in its own image. Rather than abandoning the objective of having rights of way legally and accurately recorded, the definitive map process should be simplified and take the 1929 Local Government Act highway record as its datum. The outcome of the massive loss of habitat over recent years has been the creation of overcrowded Traveller sites of longer duration in more exposed situations. The social and environmental stress that occurs as a consequence offers a pretext for a further cycle of 'tough' legislation and site denial. It arguably breaches international documents to which the UK is a signatory, including the UN Convention on Civil and Political Rights.[135]

My research indicates a loss of between 80 and 90 per cent of customarily used sites in Somerset between 1986 and 1993. Droves around the periphery of market towns have been particularly vulnerable to closure because of their proximity to anticipated urban expansion and the perceived threat of the nomad to property 'values'. With up to 50 per cent of the rural landscape being Green Belt, Special 'Landscape' Areas, Areas of Outstanding Natural Beauty or National Park, and the rest being 'open countryside', planning is undertaking social exclusion on an aesthetic basis. The 'rural idyll' of land as stereotypical pure space is employed to create 'geographies of exclusion';[136] culture as an image usurps culture as practice, and we are all culturally impoverished as a result. "There is concern that planning standards and the rules of thumb inevitably reflect the values of social groups who have been historically influential in British society. The standards may not recognise the diversity of multi-cultural society, and its plurality of culture and values".[137] Customs integrate

---

135 Article 27: "In those states in which ethnic, religious or linguistic minorities exist, persons belonging to such minorities shall not be denied the right, in community with the other members of their group, to enjoy their own culture, to profess and practise their own religion, or to use their own language".

136 Sibley, David. *Geographies of Exclusion*, Routledge, London, 1995

habitation and land, while planning contrives their separation; consequently agriculture is in crisis, country people rail at town folk and vice versa, and the poor are deprived of the common rights and practices by which their poverty could be overcome. Sustainable development is a relationship to the environment which is culturally integrated into everyday practice. It is the integrating capacities of customary practices that are a measure of their sophistication. Single Use Zoning is blind to such subtleties, such relationships being not easily definable in economic terms.

DoE Circular 1/94 aims "to provide that the planning system recognises the need for accommodation consistent with gypsies' nomadic life-style". To do this, however, the planning system has to develop the conceptual framework necessary to embrace shared usage of land and the dynamics of nomadic dwelling. Nomadism is not a stubborn anachronism but a continuing response to economic, environmental and social need. By learning from the nomadic models of land use which have evolved over the centuries, sustainable practices can be arrived at through inclusive management measures.

Customary practice necessitates the observation of certain mores, upon which reasonable people can agree as being 'common sense'. They are: respecting rights of way; keeping sites clean; and controlling dogs and other animals.[138] Sanitary arrangements can be minimal and effective. Good practice entails burying waste; expertise in the construction of composting toilets from greenwood sources offers another solution to the problem of waste treatment and is becoming popular on sites with a more secure occupancy. Reed bed planting in lane ditches could promote waste water purification.

The outcome of a massive loss of habitat since 1945 in conjunction with continuing influxes of refugees has been the creation of overcrowded, overused sites of longer duration in more exposed locations, with all the attendant environmental and social stress. Customary site use offers the opportunity for population dispersal, discreet locations, geographic choice and rotational conservation. Movement and dispersal within an inclusive management regime avoids situations escalating into crisis. A rotational conservation approach gives Travellers a custodial role, a role which has too often been thwarted by conflict.

Vacancy enables winter frosts to cleanse the soil and an undisturbed spring, summer and autumn promotes floral regeneration. The rate of environmental regeneration relates to the intensity of usage, the nature of the ground surface, and the state of drainage. This implies a bias towards small scale development for settled situations and reinforces the rationality of movement to minimise environmental impact. All Travellers cannot therefore be accommodated on all green lanes permanently. Without surface treatment, accommodation for heavy vehicles used on a daily basis becomes impractical.

The principles of nomadic land use can be adapted to derelict or unrealised development land for limited periods as a form of planning gain and to embrace parcels of agriculturally fallow land. To achieve balanced usage, practice informs us that sites of

137 Royal Town Planning Institute. *Ethnic Minorities and the Planning System*, 1993
138 Legislation already exists to impose civil standards of behaviour in regard to creating obstructions on the highway, dropping litter and controlling animals.

between four and ten dwellings with either a four or six month occupancy within a two-yearly cycle is sufficient, so it takes a minimum of four sites to make a network. The larger the number of sites and networks held in reserve, the greater the tolerance margin of the system and landscape concerned. Both sites and networks could be used in sequence.

In having networks in the orbit of market towns, access to health, education and employment opportunities are maintained, as is access to fresh ground. The sedentary population (if any) in proximity to encampments are more likely to accept a transitory presence of known duration. This approach has been working informally in Dorset for the past fifty years or more without the need for costly legal action. Most of the sites are already there; green lanes are not alien features on the landscape. Hedgerow, as well as providing a visual screen, offers protection from strong wind and sun, creating temperate micro-climates in otherwise exposed locations. Orthodox local authority site provision is budgeted at £27,000 per pitch; traditional site models could translate this into three miles of mixed species hedgerow on reinstated green lane, or 1.5 miles of new green lane, thus enabling resources to be redirected into environmental renewal.

Identifying sites which could complete, reinstate and make more accessible the green lane network would enhance the amenity for all countryside users. The high rents imposed by owners of fixed sites promote dependency on the welfare system, and so are an unnecessary drain on public resources. Customary practice avoids this poverty trap. It meets an identifiable need for Traveller site provision within the parameters of Circular 1/94 and Agenda 21. Cross-funding for tree and hedgerow planting, shelter belts, set-aside, restoring historic landscapes, and enhancing public amenities and highways will help allay costs. This integration can be further promoted by countryside skills training.[139] "[S]ince custom is the principle magistrate of man's life, let men by all means endeavour to obtain good customs. Certainly custom is most perfect when it beginneth in young years: this we call education, which is in effect but an early custom."[140] Customal skills displace capital relations, consequently formal educational institutions have not developed curricula for their transmission. Other forms of generational transmission have been disrupted by industrialisation, enclosure, and constraints placed on freedom of assembly. Thus access to information is essential, on resources, technological choices, and training and development processes, drawing on traditional herb lore and contemporary pioneers of permacultural practice and environmental regeneration.

The following options can and should be explored to identify and secure traditionally used land:

- Identifying green lanes where there is a clear case of illegal closure or encroachment.
- Local authorities using their compulsory purchase powers.[141]
- Private or highway authority acquisition of 18 metre land strips leading to existing green lane.

---

139 Such as the Woodlands Skills training programme currently being managed by Friends, Families and Travellers.

140 Bacon, Francis. *The Essays or Counsels Civil and Moral*, 1625

141 Section 24, Caravan Sites and Control of Development Act 1960

- Identifying and, if necessary, upgrading existing green lanes of appropriate width for use.
- De-enclosing agriculturally over-exploited land as a matter of public interest, creating green lanes as a necessary initial step to retard soil erosion and enhance biodiversity.
- Applying Agenda 21 principles of sustainability to the provision and enabling of sites.

Agenda 21 Section 3 talks of recognising and strengthening the role of indigenous groups, by providing technical and financial assistance for capacity building programmes to support the sustainable self-development of such people and their communities, and by developing research and education programmes aimed at achieving a better understanding of indigenous peoples' knowledge and management of the environment, applying this to contemporary development challenges. This acknowledges that customary practices are not just a replication of pre-industrial practice, but are a strategic approach to contemporary dilemmas. "Human beings are at the centre of concerns for sustainable development. They are entitled to a healthy and productive life in harmony with nature."[142]

Community development *Paul Goltz and Annie Murdoch*

Introduction *by Annie Murdoch*

The South Somerset District Council Traveller Panel was set up in August 1995 to consider all the challenges faced by Gypsies, Travellers and other nomadic groups, low-impact dwellers and settlers and the impact (real and perceived) of such lifestyles on established local communities. Nine months later, we held our seminar – a magic day which brought together representatives from different organisations and various Traveller groups, including horse-drawn, new and traditional Travellers and bender dwellers. The diverse Traveller groups constituted one third of those attending. They had a thirty minute speaking slot on the programme (five Travellers shared this slot) and took an active part in the workshops (a minimum of three in each).

The impact of the day was more than anyone could have imagined or even dreamed of. Parish and District Councillors were seen viewing Traveller vehicles during the lunch hour and involved in intense conversations with the Travellers about their lifestyles. The culmination of the day was the closing speech, where an eminent District Councillor stated, most surprisingly, that she had been won over and would give Travellers her unconditional support from then on.

One of the almost immediate results of the seminar was the appointment of a Traveller Community Worker, Paul Goltz. Paul was appointed, initially, on a tempo- rary six month contract of eighteen hours per week; with a specific remit to develop a more trusting and positive relationship between District and Parish Councils and the Traveller populations. We soon realised, however, the need for more time to be invested in this area and, consequently, the post was extended for a further short period, increased to twenty-eight hours per week.

Paul was also given the task of collecting personal and special circumstances from

---

142 Agenda 21, Principle 1

each Traveller group in the area when necessary. Unlike some of the other authorities at that time, Paul was encouraged to collect personal and special circumstances first and foremost as a way of better helping the Travellers with their planning applications and associated accommodation needs rather than as a safeguard against Judicial Review following the Wealden and Kerrier judgements. The personal and special circumstances were to be used as encouragement to the planning committees to either look favourably on the Traveller applications or defer any enforcement action until mutually acceptable alternative sites could be found for the particular groups.

While Paul was appointed as an officer of our Council, he was first and foremost to be an advocate and friend of Travellers. This, at times, meant arguing strongly against the very Authority for which he worked. This community development angle also required Paul to work closely with Parish Councils, who, along with the Travellers, have consistently argued vociferously at each of the review meetings, that Paul's post must continue. From the comments collected from both Parish Councils and the Travellers, it can unequivocally be said that both have benefited from Paul's involvement and that mutual trust has been established. Following this positive and unanimous support from all involved, Paul's post has recently been extended, on a full-time basis, to enable us to mainstream the Traveller issue and develop expertise and empathic working practices in other areas of the Council.

The philosophy behind the post has always been and will continue to be one of community development, rather than control. The idea has been to establish meaningful relationships and to work in partnership with all concerned to find mutually acceptable solutions to the accommodation needs of our nomadic minority groups. We still have a considerable way to go and a number of targets to achieve, but with Paul's help, we can continue to make the much-needed progress that the Travellers need in order to be treated equitably.

District community work *by Paul Goltz*

The Traveller Panel is still ongoing here at South Somerset and is attended by a range of people including Travellers, Parish Council representatives, the County Gypsy Liaison Officer, and Traveller Support Groups as well as members and officers of the District Council. As stated in the introduction the Traveller Community Worker post has recently been extended and I am now a District Community Worker with further remits to look into the issues facing people from the non-white population of South Somerset and those issues faced by marginalised youth.

When I started in post as the District Council's Traveller Community Worker I set out to build up a working relationship with the Travellers who were residing in South Somerset as well as networking with all the relevant agencies and support groups. Initial reactions from the Travellers to my post were positive. Because of the work done by the Traveller Panel I felt able to put over the positive approach that the District Council were taking. This wasn't always easy as most of the Travellers had memories of bad experiences dealing with local authorities. There was much discussion on how to get involved with Parish Councils. Thoughts of writing to all the Parish Councils were dismissed at this early stage, instead, I contacted individual Parish Councils when the need arose.

During early meetings with support agencies we agreed to work closely whenever possible but that there could be times when we could be in opposition. Over the months that followed we have become strong allies, developing a partnership approach to a variety of issues.

One of the initial aims of the Traveller Community Worker post was to establish a satisfactory method for undertaking investigations into the personal and special circumstances of the Travellers. Although done in accordance with the current legislation and advice, the thrust was to support and involve Traveller groups with help towards resolving their accommodation needs. I worked closely with the legal department to draw up a questionnaire designed to identify the personal circumstances of the Travellers. The next stage was to consult with Travellers from across the district and Traveller Support Agencies to see if the questionnaire felt okay to them.

Once the questionnaire had been designed I found myself involved in the collection of personal circumstances information for the first time. I took the questionnaires to the site involved and spent time with every individual Traveller, explaining the process and answering their questions. I informed the Travellers as to when I would return to collect the completed questionnaires. This I did, with the next step being to photocopy the questionnaires and return the originals to the Travellers. They then signed the photocopies to say that they were exact copies of the originals. This part of the process was done in this way as the Travellers had told me that previously they were never left with any paperwork when dealing with local authorities.

The personal circumstances information along with the lack of legal sites across the district, led South Somerset's Area West Committee to state that "In the particular circumstances of this case there should be no enforcement action till a suitable alternative site becomes available". This statement proved to be a positive guide to the Planning Inspector at the subsequent Public Local Inquiry.

Following on from this decision and the statement from Somerset County Council that they no longer had intentions of providing further sites (emergency stopping places) after having tried and failed to gain planning permissions, the-then Chairman of South Somerset's Area West Committee set up a meeting on Solutions to inappropriate Encampments and invited representatives to discuss the issues of site provision. The following paper was produced for Somerset County Council's Gypsy and Traveller Issues in Somerset Seminar held on 19 September 1998.

Solutions to inappropriate encampments

Why the meetings were set up

The 'Solutions to Inappropriate Encampments' meetings were established by Jill Shortland, then Chairman of the District Council's Area West Committee, as an informal group to promote a fuller understanding of the issues surrounding inappropriate encampments and to enable Parish Councils to be involved in, and have a sense of ownership of, the difficult process of identifying solutions to these encampments in Area West of the District Council. The idea to set up the meetings resulted from a letter which had been sent to all parishes by Chris Clarke, Leader of the Somerset County Council, and referred to consultation taking place with parishes to ascertain whether they had an ideas concerning these issues.

Six meetings have taken place so far, the first being on 26 June 1997. The meetings have involved the Chairman and Vice-chairman and other member representatives of the Area West Committee and appropriate District Council officers including the Community Initiatives Co-ordinator, Traveller Community Worker, Director of Area West, Area Planning Manager and Assistant Solicitor. Representatives of the Somerset Association of Local Councils, National Farmers Union and Somerset County Council have also been involved.

What we have been doing

In order to promote a fuller understanding of all the issues, brief presentations were made by officers on the planning, legal and social issues surrounding inappropriate encampments when a number of points were referred to including the following:

- It was felt important to distinguish between illegal sites (continued occupation once legal judgement passed) and unlawful sites (occupation when landowner objects and without necessary permissions having been obtained). It was noted that inappropriate and poorly located sites may or may not be unlawful as well.
- The Travellers in South Somerset appeared to be a fairly stable group of approximately thirty-five adults and fifteen children, some of whom had been born and bred in South Somerset. It was noted that during the summer months a larger number of Travellers passed through the District. It was also noted that whilst some Travellers passed through the district, many Travellers were forced to remain against their wish to travel because of the lack of tolerated and/or authorised sites.
- It was noted that there was only one legal site for new Travellers currently in South Somerset District (at Dommett Wood, Buckland St. Mary). However, two sites for traditional Travellers had been provided and were managed by Somerset County Council. Slough Green (near Hatch Beauchamp) in Taunton Deane District is the only other authorised new Traveller site in the county although a transit site has been approved at Glastonbury.
- It was suggested that if the traditional stopping sites were still available, the Traveller would move around. However, with many of those sites having been 'ditched' to prevent occupation, Travellers were forced to remain and occupy land unlawfully.
- South Somerset has received a total of nine planning applications for Traveller sites, three of which have come from the Dommett Wood site in the parish of Buckland St. Mary.
- A need to tackle anti-social behaviour was identified, as the actions of a few Travellers could give all a bad name. It was also recognised that the same was true for people in other forms of housing tenure.
- It has been suggested that accommodation matters could be dealt with under Housing and Homelessness legislation but it was felt that encouraging Travellers to give up their life-style by offering Council housing accommodation would be unlikely to succeed. Many Travellers had sound reasons for not wishing to return to the 'settled' community and in any event this should not be insisted upon as the District Council could offer alternative housing 'appropriate to gypsy accommodation needs'.
- Advice has been given on the implications of the Inspector's decision to grant a

temporary planning permission for three years for a Travellers' site at Dommett Wood. The Secretary of State has made it clear that an alternative site has to be found for Dommett Wood and that there was a need for a network of Traveller sites in the District. Should an alternative not be found it is possible that the site will get a permanent permission and is has been recognised that doing nothing may mean further inappropriate sites. It was noted that unless alternative sites could be found the Council could have problems at any planning appeal hearings concerning Traveller sites.

It has been agreed that the issue of Travellers needs to be managed and that the problems associated with unlawful occupation could only be solved if authorised sites could be found. However, it was seemed that a 'Catch-22' situation existed whereby, with no authorised sites in the district, Travellers were forced to occupy land unlawfully. In these circumstances, the District Council could not impose conditions to regulate and control the use of the site (this it could only do when granting a planning consent). Recent legal judgements had also made it difficult to take enforcement action in cases where planning approval had been refused, if no suitable alternative sites existed.

There is broad agreement that Parish Councils should have a central role in deciding if a site should be approved and that Travellers could help themselves by recognising the need to prove themselves as members of the community, if they want the Parish Council's support to stay. It was further noted that Travellers were subject to the same laws as everyone else and that they also had a vested interest in self policing their sites.

The need to look at both brownfield and greenfield sites as part of the solution has been discussed and there is recognition that a proactive approach would be more satisfactory in the long run, rather than an ad-hoc series of planning applications for less than ideal sites. It was agreed that brownfield sites would probably be better suited for transit or stop over purposes and greenfield sites best for longer term occupation, but with fallow or recovery spells built in. There was a general feeling that small sites would be more acceptable as they were less obtrusive and easier to control.

If new sites were to be identified there was a need for landowners to come forward with sites. It was recognised that the provision of sites could be on either public or private land and discussions have taken place with officers of the County Council with regard to the identification of land in their ownership that may be suitable. Land, predominantly smallholdings but also some woodland, has been identified but it has not been established where Traveller sites may be located. The potential for involving private landowners has also been considered. A requirement for a maximum of twelve sites was mentioned throughout the district as a whole, the idea being to find sites with local agreement.

The wider picture with regard to the issue of which tier of government should be responsible for finding solutions to the problems of inappropriate encampments has also been discussed. The consensus was that whilst these issues were best resolved at a local level, it was felt that central government should take a strong lead in defining and or clarifying the relevant national planning and social policies. Comment has also been expressed about the need to deal with the provision of sites on a County wide or regional basis rather than just at district level.

How we are progressing matters

To progress matters, separate meetings comprising smaller groups of people were held both with the Travellers, to ascertain their requirements for sites and their willingness to comply with a code (guidelines for the responsible use of sites), and with landowners, to ascertain their requirements with regard to a code. Representatives from Parish Councils met with Travellers and representatives from the Children's Society whilst representatives of the Somerset Association of Local Councils and National Farmers Union met with representatives of farmers and other landowners. Officers of the District Council acted as facilitators for both these meetings.

Arising from those meetings, officers prepared a suggested framework and conditions which would be needed to help bring about the provision of private sites by landowners and farmers. The initial suggestions reflected the priorities identified by farmers and landowners and feedback was sought from Traveller representatives on their expectations. It was felt that consultation early in the proceedings could only be beneficial and generally very positive feedback has been received. The draft framework/site conditions were considered to be broadly acceptable but needed further refinement. It was stressed that the final document should be coherent, comprehensive and in plain English that could not be misinterpreted.

Our meetings have achieved a fair degree of understanding between the parties involved and have brought representatives of Parish Councils and Travellers together. We have also made significant progress in identifying the problems and seeking solutions with the drawing up of a framework for sites and site conditions being actively progressed.

Where do we go next?

In the first instance, the site framework/site conditions document is to be drawn together by the District Council's officers. Parish Councils will then be asked to advise us should there be any refinements they would like to see incorporated. A skeleton legal tenancy agreement is also to be drawn up. The framework/site conditions will be consolidated as a document that could then be passed to landowners who show an interest in providing a site. It was felt that initially a pilot site needed to be established from which lessons could be learnt in order to make further progress. Investigations are to take place regarding the best way to attract interest from landowners in providing a site – by letter or advertisement has been suggested.

It has been questioned what the incentive would be for private landowners to provide sites. It was commented that a rent per pitch could be charged although the amount would depend on the facilities provided at a site. Any rent, however, should not be so high so as to put Travellers on benefits dependency. The Council could exercise control of sites where the land was in the local authority's ownership. On private land, however, there will need to be some form of leasing arrangement – the Council could not just assume a management role. Sites will also need to be subject to licensing and the criteria for that purpose would need to be investigated.

Taking a wider view the opinion has been expressed that pressure should be brought to bear on central government to take a lead in finding solutions to inappropriate encampments. There is a need to consider whether the provision of sites should be considered on a County wide or regional basis. These issues could perhaps be considered by the Local Government Association and the National Association of Parish Councils.

The Government has recently issued a White Paper in which they set out their vision for modernising local government in England. Amongst other things, the Government are setting up Regional Development Agencies which will work alongside voluntary regional chambers in each of the English Regions. They have also shown a commitment to move to directly elected regional government in England, where there is a demand for it. The provision of Traveller sites could perhaps be considered by any new regional chambers or governments in the future.

Other initiatives

An initial idea to produce a leaflet for Travellers regarding planning expanded into a booklet for settled and travelling communities, covering such subjects as: Applying for planning permission; South Somerset District Council's Toleration, Eviction and Planning Policies; Rights and Responsibilities; County Council Information; Health, Safety and Welfare; and Children and Education, as well as an extensive range of contacts at local, national and international levels. The booklet has gone out to a wide range of individuals, agencies and organisations as well as all the Parish Councils within South Somerset, and the feedback has been very good from all the above. With regard to applying for planning permission the booklet has proved to be extremely useful when combined with my time spent with the Travellers discussing the matter. I have felt happy that the information within the booklet is understood during the discussion and then remains with the Travellers to refer to if necessary.

Another positive initiative around the planning issue has been to develop joint-working with Enforcement Officers. This has proved to be useful for all parties as the individuals concerned are given the facts around the issue of planning at the same time as being supported by the Community Worker.

Last autumn a tangible partnership between the District Council and Somerset Health Authority was set up. A local health visitor who has worked with both traditional and new Travellers unofficially for many years has been commissioned by the Health Authority to co-ordinate a one year pilot project in South Somerset to develop an integrated approach to social health in partnership with the nomadic community. South Somerset District Council have provided a desk, telephone and administrative support. A Steering Group has been formed including the National Co-ordinator of Friends, Families and Travellers, the Children's Society's Children Participation Project, the District Community Worker, District Councillor and a Health Visitor, as well as representatives from both the Traditional and New Travelling communities.

Conclusion

There is no doubt some way to go but it is felt that significant progress has been made at a local level in tackling the issues surrounding inappropriate encampments. Further meetings of the 'Solutions to Inappropriate Encampments' Group are to be held to further discuss the above mentioned issues.

The role of the church *by Richard Trahair*

Social Responsibility Officer Mrs Kathleen Ben Rabha is assisting a Gypsy family in Salisbury District. The family owns its own land and has been living on it continually for eight years, in a caravan. This contravenes the county structural plan for land use, even though the site is very neat and clean and the family have never given anyone cause for complaint. The land is designated as open farm land; hence the family has faced eviction for all that time and legal proceedings have been continuous.

Mrs Ben Rabha has been in touch with county planning officers, who eventually agreed with the family on a move to another site. The planning officers recommended the move to the planning committee, which nonetheless turned it down because of organised local opposition – local residents feared a fall in property prices. Church involvement can still help, however, in Mrs Ben Rabha's view: Church officers need to build up and maintain good working relationships with local government officers so that when there is some kind of crisis they can build on a good existing relationship. There is also a need to work on public opinion, to reduce prejudice. The Churches at national !evel need to join the increasing number of organisations calling for changes in planning regulations to allow Gypsy families to live on land that they themselves own.

The Diocese of Salisbury is also involved in a plan to make glebe land available for temporary sites for travelling families. Glebe land is church-owned agricultural land from which local incumbents used to derive their living. Much glebe land has been sold for housing or other purposes but much still remains. I am looking closely at where glebe land may be made available for sites. Particularly promising would be small patches of unprofitable coppice which the tenant farmer is not working and which s/he does not intend to clear.

This would tie in well with the Woodland Skills project run by Friends, Families and Travellers and which has received lottery funding, whereby Travelling families learn to maintain coppices. Families would camp at a coppice, work the woodland, then move on when the work is done, to work on the next coppice. This would give work to Travelling families; keep woodland in economic production; maintain woodland in healthy condition; encourage the retention and planning of coppiced woodland; and improve relationships between settled people and Travellers when settled people can see that Travelling people are performing a service which is useful to ecology and economy. Travelling people could also teach coppicing skills to settled people, earning the respect of the settled population.

One problem with allowing glebe land to be used as sites is that glebe land is supposed to produce an income. I am investigating the possibility of housing benefit being paid to the church on behalf of Travellers using glebe land; this would produce an income and may satisfy the trustees of glebe land.[143]

---

143 For a directory of involvement in *Gypsy and Traveller matters by other churches, see the Churches* Commission for Racial Justice. Gypsies Travellers and the Churches, Interchurch House, 35–41 Lower Marsh, London SE1 7RL (£2.50), 1998

10

Eviction and criminal justice

Evictions from unauthorised encampments *by Chris Johnson*

T he powers of local authorities and the police to evict Travellers from unauthorised encampments were enormously increased by ss77-8 (for local authorities) and ss61-2 (for the police) of the Criminal Justice and Public Order Act 1994 (CJPOA). For the first time, trespass was criminalised if the trespasser failed to comply with a removal direction. Some guidance on the application of the powers under ss77-8 was given by Sedley J in *R v Lincolnshire County Council ex parte Atkinson, R v Wealden District Council ex parte Wales and Stratford*.[144] Sedley J. made it clear that, before deciding whether or not to serve a removal direction under the CJPOA s77, a local authority must make welfare enquiries of the Travellers as outlined in DoE (now DETR) Circular 18/94.[145] This will include statutory and other duties around the issues of health, education, pregnancy, children, and other "considerations of common humanity".

In *R v Kerrier District Council ex parte Uzell Blythe and Sons*,[146] Latham J. indicated that such enquiries should also be carried out where a local authority were considering planning enforcement action against Travellers. However, in *R v Brighton and Hove Council ex parte Marmont*,[147] Tucker J. stated that Circular 18/94 did not apply to an eviction under the Rules of Supreme Court Order 113, i.e. civil proceedings in the High Court. Nevertheless, he accepted that there remained statutory duties to which

144 *The Times,* 22 September 1995
145 Welsh Office Circular 76/94.
146 (1996) JPL 837
147 *The Times,* 15 and 20 January 1998

the local authority had to have regard and he re-iterated the need to take account of "considerations of common humanity".

This emphasis on enquiries seemed to be undermined by the case of *R v Hillingdon London Borough Council ex parte McDonagh*.[148] The case involved the eviction of a Traveller family from an official caravan site where they were 'squatting'. Carnwath J. stated that "the Circular was an indication of good practice imposing no legally binding obligation on the local authority moving to evict trespassers from its own land in pursuance of its powers of management under the Caravan Sites and Control of Development Act 1960." Though not reported in the Times, Carnwath J. also made it clear he was following the decision in *Marmont* and stated that a local authority must not be "blinkered" in its approach to unauthorised encampments. Nevertheless, the judgement did seem to indicate a lesser standard for enquiries in certain eviction situations.

In the unreported case of *R v Leeds City Council ex parte Maloney*,[149] which involved an eviction of Travellers using County Court Rules Order 24 (civil) proceedings, Scott Baker J. stated: "It is not necessary for me to decide the ambit of applicability of the Department of the Environment Circular 18/94 to possession actions. It is now common ground after the observations of Sedley J. in the Lincolnshire County Council case, about a local authority ignoring at its peril considerations of common humanity relating to the needs of those who are to be evicted, that it applies to this case. Failure to take such matters into account in public law may effect the validity of the decision to evict."

It seems that the conflicting opinions expressed in the above cases are resolved by the *Good Practice Guide* published by the DETR and the Home Office on 29 October 1998, *Managing Unauthorised Camping*.

The Guide follows the spirit of Sedley J's judgement. For example, it states: "Unauthorised camping cannot be dealt with in isolation. In the absence of a wider strategy towards the Gypsy and Traveller issues as a whole, the most that can be achieved is shifting people from one site to another to no one's advantage".[150]Most importantly, it emphasises throughout that enquiries must be carried out by local authorities when considering eviction: "Local authorities must consider welfare issues when deciding whether to proceed with eviction whatever the powers being used."[151] Important directions are given to local authority officers charged with carrying out the enquiries: "The specialist enquiries should also ... act as a trigger to the services involved in meeting those needs ... Reasonable attempts should be made to get information from Gypsies and Travellers who are not in at the time of the visit. Local authorities should bear in mind that Gypsies and Travellers may have varying levels of reading and writing skills. All sites should be visited on at least two occasions at different times of the day ...".

The Guide stresses the need for local authorities to carefully consider the results of their enquiries and not just to carry out an automatic, meaningless process.[152] There is also an important emphasis on 'toleration': "Encampments must be 'tolerated' where

148 *The Times*, 9 November 1998149 The Times, 9 November 1998
149 3 July 1998, CO/958/97
150 Para.3.1
151 Para.4.11; see also paras.3.3 and 6.2
152 Para.4.15

enquiries have revealed specific welfare needs ... 'toleration' can be defined as a willingness to delay initiating eviction proceedings and/or to give generous periods for compliance once proceedings have been started." Sites can be tolerated "for a matter of days, weeks, months or years, depending on the circumstances."[153] Local authorities should always consider the provision of services. Policies should be written down and arrived at after liaison with the police and relevant agencies, including Travellers and/or their representative bodies.[154] Site provision, both permanent and transit, remains an essential need and it is vital to ensure the upkeep of existing sites.

The police should not use section 61 indiscriminately. It should not be the first response in every case. "Appropriate triggers might include individual criminal activity, serious breaches of the peace, or disorder, or a significant disruption to the life of the local community." The police must avoid efforts to 'encourage' Travellers to leave turning into 'harassment.'[155] The Good Practice Guide clarifies the law on unauthorised encampments and puts to rest previous attempts to evade the need for enquiries. The Guide is essential reading for relevant officers in local authorities and police forces throughout England and Wales and for all barristers, solicitors and other advisers dealing with Travellers' issues.

The Crime and Disorder Act 1998 *by Bill Forrester*

The Crime and Disorder Act 1998 includes a number of new ideas and approaches. Home Secretary Jack Straw has described it as "the culmination of a long held ambition to empower local people to take control of the fight against crime and disorder in their area."

Particular measures include:

- Crime and Disorder Reduction Partnerships, led by councils and police jointly in each area. These must be set up and operating by April 1999.
- Crime audits, which show the type and number of particular crimes committed in particular areas, down to local wards or parishes. These must be carried out by the Partnerships.
- Measures to deal with antisocial activity. If such an 'anti-social behaviour order' is disobeyed, the person or persons disobeying it commit(s) a criminal offence. The order can be sought by local authority or police from a magistrates' court and lasts at least two years, but can be varied or ended earlier than that.
- Curfews enforceable within a particular area against children under ten, in a public place between 9pm and 6am and not under the effective control of a parent or responsible person over eighteen. A child curfew scheme is made by the local authority, but is only effective when confirmed by the Home Secretary, and must follow consultation with interested parties.
- Measures requiring a police officer to work in each Young Offenders Team.

Whenever new criminal powers are proposed, they are scrutinised by both Houses of Parliament. However, problems are most likely to appear when they start being used. It

153 Para.5.1, para.5.5
154 Paras.2.7-9, 3.4-6, 3.18-20 and 4.2-7
155 Para.6.10

is understandable that Travellers and other minority groups are going to fear that any new powers are going to be used against them. It is vitally important that all minority groups are aware of what is in the Act, and of the risks of powers being used maliciously or in ignorance by those who are prejudiced. The price of liberty is eternal vigilance.

The main risks would appear to be:

- Crime audits only measure types of crime and numbers of crimes reported. If such an audit reveals a lot of crime near a site or encampment, then, unless the culprits are known, Travellers could easily be blamed. This could lead to pressure for a site to close or an encampment to be more quickly moved. However, the crime audit might be a better alternative than current hearsay, rumour and gossip.
- The relevance of fear in any close community. If Travellers are frightened to report crime and tell on criminals, then the whole site or community may, in practice, be blamed, by use of a curfew order or general treatment by police and local authorities.
- Antisocial orders being made against Travellers, especially in housing, more easily than against others. This could be because other neighbours are either not supportive of them, or feel pressured to side with neighbours seeking to force a family out.
- Curfew orders being made over a general area which includes a site, because there are complaints about young people without anyone knowing exactly which young people are responsible for what. However, the question for most parents of any children is: do I know where my child under ten is? And should they be out till late at night with their friends at that age, wandering the area?

Kent County Council, along with others, was consulted in 1995 about the early ideas that Jack Straw had on some of the above. There is no doubt that it has been improved greatly since then. There is little doubt that antisocial activity and petty crime affect millions of people in the UK every year. My view is that everyone needs to monitor the use of these new powers closely, and that most Travellers and Gypsies (like most people) have a vested interest in crime reduction. Whatever laws are passed can give power to those who blame Travellers wrongly, and so no-one should be complacent.

Perhaps the best thing that could come out of the Partnership initiatives is joint working between police and councils on a range of matters, including the fight against the import and distribution of drugs to young people. The Act reflects the fact that the police cannot beat crime on their own. If police and local authorities can agree common approaches to the treatment of encampments, for example, Travellers could have more certainty about how they will be treated in a particular area. If various agencies can share more information, then there are risks and major confidentiality issues, but it could lead to those who commit crime (whoever they are) being less able to hide behind the communities into which they inject fear. Of paramount importance, however, is the safety of individuals who are seeking to combat crime by legitimate means.

The above paragraph contains a number of big 'Ifs'. What everyone should do next is to find out more about initiatives in their own areas, get hold of copies of publications by partnerships, and challenge allegations against Travellers which do not have any evidence to back them up. Those responsible for crime need to know that they cannot take advantage of hiding behind others and controlling them through fear and involvement.

11

Planning

An alternative planning circular: the background *by Michael Cox, Sarah Cox and Alan Masters*

Alan Masters

The aim of this document is to firstly identify the problems that exist within the current system for site provision, and secondly to explain how the solutions to those problems as set out in the revised Circular 1/94 (below) will overcome these and provide for a sound and enduring system of site provision.

Historical background – Gypsies

In the years before the First World War Gypsies and Travellers enjoyed a relatively undisturbed existence, which changed little despite the introduction of planning regulation. After the Second World War the picture began to change, first with highway and motorway construction taking away traditional stopping places on green verges and the like, then the Commons Registration Act 1960 comprehensively changing the availability of common land for winter stopping. The Act placed 'ownership' of the Commons into Local Authority or 'commoners' hands. For the first time trespass laws could be enforced against those stopping on the commons. At the same time the changes to a more modern machine-based agriculture industry meant the end of farmers' need to accommodate seasonal labour in the spring and summer months.

Gypsies and Travellers were forced to travel further afield to find accommodation, and were coming more into contact with planning regulation and court and eviction proceedings. At the same time, static 'holiday' caravan parks were proliferating, especially along the coastline. The government's response was to enact the Caravan Sites and Control of Development Act 1960, which enabled local authorities to provide pitches, and imposed licensing requirements on all private sites. However, there was no duty to provide, and little provision was made until the enactment of the Caravan Sites Act 1968.

Problems

Part II of the Caravan Sites Act 1968 placed a duty on County Councils to make public provision for Gypsies; the duty was elucidated by Circular 28/77. There was, however, no duty on District Councils, and the failure of Councils to comply with the duty and their wanton flouting of the Act even in the face of Court judgement led eventually to the repeal of the duty by the Criminal Justice and Public Order Act (CJPOA) 1994. This move, combined with Government guidance encouraging the enabling of self-provision, led to an increasing number of applications for private sites for Travelling people. However, in practice, Councils have shown a similar reluctance to allow private provision as when there was a duty to make public provision.

This has led to a growth of unauthorised sites and overcrowding on existing sites as second generation Travelling people are unable to secure legitimate pitches. The conditions on such sites are often poor in terms of basic amenities, including clean water, proper sanitation, and access to education and healthcare services. In the face of these mounting problems, many Gypsies are accepting inducements being offered by local authorities to move into settled accommodation, thus abandoning their traditional way of life. The concern is that central government and local authorities are attempting to abolish the nomadic way of life altogether and integrate Gypsies, a recognised ethnic minority, fully into the settled community.

Since the Gypsy way of life has traditionally been a nomadic one, Gypsies have always required transit sites in addition to permanent sites. The Cripps Report,[156] which gave rise to Circular 57/78, provided a comprehensive overview of this accommodation problem. One of the most important recommendations was that there should be a network of transit sites across the country. Many traditionally-used transit sites have been stopped up in modern times; this combined with the criminalisation of stopping on highways, byways and verges by the CJPOA 1994 and the unavailability of commons has led to many Gypsies and Travellers being reluctant to travel at all, or only during the summer months. Those that do travel are routinely subjected to harassment and continual cries of 'move on'.

The problem of where sites ought to be located is not a new one. Most of the traditional stopping places were on greenfield sites. With increasing protection afforded to the countryside and environment, and designation prohibitive of development, e.g. Green Belts, AONBs, SSSIs and so forth, identifying sites has never been harder (even though, as should be stressed, living in a caravan on land is a 'land use' and not operational development). Obtaining provision for mobile accommodation in Council areas – which outside of existing settlement boundaries are usually Green Belt – or with special protection has proved nearly impossible, even for Travelling people who have long-standing local connections.

---

156 Cripps, John. Accommodation for Gypsies: A Report on the Working of the Caravan Sites Act 1968, DoE/Welsh Office, HMSO, London, 1976

Current guidance

The current government guidance in respect of Gypsy site accommodation is found in Circular 1/94. The Circular requires Councils to specify in development plans either a location or a criteria-based policy with regard to site provision. The object is to make the provision of accommodation for Travelling people plan-led. The Circular also restricted site provision in Green Belt areas, reversing earlier guidance which accepted that sites may be necessary in such locations where, in exceptional cases, need outweighed other material considerations.

However, very few location-based policies have been included in plans to date, and criteria-based policies have proved difficult to comply with. There are no restrictions on the number of criteria Councils can include, what such criteria should deal with, and whether the criteria should be satisfied as a mandatory requirement before a site is deemed acceptable development or should serve as guidance only. The criteria of some Councils can even be described as perverse. Gypsies and Travellers are often able to comply with all but one criterion in a development plan, and so a site that is acceptable all but one respect falls at the last hurdle. Councils routinely use such failure to comply with one or more criterion as a peg upon which to hang refusal of planning permission.

The issue of 'need' and proving 'need' for further site accommodation has long been an identifiable problem. Councils often cite inaccurate and misleading statistics, based on the DoE/DETR biannual counts, to show that there is no further need for such accommodation in their area. It is often unclear who is included in the counts, and has been known for some time that Travelling people who are on unauthorised sites or those regularly moved on are not always included within the figures. The data gathering and record keeping of numbers and need is at present inadequate.

Councils are often reluctant to grant planning permission for sites in the face of local opposition, and there has long been concern that refusals of permission are not based on land use factors. Local opposition is often borne from prejudice or perhaps from experience of unauthorised encampments or badly-run public sites; these are, for the most part, vastly different from the private authorised sites that have found their way over the planning hurdles. This provides another reason why such private site provision needs to be encouraged by effective policies and guidance.

Revised circular solutions

The need is for more positive encouragement from central government to Councils in respect of site applications, and the formulation of a more structured approach to the need for site provision. This will have the benefit of reducing the number of unauthorised sites, releasing pitches on public sites for those who cannot afford to buy land to provide their own site. This should also have the effect of ending the pressure on poorer and next generation Travelling people to move into settled accommodation which they would not otherwise choose.

To overcome the problem of identifying 'need' on a piecemeal basis, inquiry by inquiry, guidance should be issued that would require Structure Plans and Part II of Unitary Development Plans (UDPs) to set out a strategic framework for site provision. This would include the requirement to indicate a figure for the projected scale of site provision to be made in the area as a whole, during the currency of the Plan. The Plan would need to explain how the caravan site provision figures had been derived and the assumptions underlying them. Thus this would have the added benefit of requiring Councils to obtain accurate records of numbers of Travellers and patterns of travelling in their area.

In addition the Plan should identify the type of sites required, i.e. short-term transit sites, permanent sites and sites for identifiable groups (mirroring the approach adopted by urban authorities to the provision of housing to separate ethnic groups).

The system will work much as projections for new housing for the settled populations are currently enshrined in plans, such that Councils will have to provide at least that number of pitches during the life of the plan. If a need was proved that exceeded the minimum number of new pitches recommended in the Plan then this would be no bar to further provision being made. As Structure Plans and Part I of UDPs will only specify minimum pitch numbers to be provided, problems associated with the former system of designation under the 1968 Act will be avoided.

Local Plans would be required to translate the broad policies of the structure plan into more detailed development control policies and map-based land allocations. As with the allocation of land for new housing development, the allocation of land for sites should be a duty placed upon local planning authorities through the local plan process. Location-based policies would thus become the norm in Local Plans with criteria-based policies providing opportunities for additional site provision where 'need' above that set out in the plan can be proven.

Temporary stopping as permitted development

In addition, consideration should be given for guidance to be incorporated that would restate the need to make provision for a network of transit sites. This would allow Travelling people (even those who have obtained permanent private or public site provision) to travel and continue with their cultural traditions, without the fear of losing their permanent pitch or incurring the sanctions of the criminal law.

Local authorities could be required to make provision of more transit sites (as envisaged by Cripps) and to reopen those that have been stopped up; or provision could be made to regularise the common practise whereby those unable to park at the roadside 'holiday' at authorised private sites owned by other family members. This practice could be encouraged where appropriate by altering the terms of the General Permitted Development Order 1995 to allow the residential occupation of a caravan on land without specific planning permission for a period up to 3 months, where the land is privately owned and/or where the land is already the subject of a site licence. (for further see below, in a piece by Dr Malcolm Bell). The period could be shorter where land is publicly owned. In this context it should be remembered that the siting of caravans for residential use would remain subject to regulatory control under the 1968 Act.[157] More accurate record keeping will enable Councils to monitor numbers and patterns with regard to transit site use and provide more pitches in areas where demand is high; or perhaps provide additional pitches only at peak times, thus avoiding problems of vandalism of underused facilities. Better record keeping could

157 Provision for site licences and conditions.

enable people intending to travel to an area to contact the relevant Council in advance to ascertain pitch availability.

Land allocation

Local authorities should be encouraged to use location-based policies in Local Plans and Part II of UDPs instead of Criteria-based policies wherever possible to identify appropriate land for sites. Councils are encouraged to look to their own land and land owned by public bodies. This will have the dual advantage of putting to use underused or unused land, and solve mobile accommodation problems in the short or longer term. It will also make it easier for Travelling people and their advisors to locate and purchase appropriate land on which a site can be established.[158] Guidance in respect of Green Belt land and other special sites should be reviewed. General policy would remain the same, that the need to protect the countryside and natural environment is recognised and sites would not normally be appropriate in Green Belt areas, AONBs, SSSIs and the like where housing is also not appropriate. This would not by itself exonerate local authorities from dealing with site provision in their Structure Plan. Where an extensive proportion of the land in a local authority are outside existing settlements consists of such designated land, the authority will still be required to set out a projection of need and a realistic policy for meeting it.

Where it can be demonstrated that there is a considerable unmet need (in the first instance as would be set out in the Plan) and where it is not practicable for that need to be met without allowing site provision in those areas, this would be a material consideration which might justify setting aside the general presumption against development. In such circumstances a further material consideration could be whether sites could be identified that would provide positive planning gain, such as by reusing derelict land and helping to return brown field sites and despoiled land to its former state.

Councils could be encouraged to grant permissions on a temporary basis, both on land which is awaiting development (to provide a temporary solution to an accommodation shortage) and where there is local opposition such that a temporary permission may act to quell it when a full permission is sought. This may appear to be putting Travelling people on 'probation', but is a politically and practically realistic option.[159]

Planning and sites for Travelling people: DoE Circular 1/94 revisited *by Philip Brown, Diana Allen and the Traveller Working Group on Planning*

Introduction

1.   Special considerations apply to the provision of caravan sites for Gypsies and Travellers, because of the need for such sites and the consequences of inade-

---

158 A service already exists which identifies land for commercial use and, in some cases, offers planning permission and subsidisation. See the fact sheet on *The Commission for New Towns*, Traveller Law Research Unit, Cardiff Law School.

159 Diana Allen is opposed to use of temporary permissions except on land which is to be used for other purposes, as it encourages local settled people to keep up opposition when permanent permission is sought, and leads to unfair insecurity for site residents. Well-run permanent sites, as already shown in Part 1 Chapter 3, can prove opposition unfounded.

quate provision. Travelling people only make up a small proportion of the population of England and Wales, but their land use requirements need to be met. The aim must be for every Gypsy or Traveller in a particular area to have a lawful place to stay, and to avoid the necessity for families to camp haphazardly on unauthorised sites where they are denied access to mains water, proper sanitation, education and healthcare facilities. The planning system must recognise the need for accommodation consistent with the nomadic life-style of some Travelling people.

Diana Allen

2. Section 24 of the Caravan Sites and Control of Development Act 1960, as amended by Section 80 of the Criminal Justice and Public Order Act 1994, provides that 'Gypsies' means persons of a nomadic habit of life, whatever their race or origin. The term does not include members of an organised group of travelling show people or circus people, travelling together as such. The courts have further clarified the definition of the word 'Gypsies' as meaning persons who wander or travel for the purpose of making or seeking their livelihood, and does not include persons who move from place to place without any connection between their movement and their means of livelihood. 'Travellers' have not been included in this definition. All references to Travellers in this guidance are references to Gypsies in this sense, and also include: Irish Travellers; other people who are nomadic by habit or by choice and whose sole place of residence is a caravan, bus, tent or other form of moveable structure; and Travellers who have been nomadic but are in housing due to circumstances including ill-health. The purpose for travelling should not be relevant and no strict definition should be sought.

3. The repeal of local authorities' duty to provide sites by the Criminal Justice and Public Order Act 1994 has led to more applications for private sites. Many Travelling People would prefer to find and buy their own sites to develop and manage, and the planning system should encourage them to do so. The existence of more private sites should release pitches on local authority sites for those Travelling People most in need of public provision.

4. A variety of sites will be required to reflect different forms of accommodation, including residential caravan sites for prolonged periods of occupation, and transit sites. Provision may also need to be made for on-site working. Most working Travelling People are self-employed, sometimes occupied in landscape gardening or other such occupations where on-site storage facilities may be required; others earn their living from carpet selling or supplying, fitting UPVC cladding, the use of woodland and agricultural skills or the provision of other such goods and services whereby no on-site facilities are needed. Local planning authorities need to be aware of the different accommodation and occupational needs of Travelling people when preparing their development plans. It will therefore be necessary for local planning authorities to discuss Travellers'

accommodation needs, at an early stage in the preparation of structure plans and unitary development plans, with the Travellers themselves, their representative bodies and local support groups.

Development Plans

5.   In preparing or amending their development plans, local planning authorities will be expected to make adequate provision for Travelling people choosing to reside in their areas, through the use of locational or criteria-based policies.

6.   Structure Plans and Part 1 of unitary development plans will indicate the level of provision to be made to meet the accommodation needs of Travelling people, expressed in terms of the minimum number of caravan pitches to be provided within the Plan period. Structure plans should break this total down into separate figures for each district. Any figures set should be treated as a minimum, not an end goal. As with the housing market, a vacancy rate of around five per cent is essential at any given time to ensure fluidity within the market.

7.   Structure Plans and Part 1 of unitary development plans will need to explain how the site provision figures have been derived and the assumptions underlying them. They must also contain criteria-based policies which provide a general framework to enable site provision.

8.   In deciding what level of provision is necessary it is essential for authorities to maintain accurate and up-to-date records of unauthorised encampments. It is often the case that authorities' own environmental health departments will be responsible for investigating complaints about unauthorised encampments, and their records may provide a more accurate indication of need than the biannual count published by the DETR. Support agencies such as Traveller Education Support Services (TESS), and health visitors, may also hold records of unauthorised encampments which can assist in the assessment of need. Such information will also help determine the geographical distribution of caravan site provision, but it must be borne in mind that an absence of unauthorised sites will not necessarily indicate an absence of need. In general, Travelling People will wish to locate in areas close to large centres of population, or close to major transport routes, and the distribution of provision should reflect this.

9.   Local Plans and Part II of unitary development plans should wherever possible identify sufficient locations suitable for sites, whether local authority, housing association, or private sites, to satisfy the minimum level of provision proscribed by Structure Plans or Part I of unitary development plans. Authorities will be expected to make use of the registers of unused and under-used land owned by public bodies in identifying suitable locations. Vacant land or surplus local authority land may be appropriate. Locations awaiting development in the future may also be suitable for a limited period, but will not generally be suitable for the establishment of private sites.

10. It is important that sufficient land is genuinely available in practical terms to enable the policies and proposals of the development plan to be carried forward. This means that sites must not only be free, or readily freed, from planning,

physical and ownership constraints, but must be affordable and capable of being developed economically, be in areas where Travelling people want to live and be suitable for the complete range of site provision which their communities may require. Local planning authorities should satisfy themselves, in consultation with Travelling people and their representative bodies, on the value of sites which may be regarded as being affordable.

11.   Even where sufficient sites are allocated to meet structure plan requirements, local plans must also set out clear, realistic criteria for suitable location, as a basis for future site provision. These criteria-based policies must not only indicate where sites will not generally be appropriate, but must also give a clear indication of those areas within which sites will generally be acceptable in order to reflect the positive encouragement to be given to the establishment of new sites.

Location of sites

12.   In deciding where to provide for sites for Travelling People, local planning authorities should note that most have access to private transport. While it is desirable that sites should be located reasonably close to schools, hospitals and other services, those able to develop their own site can decide such matters for themselves – as is the case for other, settled, people – in deciding where to live.

13.   Sites will generally be appropriate in rural areas, but care must be taken to minimise encroachment into the open countryside by encouraging the re-use of derelict, despoiled or previously developed land, and ensuring that sites are capable of accommodating a high standard of landscaping. Care needs to be taken to ensure compatibility with agricultural, environmental and countryside policies, as set out below.

14.   As a rule it will not be appropriate to make provision for sites in areas of open land where development is severely restricted by national countryside designations, such as AONBs or SSSIs. Locally important sites for nature conservation, designated in development plans, should also be avoided. The general principle is that any restriction or allowance applying to the development of housing should apply equally to sites for Travelling people.

15.   Gypsy and Traveller sites are not regarded as being among those uses of land which are normally appropriate in Green Belts. Green Belt should not therefore be allocated for sites in development plans. A site for development of a site could, where it is located on the edge of a settlement, be considered alongside any proposal for the adjustment of Green Belt boundaries. Such boundaries should be altered only where a demonstrable need exists for additional site accommodation and all other practicable options for location outside of the Green Belt have been thoroughly assessed and discounted, or where housing development is also considered appropriate and necessary on that Green Belt land.

Applications

16. Where a development plan contains policies relevant to a proposal for a site for Travelling people, authorities must determine the planning application in accordance with the plan unless material considerations indicate otherwise. In this regard, criteria-based site policies will be assumed to be consistent with the other policies of the plan, including policies for the control of the development of accommodation in the open countryside. Where a development plan does not include a specific site policy, application should be determined in accordance with this Circular.

17. In circumstances where insufficient sites have been granted planning permission, or identified in development plans, to satisfy the structure plan requirement, a need for additional accommodation will be presumed to exist. Even where the structure plan requirement has been met, a demonstration of need will be a material consideration which must be taken into account in the determination of planning applications.

18. Most sites will give rise to objections of one kind or another. Local objections by settled people to a proposal may prove unfounded when a well laid out and well run site is established and the site residents have settled in. Conditions on a properly equipped site are very different from those on an unauthorised encampment with no facilities. Need, and the problems arising from a lack of proper sites, are capable of being the decisive factors in the determination of planning applications, particularly where any encroachment into open countryside, or other visual harm, is capable of mitigation by landscaping. Small sites of about 0.4 ha can usually accommodate up to five pitches for individual or extended families without on-site business activities, save for within specially protected areas of countryside. There should be a presumption in favour of allowing such development.

19. Sites cannot be regarded as appropriate development within an approved Green Belt. Special considerations may, however, arise in some of the more extensive areas of Green Belt. Within areas where a substantial proportion of land outside of existing settlements is designated as Green Belt, an identified need for additional site accommodation may justify setting aside the general presumption against inappropriate development, where all other practicable options for location outside the Green Belt have been thoroughly assessed and discounted. The availability and price of land outside of the Green Belt, and the viability of purchase by Travelling people who are often unable to raise finance in the normal way, will be relevant factors in deciding whether practicable options exist.

20. Authorities should recognise that they may receive applications from Travelling people without local connections, just as non-Travellers may move to an entirely new area whether for employment or other reasons, and which could not reasonably have been foreseen in development plan policies. Authorities should not refuse private applications on the grounds that they consider existing provision in the area to be adequate, or because alternative accommodation is available elsewhere on the authorities' own sites.

Site policies in local, unitary, structure and regional plans   *by*
Rodney Stableford

Within the planning system, it remains the statutory duty of local planning authorities to review their structure, unitary and local plans at regular intervals as required by the Secretary of State of the Department of the Environment, Transport and the Regions (DETR). This provides an opportunity for the plans to be updated to take into account evidence gathered from census and survey data relating to changes and distribution in the size and characteristics of the population, inward and outward migration of population and resources, alterations to the economy, the transport needs of the planned area and the protection of its environment.

Policies are updated in all issue areas such as housing, the economy and employment, transport and the environment to meet the new problems that may be emerging over ten to fifteen years into the future. Currently, county, unitary, and local planning authorities are reviewing their plans up to the year 2011, using data gathered at national, regional and local levels. The reviews take into account the hierarchy of the planning system in that the structure plans prepared by county councils provide the strategic framework for detailed policies in the local plans prepared by the district councils, and for the control of development through decisions made on individual planning applications. Unitary authorities are responsible for all-embracing unitary plans which combine the roles of the structure and local plans within the unitary plan framework.

At the same time current central Government policy is to modify the planning system by adding a number of missing dimensions which are seen to be necessary. These include taking into account the European context; providing a national policy for projects where decentralisation of decision making is not seen to be possible; making effective arrangements for regional planning so that more issues can be resolved at that level; and making improvements to local planning through the use of economic instruments and other policy tools (e.g. subsidy, taxation and other financial incentives) to help meet emerging planning objectives. These proposals were outlined in the DETR publication *Modernising Planning: A Policy Statement by the Minister for the Regions, Regeneration and Planning*, first issued in January 1998.[160] It is within the context of these impending changes to the planning system that the following suggestions are made.

The serious and chronic shortage of authorised sites for Travellers, and the failure of the planning system to allow or enable sufficient numbers of such sites, coupled with the effects of the Criminal Justice and Public Order Act 1994 on the Traveller communities, has criminalised many families who have been left with no legal stopping place through no fault of their own. To increase provision regional planning guidance is seen as being important in setting down guidelines to local planning authorities, and the proposed Regional Development Agencies (RDAs), and Regional Assemblies (RAs) are central to ensuring their implementation.

Travellers require planning policies which are based on the principles of equality

160 Copies available from the DETR, Publications Dispatch Centre, Blackhorse Road, London, SE99 6TT tel. 0181 691 9191.

with house-dwellers, with public support for a range of provision. This should include transit sites conveniently sited near to the main routes of travel, as well as permanent sites which may be used for long or short-term stays. Policies could allow both public and privately owned sites to be enabled and would, for example, include the need for double pitches for each household for a minimum of two caravans together with their towing vehicles. Each double pitch would be provided with amenities which would include washing, cooking, and toilet provision, with full services including mains electricity, refuse collection and drainage facilities. Separate on-site working areas would also be included to allow Gypsies and Travellers to carry out their trades and earn their livelihood.

Development plans would need to give clear guidance to housing authorities on the projected growth of households among the Traveller community, and to include policies giving sites specific locations as well as criteria for site provision to be made within the time period of the development plans to meet the accommodation needs of Travellers. This would then give housing policies for Travellers the same status as those for the rest of the population.

The regional planning guidelines would provide the overall regional household projection for Travellers, and this figure would also be broken down into figures for each Development Plan to provide guidance to all the county or unitary authorities within the region when preparing their development plans. This information would need to be given as distinctly separate from but of equal status to the information relating to households with the general population who are to be accommodated in permanent dwellings.

The structure planning and unitary planning authority would, based on guidance from the Regional Policy Guidance Notes, use the household projections for Travellers, including those numbers projected to move in or out of housing, and distribute these figures on an area development plan basis. This would ensure that Traveller site needs would be included in Unitary Part II Development Plans or Local Plans as guidance to planning authorities responsible for that level of development planning.

These development plans (Local and Part II Unitary) would need to provide site specific as well as criteria-based policies if they were to be effective and enable the needs of the Traveller communities to be met within the time scale of the development plan. Regional Policy Guidance Notes would therefore set the overall site provision need in each area covered by either the Structure or the Unitary Part I Development Plan. The role of the Unitary Part II Development and Local Plan would be to provide policies which identify the locations of future sites, the number of double pitches and ancillary amenities they may accommodate in site specific terms, and to provide criteria-based policies for those sites which may be created by and provide accommodation for, as an example, an individual family or group of families.

There needs to be a monitoring process to check on non-compliance by those planning authorities who fail to provide site-specific or even criteria based policies because of, for example, local opposition and prejudice. Therefore that aspect of the local plan would need to be completed by the structure planning authority or, failing that, it would be the responsibility of the RDA or RA to implement Traveller policies required at structure and local plan level. Using the regional level would mean that politically difficult decisions could be taken sufficiently distantly from local pressures exercised by those who may be prejudiced against Gypsies and Travellers and might block proposed developments on that basis alone. It would be through the monitoring and review process that regional policy guidelines would be used as a means to detect non-compliance by the local planning authority. Action at regional level would then be seen as the way to implement policies at structure or local plan level.

The regional bodies are therefore seen as being ultimately responsible for the implementation of policies to meet the needs of the Traveller population embracing its natural growth. These policies would be based upon equality with those housing policies needed for the non-Traveller population who are in need of dwellings, but recognising that Travellers are in need of caravan sites to meet their primary accommodation needs.

Criteria based policies would need to avoid contradictory statements such as when they express the need for sites to have reasonable access to shops, schools and services yet at the same time to be some distance away from substantial residential development. It would be reasonable for the RDAs and RAs to provide guidelines, or 'model criteria', to ensure that criteria-based policies would avoid contradictory policies of this kind.

In conclusion, because of the inability and unwillingness of the majority of local planning authorities to provide planning policies which will actively encourage the creation and overcome the chronic shortage of sites for Gypsies and Travellers, the role of the regional bodies is one of major importance. Eventually it will be the directly elected RAs which will have the democratic power base to carry out their role in protecting the interests of less politically powerful minority groups such as the Traveller communities.

Meanwhile, there has for some time been strong evidence that public sector funds are being wasted in enforcement actions to evict Gypsies and Travellers who have no option but to reside on unofficial sites. Evictions result in their being forced out of one area only to be evicted then from the area into which they have moved. Considerable savings in public costs would be gained if areas for authorised pitches with ancillary amenities were identified in development plans, to give the Traveller communities the same accommodation rights as those enjoyed by the settled population. The proposals outlined above need to be implemented during the current exercise to modernise the planning process and to update development plans to meet the needs of the Traveller communities over the next ten to fifteen years.

Gypsies, race discrimination and planning *by Stephen Field*

It is supposedly unlawful for a planning authority to discriminate against a person when carrying out its planning functions.[161] Both direct and indirect racial discrimination is prohibited. A person discriminates directly against another on racial grounds if he treats that other less favourably than he treats or would treat other persons.[162] A person indirectly discriminates against another if he applies to that other a

---

161 Section 19A(1) of the Race Relations Act (RRA) 1976, as inserted by the Housing and Planning Act 1986 section 55
162 RRA 1976 section 1(1)(a)
163 RRA 1976 section 1(1)(b)
164 *Commission for Racial Equality v Dutton* [1989] All ER 306

requirement or condition which he applies or would apply equally to persons not of the same racial group as that other; which is such that the same proportion of persons of the same racial group as that other who can comply with it is considerably smaller than the proportion of persons not of that racial group who can comply with it; and which is to the detriment of that other because he cannot comply with it.[163]

The Court of Appeal has held that Gypsies are a racial group[164] within section 3(1) of the RRA 1976.The *Dutton* decision was based on the proposition that Gypsies remain an identifiable group defined by reference to their ethnic origins. There is a discernible group of Gypsies with a long shared history, which the group is conscious of as distinguishing it from other groups, and the memory of which keeps it alive. Gypsies have a cultural tradition of their own including family and social customs and manners. However, the term 'Traveller' is not synonymous with 'Gypsy' but refers to all persons leading a nomadic life, living in tents, caravans or other vehicles.

Thus, before a 'Gypsy' falls within the ambit of the RRA 1976 it is necessary for him or her to satisfy a 'cultural' and therefore 'ethnic' basis to his or her claim to Gypsy status. This requirement deprives those of a 'non-racial Gypsy' but, nonetheless, 'Traveller' life-style of the purported protection of the RRA 1976. It was held in *Dutton* that not all Travellers are Gypsies. Similarly, two 'New Age' Travellers were held not to be Gypsies, for the purposes of the Caravan Sites Act (CSA) 1968.[165] It was held that the applicants were not Gypsies, even though they adopted a nomadic way of life as their preferred life-style. The rationale for this was that there was no economic purpose to their travelling around the country.[166] Further, those of non-Gypsy and non-Traveller yet alternative life-style are offered no recognition or protection within the context of the RRA 1976.

It will be submitted in the conclusion to this paper that the current anti-discrimination legislation should, as well as actually being applied to those it purports to, but does not protect, should be extended in its application to a wider group than the present section 3(1) RRA 1976 grouping.

Even if a Gypsy satisfies the 'racial group' test such that section 19A ought to apply, it has been held[167] that since the term 'Gypsy' as used in the CSA 1968 simply meant 'persons of nomadic habit of life whatever their race or origin', it was not used in this context to mean Gypsies as a racial group.

Further, Runnymede's local plan policy, since the borough's quota for Gypsy caravan sites had already been exceeded, that the council would not agree to further Gypsy sites or pitches, was not discriminatory.

It was held not to be directly discriminatory, since the word 'Gypsy' was used in the non-racial sense of the CSA. And it was held not to be indirectly discriminatory since it did not accord to Gypsies a treatment less advantageous than to other ethnic groups, but marked a shift from treating Gypsies as having a special status, to treating them in the same way as everyone else. The policy of not allowing further caravan sites or pitches applied equally to Gypsies and non-Gypsies.

The obvious counter argument to this train of thought is that Runnymede's local

---

165 'Gypsies' being defined in section 16 of that Act as 'persons of nomadic habit of life whatever their race or origin'.

166 *R v Dorset County Council, ex parte Rolls and Another* [1994] EGCS 13

167 *R v Runnymede Borough Council, ex parte Smith* (1994) 70 P and CR 244

plan policy of not agreeing to further Gypsy sites or pitches was indirectly discriminatory. Such a policy is indirectly discriminatory since it applies a condition – of not residing in a mobile home or caravan – which is applied equally to non-Gypsies seeking planning permission for their home, but which is such that the proportion of Gypsies who can comply with it is considerably smaller than the proportion of non-Gypsies who can comply with it. Further, the policy is to the detriment of Gypsies because it makes it harder, in some cases impossible, for Gypsies to find themselves a home than it is for non-Gypsies, yet Gypsies cannot comply with it without giving up a central part of their shared, racial culture and tradition (e.g. residing in rural areas on or near to the roadside which represents the ethos of 'racial-Gypsy' living).

The proffered justification is that since Gypsy sites are (supposedly) more environmentally intrusive than permanent housing, the policy is justified on the basis that the environment should be protected.

However, if the provisions of the RRA 1976 are to be given effect, then the statutory requirement to avoid discrimination must be permitted to 'trump' purported planning amenity, just as the avoidance of discrimination in the case of motor-cyclist Sikhs and crash helmets allows the avoidance of discrimination to 'trump' safety issues.

Circular 1/94 states that Gypsy sites are not regarded as being among those uses of land which are normally appropriate in Green Belts. Again, the effect is clearly indirectly discriminatory, in the way outlined above. Again, however, planning policy justifies allowing permanent housing in Green Belts but not Gypsy sites on a basis that is irrespective of the race of those to whom the policy is applied.

The problem which needs addressing is thus not limited to the law relating to race, at least insofar as 'racial' Gypsies are concerned, but with British planning policy and planning case law in its failure to comply with the provisions of the amended section 19A of the RRA 1976.

Attempts to argue that British planning policies regarding Gypsies are unlawful under the European Convention on Human Rights (ECHR) have been no more successful than the *Runnymede* argument.[168] Mrs Buckley was refused planning permission for the three caravans on her site. Her appeal against this decision failed. The Inspector's report contained the following remarks: "It is therefore clear in my mind that a need exists for more authorised spaces ... Nevertheless, I consider it important to keep concentration of sites for Gypsies small, because in this way they are more readily accepted by the local community."

The Inspector would doubtless maintain that s/he used the word 'Gypsies' solely in the non-racial sense of 'persons of nomadic habit of life whatever their race or origin'. If the word were being used in its racial sense, the objection would be obvious. No planning authority would dare limit the concentration of homes for any other racial minority on the basis that in this way they would be more readily accepted by the local community!

Mrs Buckley claimed that the subsequent Criminal Justice and Public Order Act (CJPOA) 1994 criminalisation of 'unauthorised camping' discriminated against

---

168 Buckley v UK 23/1995/529/616, [1996] JPL 1018

Gypsies by preventing them from pursuing their traditional life-style. The European Court of Human Rights did not adjudicate this issue since the Act had never been applied to her. Clearly, this leaves open the possibility that the Court will find in favour of an applicant who advanced such an argument to whom this Act has been applied.

Mrs Buckley also claimed that since she was prevented from living in caravans on her own land with her family and from following a travelling life, there was a violation of her right under Article 8 of the ECHR to respect for her private and family life and her home.

The Court held that the refusal of planning permission, pursuant to the Town and County Planning Act 1990, did constitute interference by a public authority with Mrs Buckley's right to respect to her home.

However, the Court also held that the procedural safeguards provided for in the regulatory framework afforded due respect to the applicant's interests under Article 8. The special needs of the applicant as a Gypsy following a traditional life-style were taken into account. Both the Inspector and later the Secretary of State weighed the applicant's interest in being allowed to live in a caravan on her land against the general interest of conforming to planning policy. Further, the interference with Mrs Buckley's rights had been pursuant to legitimate aims on the part of the British Government – furthering highway safety, preserving the environment and public health.

Mrs Buckley also argued that Article 14 which requires that the rights and freedoms set out in the ECHR shall be secured without any discrimination on racial and other grounds had been violated. However, in *Buckley* the Court found that since there had been no violation of Article 8, the issue of violation of the right set out in Article 8 on racial grounds did not arise. There was thus no violation of Article 14 taken together with Article 8. (It is a familiar point that Article 14 does not prohibit racial discrimination per se. Rather it merely prohibits discrimination with respect to the other rights and freedoms enshrined in the Convention).

In a domestic case the High Court have refused to adjudicate on an alleged violation of Article 8 and its discriminatory effects on the basis that the issue was belatedly raised. Again, the courts have shown a lack of willingness to give any teeth to anti-discrimination law. In conclusion, the flawed rationale that British planning policy regarding the stationing and use of residential caravans is not discriminatory can be illustrated by an analogy with a similarly flawed proposition. The effect that a policy of prohibiting persons from sleeping at night under Waterloo Bridge is said not to discriminate against the homeless on the basis that all persons sleeping at night under Waterloo Bridge would be prohibited from doing so, homeless or not.

It is submitted that it can be seen from both the European and domestic perspectives. The problem which British planning policy imposes on 'racial' Gypsies requires not reform of the notion of race, rather a sea-change in British planning policy itself, and in the judicial approach to the issue. In the first instance, those Gypsies who fall within the current and restrictive section 3(1) definition of 'racial' Gypsies should be forthwith afforded the protection of the Act in planning law policies and decisions. The problem that Gypsies face is simply that British planning policy gives more weight to the various planning factors mentioned above than it does to their distinctive and traditional form of life.

It is further submitted that judicial decisions which give convenient sway to the various possible definitions of 'Gypsy' and 'Traveller' when consistently finding against 'racial' Gypsies and 'non-racial' Gypsies – depending on the status of the affected party – involve an element of intellectual gymnastics and are contrary to the statutory scheme of the RRA 1976. If that proposition is correct, then Parliament might readily amend the Act, and/or the Department of the Environment, Transport and the Regions might readily amend planning policy guidance to incorporate and enshrine the spirit and letter of anti-discrimination legislation.

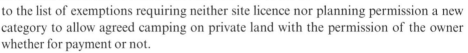

Further, if planning law is to recognise the legitimacy of diversity, 'non-racial' Gypsies and Travellers and, indeed, any person seeking to pursue an 'alternative' life-style in what purports to be a pluralistic society, should be afforded legal protection. In order to achieve this aim, section 3(1) of the Race Relations Act might reasonably be extended to a broader class, ideally in accordance with the ECHR Article 14 model.[169]

Amendment of the General Permitted Development Order *by Dr Malcolm Bell*[170]

The GPDO gives deemed planning consent to those sites listed in it which did not need a site licence. One could add to the list of exemptions requiring neither site licence nor planning permission a new category to allow agreed camping on private land with the permission of the owner whether for payment or not.

It is important that such sites should not count towards nor be considered as meeting the need for all-year permanent and transit sites.

It is suggested that either a new Class C be drafted as follows:

Part 5

Caravan sites

Class A
Permitted A. The use of land, other than a building, as a caravan site in the development circumstances referred to in paragraph A.2.
Condition A.1 Development is permitted by Class A subject to the condition that the use shall be discontinued when the circumstances specified in paragraph A.2 cease to exist, and all caravans on the site shall be removed as soon as reasonably practicable.
Interpretation A.2 The circumstances mentioned in Class A are those specified in paragraphs of Class A2 to 10 of Schedule 1 to the 1960 Act (cases where a caravan site licence is not required), but in relation to those mentioned in paragraph 10 do not include use for winter quarters.

> **Class B**
> **Permitted** B. Development required by the conditions of a site licence for the time development being in force under the 1960 Act.
>
> **Class C**
> **Permitted** C. The use of private land, other than a building, for not more than three development calendar months in total in any calendar year, as a caravan site for the purposes of a Gypsy site with the permission in writing of the owner whether for payment or not. 'Gypsy' shall have the meaning given in Section 16 of the Caravan Sites Act 1968.

or as an alternative, a new paragraph 10A of the First Schedule of the Caravan Sites and Control of Development Act 1960 which would require amendments to Part 5 of the GPDO thus:

> **Interpretation** A.2 The circumstances mentioned in Class A are those specified in paragraphs of Class 2 to 10A of Schedule 1 to the 1960 Act (cases where a caravan site licence is not required), but in relation to those mentioned in paragraph 10 do not include use for winter quarters.

and the insertion of a paragraph 10A of the 1960 Act stating:

> **Gypsy Sites** 10A. Subject to the provisions of paragraph 13 of this Schedule, a site licence shall not be required for the use of land as a caravan site for the purposes of a Gypsy site for not more than three calendar months in total in any calendar year. Permission will be required in writing of the owner of the land whether for payment or not. 'Gypsy' shall have the meaning given in Section 16 of the Caravan Sites Act 1968.

From Defining Rural Sustainability, *a report produced by the Rural Planning Groupof The Land Is Ours (TLIO)*

Fifteen Criteria for developments associated with sustainable land-based rural activities:

1. The project has a management plan which demonstrates:
   a. how the site will contribute significantly towards the occupiers' livelihoods;
   b. how the objectives cited in items 2 to 14 below will be achieved and maintained.

2. The project provides affordable access to land and/or housing to people in need.
3. The project provides public access to the countryside, including temporary access such as open-days and educational visits.
4. The project can demonstrate how it will be integrated into the local economy and community.
5. The project can demonstrate that no activities pursued on the site shall cause undue nuisance. to neighbours or the public.
6. The project has prepared a strategy for the minimisation of car use.
7. The development and any buildings associated with it are appropriately sited in relation to local landscape, natural resources and settlement patterns.
8. New buildings and dwellings are not visually intrusive nor of a scale disproportionate to the site and the scale of the operation; are constructed from materials with low embodied energy and environmental impact, and preferably from local or traditional materials; and are in keeping with local vernacular styles unless environmental considerations or the use of reclaimed materials determine otherwise. Re-use and conversion of existing buildings on the site is carried out as far as practicable in conformity with these criteria.
9. The project is reversible, insofar as new buildings can be easily dismantled and the land easily restored to its former condition.
10. The project has a strategy for minimum generation, maximum on-site re-use and recycling, and minimum export of waste.
11. The project has a strategy for energy conservation and the reduction of dependence on non-renewable energy sources.
12. The project aims over time for the autonomous provision of water, energy and sewage disposal and where it is not already connected to the utilities, shall make no demands upon the existing infrastructure.
13. Agricultural, forestry and similar land-based activities are carried out according to sustainable principles. Preference will be given to projects which conform to registered organic standards, sustainable forestry standards or recognised permaculture principles.
14. The project has strategies and programmes for the ecological management of the site, including :
    a. the sustainable management and improvement of soil structure;
    b. the conservation and, where appropriate, the enhancement of semi-natural habitat, taking into account biodiversity, biomass, indigenous species, and wildlife corridors;
    c. the efficient use and re-use of water, as well as increasing the water holding capacity of the site;
    d. the planting of trees and hedges, particularly in areas where the tree coverage is less than 20 per cent.
15. The project can show that affordability and sustainability are secured, for example, by the involvement of a housing association, co-operative, trust or other social body whose continuing interest in the property will ensure control over subsequent changes of ownership and occupation.

12

Health, social and other services

Service provision to Traveller sites *by Debbie Harvey*

There have been ongoing problems with the provision of water, toilets and refuse collection to temporary, unofficial Traveller sites. Different local authorities have different policies around the provision of these services; some may provide water and toilets on all sites in their area, others may provide one or other if requested to by Travellers on the site. Others refuse to provide any services at all, usually with the excuse that they don't want to be seen by the general public to be encouraging Travellers to stay if any services are provided. Within some authorities it is unclear with which department the responsibility to provide such services lies.

There are many different issues that arise when considering the provision of these services to temporary sites: whether Travellers themselves want all or some services on-site; whether there are children, pregnant women or adults with health or other particular needs on-site; and the way in which services are provided.

With respect to water, there have been problems with the hygiene of water in bowsers. Standpipes seem to be a safer and more hygienic option where this is possible. Portable toilets can be problematic, especially if they are shared by a large number of people. Sometimes they are not emptied frequently enough or cleaned thoroughly, and they may soon become a source of infection and a danger to health.

Refuse collectors often refuse to collect the rubbish from Travellers sites. Rubbish may then build up on sites and may attract rats or be strewn around by animals. Travellers often request a skip when they are about to vacate a site so that they can leave the site clean. However, this request is usually refused and consequently sites are often left in a mess if people have to leave quickly.

A variety of health problems may result from lack of water and poor sanitation, including skin diseases such as Impetigo and Scabies, and Gastro-enteritis, Hepatitis and other infections.

Various pieces of legislation and guidance relate to the provision of services to temporary or unofficial sites. Circular 18/94 says that authorities should consider tolerating Gypsies' presence and could examine ways of minimising the level of nuisance on such tolerated sites, for example by providing basic services for Gypsies such as toilets, a refuse skip and a supply of drinking water.

The Children Act 1989 gives every local authority a general duty to promote the welfare of children in their area who are in need, and so far as it is consistent with that duty to promote the upbringing of such children by their families by providing a range and level of services appropriate to those children's needs.[171] Various terms are defined for the purpose of that section. A child is in need if he is unlikely to achieve or maintain or to have the opportunity of achieving or maintaining a reasonable standard of health or development, without the provision for him of services by a local authority under Part III of the Act, or his health is likely to be significantly impaired or further impaired without the provision for him of such services. However, all of these provision are discretionary (authorities are told that they may rather than that they must), and there are no known examples of the use of the Children Act 1989 to persuade local authorities to provide water or toilets for families on sites.

The United Nations Convention on the Rights of the Child states in article 24(2) that State Parties shall take appropriate measures to "combat disease and malnutrition in the framework of primary healthcare through, inter alia, the application of readily available technology and through the provision of adequate nutritious foods and clean drinking water, taking into consideration the dangers and risks of environmental pollution." The UK government has ratified the Convention but unfortunately we do not seem to have the power to force the government to implement it in each case.

A Report from the Chartered Institute of Environmental Health[172] states that "Emergency and temporary unofficial encampments can threaten public health. Local authorities must mitigate against this by providing basic sanitation, wholesome water and by removing refuse".

Access to drinking water and basic sanitation are things that everyone should have as a right, not under discretionary provision. Children and pregnant women are especially vulnerable and drinking water and toilets should always be provided for them if requested. In addition, it would be far easier for everyone if the same local authority department was always responsible for the provision of these services, countrywide; preferably the department with overall responsibility should be Environmental Health Departments.[173] They should be responsible for responding to requests for services on sites and co-ordinating the provision of such services as appropriate. The law as it stands is reasonably good but all too easy to ignore. Law reform in itself is insufficient if authorities continue to feel that they owe little or no duty to Travelling people in their areas.

Equity in health service provision *by Jim Spiller*

We have been collecting material with the purpose of highlighting the effect of the Criminal Justice and Public Order Act (CJPOA) 1994 on Traveller health. Without doubt, where the Act has been enforced then the opportunity to access healthcare, the conditions for safe and sanitary environmental health, and the stress resulting from

---

171 Section 17(1)

172 Travellers and Gypsies: An Alternative Strategy, 1995

173 Some delegates at the 1999 Conference expressed the concern that giving such responsibility to EHOs would be inappropriate as it would create an unfortunate analogy with 'pest control'.

the infringement of the rights of families and children has denied a significant number of Travellers their equitable share of statutory healthcare provision. However, the introduction of the CJPOA has in most cases only served to aggravate a situation that extends much further back than the last four years. The history of agency provision for Travellers is a litany of fragmented, provisional and often poorly financed services, reflecting a lack of committed response and serious intent at all levels.

Three years ago, the Anglia Gypsy Traveller Health Inofrmation Project (AGTH-IP) were considering some research to look at health issues as they affected Travellers in East Anglia, as part of an NHS funding bid. Reviewing material that we had on file at that time, we trawled over sixty reports, papers, and research items. The earliest piece was from 1975, the most recent 1996.[174] Despite the twenty-year difference, we found a remarkable consistency in the fundamental problems identified and the recommendations that followed; in fact, barely any difference at all. Also, given the extraordinary amount of material, the same issues not only appeared with great consistency, but they were, in essence, few in number. In collating material for the Traveller Working Group we revisited this earlier work and also included additional material that has appeared since. We also received a number of current case representations from Travellers and Health workers in the field, and other members of this group. The emphasis of the needs identified and the subsequent recommendations vary, reflecting the changes within the provider agencies, but for the most part, the same basic issues fell into the same few well-worn ruts.

The 1997 Conference held by the Traveller Law Research Unit of Cardiff Law School addressed health and social care provision, and reflected exactly the same needs for reform, based upon the principles of valuing cultural diversity and equality of access to health and social services. The recommendations made by the National Association of Health Workers with Travellers (NAHWT) in the Report of that Conference are outlined in Part 1 Chapter 7. The conference also referred to a comprehensive 1993 report on the health of Travellers from Northern Ireland by Pauline Ginnety. In it she also reminds us that the health of people is determined by more than simple access to health services since social, economic and environmental factors play a larger part. While full and open access for Travellers to both curative and preventative services must be the goal of health policy makers it must be combined with an advocacy role with other public agencies to secure improvements in the economic, environmental and educational aspects of Travellers lives.

Referring to the issues discussed at the Traveller Working Group, and as a starting point for assembling feedback and identifying suggestions for reform, the following themes were suggested:

1. Access to health: it was suggested that some national research be undertaken with a view to establishing how positive links can be fostered between healthcare providers and Travellers.
2. Efforts should be made to ensure that Travellers have some input to the new Primary Care Groups, and to the formulation of health impact statements and health improvement programs in general; bearing in mind the connection between poor health and social exclusion.

---

174 See *AGTHIP Review*, January 1997

3.   'Health' includes environmental health, access to water, toilets, rubbish collection, etc.
4.   Health and safety and site security are key to good health or lack of it.
5.   Equal opportunities for Travelling people as an ethnic minority need better development and protection.
6.   There are pros and cons to having specialist Traveller workers such as health visitors.
7.   There is a need for multi-agency training and working, backed up by unequivocal commitment, and a need for stronger policy guidance from central government to achieve all of the above.

We have also received a number of current statements, anecdotes and case reports that support the need to address these issues. We made several approaches to our NHS Regional Area office (Oxford and Anglia) and to the Ethnic Health Dept of the NHS in London for copies of policies regarding Travellers. So far we've received nothing, and have been told by some sources that no such policies exist.

Much of the material that I have presented so far has, in the main, been based upon research addressing Traditional Travellers. The issues affecting New Travellers are, in important respects, different. For the most part New Travellers know how the health systems of the settled majority work. They are familiar with the processes of primary and secondary care. Health promotion and information material is accessible to them. They share the same culture as the providers of the services they use.

We received accounts from Friends and Families of Travellers Support Group (FFT) of 106 incidents affecting Travellers since 1994, mostly relating to site evictions, prosecutions and authority actions. FFT does not differentiate between Traditional and New Travellers. Their recent piece of research, the *Report of the Pilot Health Promotion Project with Travellers in Dorset*, recognises that the Travelling community is an extremely diverse group of people, with, as a consequence, a wide range of differing needs which are quite specific in terms of healthcare provision. In presenting a common raft of issues it might be necessary to acknowledge the differences in order to determine the specific needs of each community.

Our remit was to collect and collate data to substantiate the health issues in the case for reform. Good healthcare practices do exist in parts of the country, in various parts of the system. It has existed in the past and has been lost. It would be possible now to identify it, and if there is the will to do so, build it into a national policy. It is felt by the Traveller Working Groups that it is impossible to do this without some more enlightened and far-reaching policy enabling appropriate accommodation for Travelling people.

An elderly Gypsy Traveller in Cambridgeshire says: "When I first started having trouble with my breathing, I'd go to the doctors and they give me some pills or some medicine, never gave me no tests, they send me away. They never said nothing about Asthma. It went on for years and years, and I got worse and worse. When I came down here to Cambridge and saw this Doctor, straight away she said you've got Asthma. She put me on pumps and the steroids. She got the tests done. Now, it's taken some time, but my breathings better, it ain't one hundred per cent, it never will be, but I can walk about now. With my regular check-ups, taking my pills and pumps I'm able to manage. But I want to tell other Travellers, don't do what I did. Letting them put you off all the time. Stand up for your rights, and if the doctor won't see you, or they don't want you there, find a doctor that do. Stand up for your rights and you'll get them."

Travellers and health: a case study *by Penny Ballinger*

A and B are Romany Travellers. Neither has a level of functional literacy or basic numeracy and budgeting skills to make the transition into housing without a lot of support. At a time when they were having difficulties in housing association property, they were dependent on the limited literacy skills of a daughter, then thirteen years old. Although their children were on the Child Protection Register when they moved into the area, they were not allocated a qualified social worker, but a young and unqualified family support worker. Clearly, there were difficulties for this young lady in engaging with the family, and also identifying and responding holistically to the family's needs and problems.

When A and B married, documentation to activate housing benefit was not completed and the family were also getting into difficulties with fuel bills and budgeting quarterly bills. They had missed out on a basic settlement advice and support package. Instead, the functionally illiterate mother was endeavouring to sort out finances with her thirteen year old daughter. The family got further and further into debts, and the consequent escalation of domestic arguments and violence became the prominent focus of the statutory agencies attention.

The housing association, communicating with the family in writing, began to institute proceedings to evict them. At this stage, there appears to have been no dialogue between the statutory agencies and the distant landlord to attempt to resolve issues or advise the family on dealing with the problems which were accumulating. It is extremely unlikely, given their functional illiteracy, that they had much understanding of either their tenancy agreement nor the correspondence from the landlord as to how they had transgressed it. They did engage the services of a local solicitor, but they seem to have been very unfamiliar with what he was actually doing on their behalf; and when he finally was unable to activate the legal aid system to pay for his work to forestall the eviction, he failed to inform them, so that they effectively got one and a half hours notice of their impending eviction and many of their possessions were lost in the ensuing chaos.

After leaving the house and feeling that the temporary accommodation offered them in a hostel was unsuitable, the family resorted to the Traveller way by taking to the road. Inevitably, because of restrictions on unofficial encampments, they could only find a park-up on a farm which, though not an authorised site, offered them access to water and a secure place to stay, in exchange for paying over their family child benefit allowance. However, the difficulties existing outside the housing benefit system and the family's lack of prospects to be considered for housing in the area, together with the conditions on the site – acknowledged by the local council's Traveller department to be "very poor, and if we could we would like to shut the place down" – put the family back on the road.

In mid-February they returned to the previous area and gained access to a public site by following two other caravans on. The sites department would not make their tenancy legitimate because, even though there were vacant plots on that site, and two other sites in the area, the family had not gone through the proper procedures for obtaining a plot, because they believed they would be refused. At this stage, they did not have access to potable drinking water, or a utility block where the children could be washed or bathed, and yet the composition of the family included a four-month old baby and a teenager who had recently undergone an appendectomy. Interventions by the statutory services with the sites department suggesting legitimisation of the encampment, and the provision of basic amenities such as water, were unsuccessful.

The department then successfully applied to the court for repossession, and boarded up the utility blocks so that the family could have absolutely no opportunity to access water or electricity. The father was also charged with forcing the utility block door in order to gain access to water for the family. It was only through the aegis of a new solicitor that the family were, at the eleventh hour, found temporary accommodation in the locality. Now they are in urgent need of accommodation and support networks to help them become successful and competent parents and tenants. This is the role of the social accommodation and health and social support statutory agencies, and there is a definite need for an improvement in the model of support offered to this family and families like them.

The difficulties of settlement of the long-term homeless has been researched and well documented and there are instances of impressively good practice in some areas when working with people in this socially excluded group. However Traveller settlement has not been investigated, and the reasons that some Travellers fail in housing have never been examined. It is assumed that these Traveller families are simply dysfunctional and will not cope and this often appears to be an excuse for not wasting time and resources on them. But realistically, this is not a good enough response to members of the largest ethnic minority in the county. There are now several case studies of other Traveller families being bounced between the housing and sites departments, neither of whom want to take on the responsibility of accommodating them. if the basic needs – water, warmth, security and a place to stay – are not met, then interventions aimed at addressing needs further up the hierarchy are broadly meaningless.

A and B need accommodation and support in that accommodation, so that the family, and particularly the children, can achieve their potential; so that the child with special needs can get appropriate educational support, and so that the parents can be supported to become, themselves, supportive and competent parents. Any decision about their long-term housing needs should take into account not just the family's difficulties functioning within housing, education and social support and systems, but the deficiencies of the systems themselves, and harm perpetrated on the family by the systems' inflexibility. Any social accommodation system which denies children a roof over their heads, or access to drinking water because of the parents' functional illiteracy or failure to follow the correct procedures, has got to be fundamentally unsound in a county of comparative affluence.

Inter-agency working *by Sarah Cemlyn and Rachel Morris*

"In the early stages of support in Traveller Education, mistakes were sometimes made by staff in seeking to resolve the range of difficulties faced by families in being unable to access health and welfare care. Staff sometimes operated alone and unsupported, unsupervised and unaccountable, frequently undermining their own skills and expertise as educators. They also inadvertently 'covered up' for the lack of provision by other service deliverers. Links made with Health Visitors and other public service personnel were often at an informal level, dependent on the individuals involved and not on the policies and practices of the organisation. Liaison was often passive as a result of being personal contact, not rooted in organisational or planned intervention.

Sarah Cemlyn

"Models of partnership began to emerge in the mid 1980s with the negotiated involvement of policy makers, budget holders, management and field staff from a range of agencies, organisations and departments working out together common aims and objectives, communication and support links and setting personal targets in their respective organisations. Interagency partners identified the rules of the partnership and recognised not all held the same amount of power, nor were, necessarily, equal, but each agreed an active participation based on a need for fairness and a natural sense of justice. Interagency partnerships vary. It may be a partnership initially between Health and Education which develops to include Environmental Health, Planning and sometimes Youth Services, Police, etc. Interagency partnerships work towards cohesive and accountable provision through policy, planning, liaison, communication and mutual support. The principle of interagency partnership is that the partnership way is stronger and more effective than any one agency delivering alone, in isolation."[175]

It is essential to efficiency, best value and best practice that service delivery be integrated, therefore working towards good inter-agency (IA) practice and procedure is also paramount. Most IA structures are informal and operate on an ad-hoc basis, so the objectives of these structures vary. Some operate for the exchange of information, others for the mutual support of co-workers, the co-ordination of service provision, or a 'one stop shop' access point for service users. There is a need for some formalisation and explication of these structures if they are to be used most effectively, and if service users are to gain the maximum benefit. To this end, it might useful in some areas to set up forums of field workers and service users to explore the potential structure and benefits of an IA platform.

During the process of developing a more formal IA working practice, any anomalies within existing practice can be exposed, modes of working can be professionalised, service users can be consulted as to their needs and preferences, and through this ways can be found to support the voices of service users. By creating field worker and service user forums, cohesive mechanisms can be found for the raising of issues, planning, and redress. Often field workers find themselves simply caught in a cycle of repeatedly facing the same issues without agency management taking on board the need for strategic resolutions; minutes and reports from more formalised IA structures can be tool to overcome this problem.

Developing IA relationships with members of the police forces can also be produc-

175 *Partnerships* information sheet, issued by the National Association of Teachers of Travellers (NATT), 1998

tive, although there are specific issues and problems which require discussion and agreement; for example, the relationship of forum members may need to change by common agreement where police raids of Traveller sites are concerned. However, the relationships can be highly beneficial when such a raid has taken place and future best practice may need to be discussed, developed and agreed. There may of course be times and/or areas where direct police involvement in fora may not be thought appropriate. The composition of a forum is a matter for early and careful consideration.

Various models are used by Social Services Departments (SSDs), although they are perhaps the least engaged with Travellers and little research has been done into these models. For example, research has shown that of those SSDs which responded to research (less than 50 per cent of departments in England), "mechanisms relating to Travellers were established with education departments by 17 (50%) of the social services departments in the first sample, by 13 (38.2%) with health authorities and trusts, and by 10 (29.4%) with police authorities and housing departments. Links with other named departments ranged between eight (23.5%) with environmental health and planning, four (11.8%) with highways and property departments and voluntary agencies, and one (2.9%) with leisure. Inter-departmental liaison groups were the most frequently reported mechanism."[176]

Some SSDs have vicarious contact with Travellers via contact with the voluntary sector. If this method of working is to continue then ground rules for such relationships should be developed and formalised. SSDs cannot always get involved in outreach work, which is particularly important in relation to Travellers, but they can assist and learn from those who undertake such activity. All agencies – but Social services in particular – need to develop more active involvement in IA mechanisms, especially in relation to community based and 'preventative' work; perhaps building on or employing the best practice from their well-established IA mechanisms for dealing with child protection issues in the settled community.

Fora and their benefits should be formally recognised by the agencies involved and this recognition should be integrated into decision structures. This also has intra-agency implications, in that the knowledge by management of field working issues in relation to Travellers can be improved. Most areas in England have a forum, but it is not always entitled or understood as such. A forum should include regular meetings between field workers and middle management, at least twice a year but preferably quarterly, to discuss strategies and resources. Where Gypsies and Travellers are concerned, using regular agenda slots during the more formalised meetings of Joint Consultative Committees to introduce Traveller issues may be appropriate, in order that senior management and political leaders are able to discuss the issues around responsibilities, roles and resources, and seek solutions. 'Buck passing' is a common problem inhibiting access to services.

Calling Gypsies and Travellers 'service users' in this context may be using an overly optimistic term, as often appropriate services are not sufficiently available for them or they may feel unable of unwilling to access what services are available, if they are

---

176 Cemlyn, Sarah. *Summary of Report: Policy and Provision by Social Services for Traveller Children and Families – a Research study,* the Nuffield Foundation and the School for Policy Studies, the University of Bristol, 1998. p.3

aware of them, for a number of complex reasons. The resource implications of attempting to give Gypsies and Travellers a greater voice in the design and delivery of services which they made need are also not simple, and the success of such attempts may depend in some part on geography: improving such relationships can be easier in areas where a voluntary sector organisation is already building bridges, i.e. Gypsy and Traveller support groups in Cardiff, Sheffield and London. Nonetheless, despite the difficulties, service providers need to be aware of the desirability of consultation and dialogue, and the necessarily long-term nature of doing so. Enhanced IA mechanisms can work against Traveller interests if their views are not somehow built in; an IA Forum can become a fortress if not set up on inclusive and progressive principles.

The pitfalls of such working practices are, however, manifold. If workers themselves feel muted, then Travellers are likely to have even more difficulty making their voices heard. Travellers may come to feel that such processes are pointless and so they will, indeed, be counterproductive in confirming Travellers' fears that they are not listened to. There is also the constant danger of seeking involvement in what is basically a non-Traveller agenda, i.e. tokenism. There are a number of potentially useful models for developing such practices:[177]

1.   Set up a separate Traveller Forum, with support as needed, where Travellers can identify their own issues and priorities. These can then be fed into a parallel non-Traveller Forum, or one involving both Travellers and non-Travellers, and this second forum can refer back and be accountable to the Traveller Forum. This model seems to have been useful where voluntary projects such as those mentioned above exist, but would need adapting for an IA context. The important principle is to find ways for Travellers to have their own voice, and then to create channels where it can be transmitted and not just heard but listened to.

2.   Professionals set up a forum in such a way that Travellers' concerns can be acted on quickly, that is, whereby links with appropriate management levels are built in. Travellers can then be invited to the forum to express their concerns with some hope that they will be taken seriously. This is a 'surgery' model and it has operated in Gloucester (where the key professional figure, an Education Welfare Officer, is himself a Traveller).

3.   Credibility and appropriate means of communication are clearly enhanced by the employment of Travellers. There a number of ways this is being developed, particularly, it would seem, through the recruitment of child care workers and school assistants. There are also Traveller workers at other levels e.g. the community development worker in Stockton on Tees (formerly Cleveland), and another on a temporary basis in Bromley. Doubtless there are other examples in England and Wales of which we are unaware. Examples from outside Britain are probably more widespread and developed, such as the Republic of Ireland, through the work of Pavee Point and others, and Roma mediators in other European countries. The importance of continuing moves in this direction

---

177 For greater detail in this area, see the chapter by Cemlyn, Sarah. *Groupwork as a Tool in Working with Gypsy and Traveller Culture*, in Musty, T. and Brown, A., Editors. Race and Groupwork, Whiting and Birch, London, 1997. pp.110-31

cannot be overemphasised, in addition to providing high quality and appropriate training for Gypsy and Traveller workers.

It is important to remember that the key importance of IA working, in addition to co-ordinating and making more compatible and efficient the provision of a range of services, is that it is a mechanism for the human voice. It is all too easy to get caught up in structural issues and forget that the IA mechanism is a means of removing barriers and developing common understandings. Bureaucracy and creativity must be integrated and balanced. IA fora members need to think like nomads: explore, be curious, avoid politics, move on, develop, share, be flexible and resourceful, and take what is needed from what is found without getting caught up too much in systems.

Gypsies, Travellers and social security in Britain *by Colin Clark*

About the Department of Social Security and the Benefits Agency

The British system of social security provides over thirty distinct cash benefits which cover a wide range of circumstances and situations. It is the Department of Social Security (DSS) that has overall responsibility for the development and monitoring of the system whilst the implementation, delivery and administration of benefits is devolved to the five executive agencies that the DSS created in the late 1980s and early 1990s as part of the 'Next Steps' New Public Management programme. The main aims of this reorganisation was to cut running costs, 'target' benefits more effectively to those considered to be 'most in need' and to improve service delivery by detailing areas of responsibility and accountability for the different agencies.

One of these five agencies, the Benefits Agency (BA), deals with contributory and means-tested benefits such as Income Support, Job Seekers Allowance, Incapacity Benefit,[178] Child Benefit and the Social Fund. There are a number of different organisations that are involved in the administration and payment of certain benefits. Local authorities or district councils, for example, deal with Housing Benefit and Council Tax whilst employers are responsible for the delivery of statutory sick pay. Administration procedures vary enormously and the rules and regulations covering entitlement can be very complicated. In the case of discretionary benefits such rules and regulations can be open to misinterpretation.[179] This is certainly the case when it comes to examining how the social security system has traditionally treated Gypsies

---

178 Housing Benefit, in relation to Gypsies and Travellers, has always been a problematic benefit. See, for example, B. Adams et al. *Gypsies and Government Policy in England: A Study of the Travellers' way of Life in relation to the Policies and Practices of Central and local Government*, Heinemann, London, 1975. pp141-2

179 See Cooper, S. *Observations in Supplementary Benefits Offices: the reform of Supplementary Benefit* (Working Paper C), Policy Studies Institute, London, 1985

and other Travellers (so-called 'transitory claimants'[180]) in the UK.

Racism, ethnicity and social security

Eligibility for social security has two main elements to it. Firstly, there are the formal rules and regulations that govern provision of benefits. Secondly, there are the perceptions of eligibility that are held by claimants and potential claimants. The contributory principle within social security, whereby National Insurance benefits are linked to earnings, gave rise to a set of rules of eligibility which disproportionately excludes those people who are in intermittent or low paid work, those with a higher risk of unemployment and recent migrants. This policy was established on the assumption of a white male norm so it formally excluded many of those in minority ethnic groups from the social citizenship rights to such benefits.

From at least the Victorian era onwards, regulation to exclude a whole range of so-called 'Alien' groups from welfare benefits is evident.[181] Poor Law policies, pensions law, aliens legislation as well as National Insurance criteria incorporate such practices. The 'dangerous classes'[182] (Black, Asian, Irish, Jewish, Gypsy, etc.) were perceived as a threat to the jobs and wages of those in the emerging Trade Unions. In many ways, post-war welfare reforms and immigration policies continued to institutionalise racially exclusionary rules that determine eligibility to social security and other welfare benefits. Such rules include residence tests, rules on 'recourse to public funds' and sponsorship conditions.[183] Racism in welfare state and social security policies today need to be seen and understood in a much wider context. Such 'normalised racism' needs to be viewed as an expression of the wider integration of racism, historically, in nationalist discourses and in gendered ruling-class conceptions of subordinate (or indeed 'dangerous') classes. In other words we need to appreciate the complex route that led to the current state of affairs: the nation-state, class relations, gender relations, colonial relations and their mixing with the very idea of 'race' both as a concept and an actuality. As context for the following discussion, there is a direct connection between these complex sociological issues and the rules and regulations of the current social security system in Britain, and how Gypsies and other Travellers experience it.

The last two decades

Studies of social security have generally not paid a great deal of attention to issues of racism and ethnicity. Despite the advice of the Home Affairs Committee in 1981, the DSS refused throughout the 1980s to commission or support any substantive research to investigate what connections there were between ethnicity, racism and access to the

---

180 Employment Services. *Advising Clients: dealing with bulk claims from transitory clients*, Circular 83/6, September 1992

181 See Williams, F. *Social Policy: A Critical Introduction*, Blackwell, Oxford, 1989 and also Holmes, C. *John Bull's Island: Immigration and British Society 1871-1971*, Macmillan, London, 1988

182 Morris, L. *Dangerous Classes: the Underclass and Social Citizenship*, Routledge, London, 1994

183 See Solomos, J. and Back, L. *Racism and Society*, Macmillan, London, 1996

social security system. However, in the early 1990s the DSS (and the BA particularly) started to interest itself in what it termed 'serving the needs of the local community'. The impact of the various public sector 'Customer Charters' was being felt within the DSS. By 1993 a report had been published looking at the 'information needs' of ethnic minority groups.[184] The focus of this study was quite narrow however and there was little in the report in terms of fresh evidence. Indeed, it tended to stick close to the dominant theme in the existing literature which argued for increased resources being put into basic linguistic initiatives; that is providing interpreters and translated materials and the like. However, one of the recommendations did go a little further than this and suggested that closer co-operation between the voluntary sector, local authority welfare rights services and the BA might produce a better all-round quality of service for people using the social security system. This tripartist approach to delivering a 'quality service' has, in theory at least, been one avenue that the BA has been keen to explore in the last five or six years with the emphasis on good 'customer service'.

One other consistent theme in the limited literature on racism, ethnicity and social security has been the nature of anti-Black and anti-Semitic sentiments amongst staff working in local benefit offices.[185] Due to the use of negative racial stereotypes, Asian and Jewish people can, for example, be viewed as wealthy and assertive in gaining information and access to benefits. The Cooper study from 1985 noted a variety of such assumptions being made in a number of different settings. One of these settings was an unofficial Gypsy Site where the visiting officer was calling on a pregnant Gypsy woman who had made a claim for a one-off payment (under the then Supplementary Benefits scheme). As the DHSS officer and Cooper approached the site, he commented to the researcher that "they [Gypsies] all look after their own so we'll be out of here quick". Such racist sentiments can lead to many claims being disregarded out of hand (as above) or subject to racially discriminatory scrutiny and high levels of unwarranted suspicion. I will say more on this later in relation to Gypsies and the often automatic assumption of fraud when new claims are being made.

This scrutiny, in turn, feeds into racially determined demands for extra documentation to establish eligibility for benefits. This is particularly the case in relation to proving one's age, marriage, children's births and immigration status. The practice of passport checking, in this context, is often erratic and unjustifiable to independent eyes. Likewise, stereotypes and racial assumptions are often made in terms of family structures or the cultural characteristics of different ethnic minority families (as noted above in the example of the Gypsy woman).

A Commission for Racial Equality study from the mid-1980s illustrated that exclusion from benefit can occur on the basis of misrecognition and misinterpretation of circumstances such as capital held overseas, pooling of household income, family separation and divorce.[186] More recently, a study looking at the experiences of Irish

---

184 Bloch, A. *Access to Benefits: The Information Needs of Minority Ethnic Groups*, Policy Studies Institute, London, 1993185 See Cooper, S. *Observations in Supplementary Benefits Offices: the reform of Supplementary Benefit* (Working Paper C), Policy Studies Institute, London, 1985

186 Commission for Racial Equality. *Submission in Response to the Green Paper on the Reform of Social Security*, London, 1985

claimants in Britain found that discrimination occurred on a number of fronts, especially the demanding of exceptional identification requirements to support a claim.[187]

Gypsies, Travellers and social security

Recorded and anecdotal evidence has long suggested that Gypsies and other Travellers have not received fair treatment when attempting to access the social security system to claim benefits.[188] For some, this discriminatory treatment is because they follow a nomadic life-style. For other Travellers, this treatment could be as a result of both their nomadism and their ethnicity (e.g. Irish Travellers in London).[189] One of the most fundamental problems arises when Gypsies and other Travellers first attempt to register with the Benefits Agency to make a fresh claim. Often, the many forms of identity required by the BA, i.e. passport, driving licence, birth certificate, etc., are not always available to the Traveller family. A case in point is the example of Irish Travellers and their cultural norms; more emphasis is given to baptismal certificates rather than birth certificates and these are commonly not accepted as proof of identity by the BA. It is of some concern, then, that the Government has recently announced its intention to introduce new procedures to fight fraud: "Officials will demand proof of identity for all claimants and will accept only originals of documents such as birth certificates".[190]

Another factor here is that often, for a local BA office, any increase in claims from Traveller families will lead to a referral to the Fraud Section to check the claims over to ensure that they are not fraudulent. Often this is done for no other reason other than they are perceived as 'Travellers' and live in caravans. In other words, there is often an assumption of fraud before the claim has even begun to be processed.[191] In the mid-1980s a 'Nomadic Claimants Working Party'[192] was established within the then Department of Health and Social Security (DHSS) to look into and report on Travellers and social security. Though they were primarily interested in the new situation that was developing regarding the movements and activities of New Travellers and social security, they also concerned themselves with Gypsies.

The report made a series of recommendations, one of the most important being the use of a special index of 'nomadic claimants' and using separate case papers which would record details of evidence of ID and a physical description of the claimant. An

187 Patterson, T. Irish Lessons: Irish Claimants in Britain in Context, *Benefits,* 1994(9). pp12-5

188 See, for example, Clark, C. *'New Age' Travellers: Identity, Sedentarism and Social Security* in Acton, T., editor. *Gypsy Politics and Traveller Identity,* University of Hertfordshire Press, Hatfield, 1997

189 See Action Group For Irish Youth. *Identity Crisis: Access to Benefits and ID Checks*, London, 1993190 *The Times,* 24 March 1999. The government document *A New Contract for Welfare - Safeguarding Social Security,* was unveiled on 23 March 1999.

191 This was also found to be the case for other ethnic minority groups: see National Association of Citizens Advice Bureaux (NACAB). *Barriers to Benefit,* London, 1991; The special issue of the journal Benefits (number 9, 1994) which had a number of articles looking at racism and social security ; Law, I. et al. *Racial Equality and Social Security Delivery: summary report to the Joseph Rowntree Foundation, Sociology and Social Policy,* Working Paper 10, University of Leeds, 1994

192 Department of Health and Social Security. *Nomadic Claimants Working Party: Final Report,* DHSS (RD9), March 1986. This report was also drawn upon in the 1990s by the Benefits Agency when it wrote and distributed a 1993 Circular on 'New Age Travellers' (Income Support Bulletin 24/93).

'Itinerant Caravan Dwellers Information Card' was being used in the London North Region for a time following the guidance given by the Working Party. It is very likely that this type of card was used in other offices around the country though this has not been proven.

The Verification Framework pilot projects under the Social Security Amendments (Fraud) Act 1997, anti-fraud administrative systems testing minimum standards for collection of evidence and ongoing verification of claims, originally identified – but no longer do so – Travellers and 'persons from abroad' as high-risk claimant groups.[193] Like other large organisations and companies in both the private and public sector, the BA has steadily moved towards computerisation of its systems and databases in the late 1980s and 1990s. For many Gypsies, Travellers and other nomadic claimants this has not made claiming any easier however as often their cases are taken 'off-line' to be dealt with clerically as if they move on quite frequently the system cannot cope with this[194.] A number of hurdles are still faced and the main one is still proving identity. Since 1 May 1997 the new Labour government has initiated a whole series of changes to the welfare state and the social security system in particular. It is still too early to say exactly how 'New Deal', 'Welfare to Work' and other such reforms will impact on Gypsies and Travellers and more research needs to be undertaken in this area.

Recommendations

On the basis of my own research and other studies that have been conducted in the 1980s and 1990s I would wish to make the following three key recommendations:

1.   Research has shown that a number of groups experience difficulties in accessing and taking up the services that the BA offers. A number of these difficulties stem from issues surrounding the proving of identity. Currently, the claimant is assumed to be potentially fraudulent until proven genuine.

    The onus to prove or disprove ID should be shifted from the claimant to the Benefits Agency

2.   Research has shown that the discretionary powers that are available to staff (or 'street level bureaucrats' as Michael Lipsky would call them[195]) in local offices can lead, in certain circumstances, to a high degree of inconsistent service and practices regarding the verification of identification and the treatment of the claim more generally.

    The BA should review its discretionary powers to assess ways of making the ID requirements more appropriate to different sections of the population. The BA should lift any 'blanket bans' it may have on specific forms of ID.

193 Unpublished letter from the Department of Social Security to Henry McLeish MP, 29 December 1998

194 See Clark in Acton (1997)

195 Lipsky, M. *Street-Level Bureaucracy: Dilemmas of the Individual in Public Services,* Russell Sage Foundation, New York, 1980

3.   As an organisation that promotes equality of opportunity, the BA must recognise the principles of racial equality and non-discriminatory practice when it comes to dealing with claims from the Gypsy and Traveller communities.

The social security system generally, and the BA specifically, should ensure that the needs and experiences of Britain's oldest ethnic minority groups are included in all non-discriminatory and racial equality initiatives. The BA should also listen and consult with Gypsies and other Travellers in terms of its annual National Customer Surveys.

Afterword

Speech by Hugh Harris, CRE Deputy Chairman, at the Second Conference on Traveller Law Reform, London, 17 February 1999

T his excellent conference is a sign of the times and it is an honour to be able to address you in the name of the Commission for Racial Equality. The number of people who have come together to debate the issues, the detailed documentation drawn up by participants and the hard working team at the Cardiff Law School, all point to what is becoming more and more obvious – there is a quickening of pace around Traveller and Gypsy issues which is long overdue. It is long overdue because as we have heard today there is great deal of need. The Traveller and Gypsy community is one that has suffered much and yet whose concerns have often been marginalised.

And a society which allows any group to suffer the discrimination and the regular, day in day out expressions of bigotry and prejudice to which the Traveller and Gypsy community is subject, is a society which will not be able to deliver equality and fairness for everyone. Everyone concerned with the great, central theme of this Government – moving toward a more inclusive and cohesive society – must keep their eyes on one of the tests of success in that task: the treatment of Travellers and Gypsies in modern Britain.

There are many, not least the organisations of Travellers and Gypsies themselves, who have ensured that our eyes are being kept firmly on that target. But I think that everyone owes a special debt of gratitude to the team at Cardiff Law School. Their work has not only brought us together today but it has played an important part in that quickening of pace which is laying the foundation stones for some real advances in the next few years.

From the CRE we would like to congratulate the Joseph Rowntree Charitable Trust for the way they have funded the work of Rachel and her colleagues. I am sure everyone here today would want to join us in saying that we hope the Trust – and other bodies – will keep up that vital support and ensure that we can be certain of much more of the sort of work which has led to this conference and the good work which will come out of it.

One thing which is very important about this work is the way in which it is bringing people together. For instance, alongside the work of the Cardiff team, there is the initiative launched by the Brent Irish Advisory Service Irish Travellers Project which is bringing together the basis for a national Irish Travellers Movement. Bringing together the different strands of the Traveller and Gypsy community is something which will help directly to raise the profile of this issue and significantly improve the impact of the work all of us are committed to.

From the CRE we ourselves have taken what is for us a unique initiative. Everyone will be aware of the sometimes appalling coverage of Travellers and Gypsies in the media. Stimulated by a roundtable initiative from the Cardiff team, we consulted on and drew up a short good practice guide for the media. Just before the end of last year we circulated copies to every newspaper editor in England, Scotland and Wales, whether for a national daily or a local free newspaper.

We want this guide to be taken up by all who are concerned about poor media coverage of Travellers and Gypsies. We want them to use it to back up complaints to individual titles and to bodies like the Press Complaints Commission. I hope you all have copies – and if you have suggestions about who would be able to make good use of copies, please let the CRE Media Office know and we will ensure that they are dispatched.[95]

It is part of the contribution that the CRE can make to creating a proper climate in which people feel able to assert their rights and see them fulfilled. The Race Relations Act is being used more. There has been an increase in the number of complaints coming to us – and we have the impression an increase in the number of cases being handled by other agencies. In addition there are some excellent examples of good practice being developed by different agencies and local authorities – examples that are still too few, but they show what can be done if a local authority uses imagination and initiative even against the background of scarce resources and limited rights in law.

Developing that law is going to be of great importance. The CRE tabled important proposals to the Government last year for improvements in the Race Relations Act. Many of these would, if implemented, be of direct assistance to Travellers and Gypsies in securing their rights. We hope to hear soon from Government, perhaps soon after next week's publication of the McPherson inquiry Report on Stephen Lawrence, what Government will be doing about those proposals.

But whether we get a better law or not, what will count is the way in which all of us work together to fulfil the promise of this excellent conference. That through targeting the issues clearly, marshalling our arguments well, and ensuring that we use every possibility, every opening, to pick away at a problem which remains a standing indictment of British society, we can make significant, measurable progress, in ensuring that one of the most excluded groups in British society is able to play a full and rewarding part in the Britain of the future.

---

95 The guidelines are at Appendix 3.

Appendices

Appendix 1: Traveller working group contributors

Dr Thomas Acton, Professor of Romani Studies, School of Romani Studies, University of Greenwich

Susan Alexander, Co-ordinator, Advice and Information Unit, Friends, Families and Travellers (FFT)

Diana Allen, Solicitor, Lance Kent and Co., Hertfordshire

Anne Bagehot, Secretary, the Gypsy Council for Education, Culture, Welfare and Civil Rights

Penny Ballinger, Liaison Health Visitor for Travellers, Herefordshire Community Health Trust

Sue Bates, Legal Department, South Somerset District Council

Charles Beresford-Webb, Planner

Lyn Bickle, Health Visitor, Gwent Community Health NHS Trust

Philip Brown, Associate, Bolton Emery Partnership Chartered Town Planners, Macclesfield

Anne Burn, Gypsy Liaison Officer, Oxfordshire County Council

Iain Cairns, Gypsy Liaison Officer, Somerset County Council

Russell Campbell, Solicitor, Shelter

Sarah Cemlyn, Lecturer and Researcher, School for Policy Studies, University of Bristol

Angela Chapman, Co-ordinator of Traveller Support, Bromley

Sheila Clarke, Gypsy Liaison Manager, Essex County Council

Noel Clarke, Researcher, (author of report on Travellers for Bridge Housing Association)

Sandra Clay, Advisory Group, the Traveller Law Research Unit, Cardiff Law School / County of Cardiff Traveller Education Service

Luke Clements, Co-Director, Traveller Law Research Unit, Cardiff Law School

Clara Connolly, formerly at the Commission for Racial Equality

Michael Connors, Irish Traveller Project, Brent Irish Advisory Service, London

Katherine Constable, Teacher for Travellers, Somerset

Sarah Cox, Barrister, Holborn Chambers, London

Michael Cox, Principal, Michael Cox Associates Planning Consultants, West Sussex

Joanne Davis, Secretary, National Association of Health Workers with Travellers (NAHWT)

Val Dumbleton, Specialist Health Visitor for Travelling Families and Ethnic Minorities, Northampton

Tom Duncan, The Planning Exchange, Glasgow

Sylvia Dunn, National Association of Gypsy Women

Mr Chris Esdaile, The Community Law Partnership, Birmingham

Stephen Field, Barrister, 10/11 Gray's Inn Square, London

Bill Forrester, Gypsy Liaison Officer, Kent County Council, Chair of ACERT and NAGTO

Florence Garabedian, Scottish Gypsy Traveller Association

Paul Goltz, Traveller Community Worker, South Somerset District Council

Imogen Hale, Travellers Advice Worker, Leeds Citizens Advice Bureau and Travellers Advice Line

Lynne Hartwell, Health Visitor, Leicester

Debbie Harvey, Traveller Support Worker, the Children's Participation Project, the Children's Society

Dr Derek Hawes, formerly of the School for Policy Studies, University of Bristol

Officer Jack Hawkins, Gypsy Liaison Officer, HM Prison Cardiff

Imogen Hinton, Gypsy Liaison Officer, Gloucestershire County Council

Ian Holding, Gypsy Liaison Officer, Bristol City Council

Mr Terry Holland, Gypsy Services Manager, Buckinghamshire County Council

Pat Holmes, Co-ordinator, West Midlands Consortium Education Service for Travelling Children (WMESTC)

Dr Robert Home, Planning Consultant, London

Helen Hoult, Health Visitor for Traveller Families, Wolverhampton

Liz Hughes, Traveller Support Worker, the Children's Participation Project, the Children's Society

Poppy Hughes, Manager, Public Accountability, BBC

Jane Jackson, Traveller, South London Travellers Project

Mike Jempson, PressWise

Mr Chris Johnson, Travellers Advice Team, The Community Law Partnership, Birmingham

Tim Jones, Barrister, St Philips Chambers, Birmingham

Elizabeth S Jordan, Director, Scottish Traveller Education Project, Faculty of Education, Edinburgh

Christine Kelly, Traveller, South London Travellers Project

Dr Donald Kenrick, Advisor in Education and Planning, the Romany Guild

Andrew Ketteringham, Communications Director, Broadcasting Standards Commission

Peter Kingshill, Solicitor, Peter Kingshill and Co, London

Josie Lee, the Gypsy Council for Education, Culture, Welfare and Civil Rights

Michelle Lloyd, Development Worker, Traveller Section, Save the Children Fund, Scotland

Brenda Lloyd-Jones, Traveller Policy and Co-ordination Officer, South Gloucestershire Council

Liz Loufti, Advisory Council for the Education of Romany and other Travellers (ACERT)

John Malone, Paid Service Unit, South Gloucestershire Council

Alan Masters, Barrister, 10/11 Gray's Inn Square, London

Trish McDonald, Senior Advisory Teacher, WMESTC

Fran McGeown, WMESTC

Madge Meyrick, Health Visitor, Pontypool, Gwent

Frank Milne, Traveller Services Manager, Carmarthenshire County Council

Richard Morran, Development Worker, Traveller Section, Save the Children Fund, Scotland

Rachel Morris, Research Associate, Traveller Law Research Unit, Cardiff Law School

Annie Murdoch, Councillor, South Somerset District Council

Dr Angus Murdoch, Travellers Advice Team, the Community Law Partnership

Mr Chris Myant, Head of Media, Commission for Racial Equality

Jackie Nesbitt, Head of Service, Essex Traveller Education Service

Mary O'Dwyer, Irish Travellers Project, BIAS

Nora O'Sullivan, South London Travellers Project

Clare Paul, Planner, London

Liz Payne, Planning Policy, South Somerset District Council

Joan Payne, Manager, Bromley Gypsy and Traveller Project

Sarah Rhodes, Team Leader, Traveller's Health Project, Bristol

Susan Roberts, External Affairs Consultant, Press Complaints Commission

Frieda Schicker, Project Co-ordinator, London Gypsy and Traveller Unit

Claire Sephton, Solicitor, North Kensington Law Centre

Erik Shopland, Director, Sussex Racial Equality Council

Nicola Simpson, Assistant, Michael Cox Associates

Des Smith, McGrath and Co Solicitors, Birmingham

Richard Solly, Education Secretary, Churches Commission for Racial Justice

Heather Spiller, Anglia Gypsy Traveller Health Information Project

Jim Spiller, Anglia Gypsy Traveller Health Information Project

Irene Spring, Senior Education Welfare Officer, South Gloucestershire LEA

Rodney Stableford, Secretary, Staffordshire and Shropshire Gypsy Liaison Group

Ron Stainer, Secretary, Avon Travellers Support Group

George Summers, Gypsy Liaison Officer, Hampshire County Council

Mark Sutton, Traveller / Nurse, Somerset

Madeleine Tearse, Policy Department, Save the Children Fund

Margaret Thompson, Assistant Programmes Director (Midlands), Save the Children

Tony Thomson, Friends, Families and Travellers (FFT), Glastonbury

Richard Trahair, Property Secretary, Salisbury Diocesan Board of Finance

John Treble, Somerset Association of Local Councils

Patrice van Cleemput, Health Visitor for Travellers, Community Health Sheffield NHS Trust

Leanne Weber, Institute of Criminology, University of Cambridge

Susan and Derek Whittlesey, Gypsy Travellers, East Sussex
Kanta Wild-Smith, Co-ordinator, National Association of Teachers of Travellers
Nicola Williams, Site Liaison Officer, North Somerset Council
Toby Williams, Planning Project Co-ordinator, ACERT
Sarah Williams, McGrath and Co Solicitors, Birmingham
Mark Wilson, Planning Policy Officer, Woking Borough Council
Ms Franqui Wolf, Friends, Families and Travellers (FFT)

Appendix 2: 2nd Conference on Traveller Law Reform delegates and participants

Anna, Earth Circus Network
Professor Thomas Acton, Professor of Romani Studies, University of Greenwich
Deborah Adams, Site Warden, London Borough of Hillingdon
Bob Adams, Research and Information Officer, Milton Keynes Council
Susan Alexander, Co-ordinator, Advice and Information Unit, Friends, Families and Travellers
Diana Allen, Partner, Lance Kent and Co. Solicitors, Hertfordshire
Annie Anwar, Community Development Worker, London Gypsy and Traveller Unit
Rachel Auckland, Research Co-ordinator, Travellers' School Charity
Lord Avebury, House of Lords, Westminster
Anne Bagehot, Secretary, the Gypsy Council for Education, Culture, Welfare and Civil Rights
Annie Bailey, Gypsy Site Warden, Mid Bedfordshire District Council
Ian Baldwin, Development Advice Officer, Staffordshire County Council
Penny Ballinger, Health Visitor for Travellers, Herefordshire Community Health Trust
Cheryl Barrott, Sheffield
Joan Batstone, Health Visitor, Traveller Health Project, Taunton and Somerset NHS Trust
Lucy Beckett, Head of Service, Advisory Service for the Education of Travellers (ACERT)
Elizabeth Beer, Widening Participation Project (Travellers), Bosworth Community College, Leicestershire
Angela Bell, Support Teacher, Surrey Traveller Education Service
Malcolm Bell, Planner, Ward Hadaway Solicitors, Newcastle Upon Tyne
Kathleen Ben Rabha, Social Responsibility Officer, Social Responsibility in Wiltshire
Camilla Berens, Journalist, London
Inspector Adrian Bloor, Staffordshire Police
Denise Bollands, Development Worker, Workers Educational Association, Stockton-on-Tees
Felicity Bonel, Co-ordinator and Advisory Teacher, Greenwich Traveller Education Service
Rosie Booth, Derbyshire Gypsy Liaison Group
Jake Bowers-Burbridge, Essex

Philip Brown, Planning Associate, Bolton Emery Partnership, Cheshire

Narinder Buaal, Senior Advisor, Sandwell Citizens Advice Bureau

Sal Buckler, Community Development Worker,   Workers   Educational Association,

Pauline Burton, Travellers and Gypsy Liaison Officer, Private Sector Housing, Leicester City Council

Pam Byatt, Citizens Advisory Group on Travellers, Milton Keynes

George Calder, Development Co-ordinator, Scottish Traveller Consortium

Roger Callow, Gypsy Liaison Officer, Sevenoaks District Council

Patricia Carey, Womens Worker, Irish Travellers Project, Brent Irish Advisory Service (BIAS)

Sarah Cemlyn, Lecturer and Researcher, School for Policy Studies, University of Bristol

Sally Chandler, Co-ordinator, Traveller Education Service, London Borough of Hillingdon

Colin Clark, Lecturer in Social Policy, Department of Social Policy, University of Newcastle

Emily Clark, Community Development, Stockton-on-Tees Council

Sheila Clarke, Gypsy Manager, Essex County Council

G Sandra Clay, County of Cardiff Traveller Education Service / Advisory Group, the Traveller Law Research Unit, Cardiff Law School

Fran Clayton, Welfare Rights and Housing Adviser, Irish Women's Centre, London

Eirlys Cleaves, Area Co-ordinator, Milton Keynes Traveller Education Service

Charles Constant, Citizens Advisory Group on Travellers, Milton Keynes

Sarah Cox, Barrister, Holborn Chambers, London

Michael Cox, Principal, Michael Cox Associates, West Sussex

Steven Cragg, Barrister, 2 Garden Court Chambers, London

Kathleen Cresswell, Co-ordinator, Bolton Education Service for Travellers

Michelle Cummings, Student Placement, Friends, Families and Travellers (FFT), Glastonbury

Helen Currie, Thames Valley Consortium Traveller Education Service, Reading

Caroline Dann, West Cornwall Children's Project, The Children's Society

Richard Davis, Race Equality Unit, Home Office

Joanne Davis, Secretary, National Association of Health Workers with Travellers (NAHWT)

Francesca Del Mese, Pupil Barrister, Watford

Christine Diamondopoulos, Development Worker, Buckinghamshire Gypsy and Traveller Project

Margaret Donaghy, Director, Traveller Movement (Northern Ireland)

Federica Donati, Policy Section, Advocacy Unit, Save the Children Fund, London

Jack Doonan, Traveller Liaison Consultant, Jayder Public Relations, Milton Keynes

Brenda Downes, Lambeth Traveller Education Service

Angela Drakakis-Smith, PhD student, Department of Sociology, Bristol University

Tom Duncan, The Planning Exchange, Glasgow
Sylvia Dunn, National Association of Gypsy Women
Susan Durrant, Traveller Education Welfare Officer, Kent County Council
Anna Eldred, Teacher, South East Area, Surrey Traveller Education Service
Alan Evans, Head of Service, Nottinghamshire Equality Education Service
Christine Farley, Assistant Education Officer, Northumberland Local Education Authority
Harry Fletcher, Assistant General Secretary, National Association of Probation Officers
Sheila Forrest, Head of Service, Bedfordshire and Luton Traveller Education Service
Bill Forrester, Head of Gypsy Unit, Kent County Council / Chair of ACERT / Chair of the National Association of Gypsy and Traveller Officers
Bill Forster, University of Hertfordshire Press
Mike Foy, Gypsy Liaison Officer, Halton Borough Council, Cheshire
Eli Frankham, President, National Romani Rights Association / Advisory Group, the Traveller Law Research Unit, Cardiff Law School
John Galvin, Partner, Rogerson Galvin Solicitors, Manchester
Jim Glackin, Equality Development Officer, Commission for Racial Equality (Northern Ireland)
Margaret Greenfields, Research Student, Bath
Imogen Hale, Travellers Advice Worker, Leeds Citizens Advice Bureau
Steve Hancock, Divisional Environmental Health Officer, Swansea Council
Rosalind Hardie, Equalities Policy Officer, Association of London Government
Hugh Harris, Deputy Chair, Commission for Racial Equality
Debbie Harvey, Traveller Support Worker, Children's Participation Project, Children's Society
Officer Jack Hawkins, Gypsy Liaison Officer, HM Prison Cardiff
Brian Hicks, Traveller Liaison Officer, East Cambridgeshire District Council
Harry Hill, Traveller Enforcement Officer, Birmingham City Council
Andrew Hipworth, Legal Department, Hertfordshire County Council
Jill Hoggans, Youth Worker, South Gloucestershire Youth Service
Joanne Holbrook, National Association of Probation Officers
Ian Holding, Gypsy Liaison Officer, Bristol City Council
Terry Holland, Gypsy Services Manager, Buckinghamshire County Council
Liz Hughes, Traveller Support Worker, Children's Participation Project, The Children's Society
Richard Hulks, Gypsy Liaison Officer, Hampshire County Council
Margaret Hutchinson, Service Co-ordinator, Leicestershire Traveller Education Service
Trevor Isbell, Citizens Advisory Group on Travellers, Milton Keynes
Sergeant Arthur Jackson (Community and Travellers), Staffordshire Police
Chris Johnson, Travellers Advice Team, The Community Law Partnership, Birmingham
Steve Jones, Training Development Worker, The Groundswell Project, National Homeless Alliance
Myles Joyce, Enforcement Planner, London Borough of Havering

Frank Kane, Principal, Department of Environment (Northern Ireland)

Rosemary Keenan, Deputy Director, Catholic Children's Society (Westminster)

Donald Kenrick, Advisor in Education and Planning, the Romany Guild

Ann King, Nurse, Maidstone

Peter Kingshill, Partner, Peter Kingshill and Co. Solicitors, London

Martin Kovats, Organiser, Roma Refugee Organisation, London

Jackie Law, Police Constable, Metropolitan Police

Robert Lee, Widnes, Cheshire

Mary Lee, Site Warden, Widnes, Cheshire

Pauline Leeson, Commissioner, Commission for Racial Equality (Northern Ireland)

Penny Lenton, Department of Property, Leicestershire County Council

Michelle Lloyd, Development Worker, Traveller Section, Save the Children Fund, Scotland

Brenda Lloyd-Jones, Traveller Policy and Co-ordination Officer, South Gloucestershire Council

Delia Lomax, Research Fellow, School of Planning and Housing, Edinburgh College of Art

James Lowe, Sites Officer, Worcestershire County Council

Lisa Lowe, Essex

Brigid MacNeely, Playgroup Leader, Catholic Children's Society (Westminster)

David Maggs, ISR Traveller Project, Churches Cncl for Industry and Social Responsibility, Bristol

John Malone, Travellers Support Officer, South Gloucestershire Council

Alan Masters, Barrister, 10/11 Gray's Inn Square, London

Norbert McCabe, Senior Warden, Gypsy Section, Hertfordshire County Council

Suzanne McCallum, Research and Information Officer, Scottish Human Rights Centre, Glasgow

Brian McCarthy, Co-ordinator, Action Group for Irish Youth, London

Trish McDonald, Senior Advisory Teacher, West Midlands consortium Education Service for Travelling Children (WMESTC)

Kevin McGowan, Travelling Peoples' Liaison Officer, North Lanarkshire Council

Eileen McGroary, Environmental Health Officer, London Borough of Camden

Fiona McLean, Principal Equalities Officer, London Borough of Southwark

Mary McMahon, Co-ordinator, Belfast Traveller Sites Project

Derek McNish, Gypsy Liaison Officer, Swindon Borough Council

Alistair McWhirter, Assistant Chief Constable, Wiltshire Constabulary

Carol Mellors, Senior Teacher, West Kent Traveller Education Service

Peter Mercer, President, the Gypsy Council for Education, Culture, Welfare and Civil Rights and Advisory Group, the Traveller Law Research Unit, Cardiff Law School Alan Miles, Traveller Liaison and Development Worker, Northamptonshire County Council

Frank Milne, Traveller Service Manager, Carmarthenshire County Council

Nicolas Mitchell, Principal, Nicolas Mitchell Site Management, Bedfordshire

Peter Moore, Director, Sheffield Racial Equality Council

Judith Moreton, Chairperson, National Association of Health Workers with Travellers (NAHWT)

Richard Morran, Development Worker, Traveller Section, Save the Children Fund, Scotland

Annie Murdoch, Councillor, South Somerset District Council

Angus Murdoch, Travellers Advice Team, The Community Law Partnership, Birmingham

Verity Nelson, Head of Project, Traveller's Training Project, Bosworth College, Leicestershire

Alan O'Carroll, Advice Worker, Travellers Outreach, Cairde na nGael, London

Mary O'Dwyer, Irish Travellers Project, Brent Irish Advisory Service

Lin Patrick, Gypsy Policy Officer, Department of Environment, Transport and the Regions

Julian Pheby, Solicitor, Ison Harrison and Co., York

Stephen Pittam, Deputy Trust Secretary, Joseph Rowntree Charitable Trust

John Pooley, Education Social Worker, North Yorkshire and York Traveller Education Service

Seema Rani, Outreach Worker, Sandwell Citizens Advice Bureau

Fiona Read, Education Welfare Officer, Derby and Derbyshire Traveller Education Service

Nicola Redwood, Teacher, Hillingdon Traveller Education Service

Sarah Rhodes, Team Leader, Traveller's Health Project, Bristol

Ian Richardson, Parks and Estates Manager, Milton Keynes Parks Trust

Susan Roberts, External Affairs Consultant, Press Complaints Commission

Karen Ryan, Liaison Officer, Cardiff Gypsy Sites Group

Beth Samphire, Health Visitor, Travellers Health Project, Bristol

Frieda Schicker, Project Co-ordinator, London Gypsy and Traveller Unit

Pauline Schofield, Project Co-ordinator, Birmingham Irish Community Forum

Alison Self, Peripatetic Teacher, Surrey Traveller Education Service

Erik Shopland, Director, Sussex Racial Equality Council

Nicola Simpson, Assistant, Michael Cox Associates, West Sussex

David Smith, Traveller Research Projects, Leicester

Richard Solly, Education Secretary, Churches Commission for Racial Justice

Anne Spalding, Liaison Officer, Truro Diocesan Council for Social Responsibility

Siobhan Spencer, Secretary, Derbyshire Gypsy Liaison Group

Heather Spiller, Anglia Gypsy Traveller Health Information Project (AGTHIP), Norfolk

Jim Spiller, Anglia Gypsy Traveller Health Information Project (AGTHIP), Norfolk

Rodney Stableford, Secretary, Staffordshire and Shropshire Gypsy Liaison Group

Andrew Standen, Policy and Planning, Thames Valley Police, Milton Keynes

Hannah Starkey, Community Development Worker, Cardiff Law Centre

Nathan Still, Travellers Liaison Officer, London Borough of Hounslow

Edmund Stoner, Student, London

Christopher Stovold, Journalist, Oxford

Inspector Robert Strong, Public Order Policy, Metropolitan Police

Julia Summerfield, Planning Officer, Cannock Chase District Council

George Summers, Gypsy Liaison Officer, Hampshire County Council

John Taylor, Senior Environmental Health Officer, Bexley Council, Kent

Madeleine Tearse, Policy and Strategy Adviser, Save the Children Fund, London

Margaret Thompson, Assistant Programmes Director (Midlands), Save the Children Fund

Janet Timmins, Teacher Adviser, Hampshire Traveller Service

John Treble, Somerset Association of Local Councils

Patrice van Cleemput, Health Visitor for Travellers, Community Health Sheffield NHS Trust

Robert Vanderbeck, Department of Geography, University of Sheffield

Penny Vincent, Community Development Worker, North Staffordshire Health Promotion

Nigel Walker, Cornwall

Debbie Walmsley, UK Grants Officer, Comic Relief

David Watkinson, Barrister, 2 Garden Court Chambers, London

Patricia Weale, Gypsy Services Unit Manager, Worcestershire County Council

Alison Webster, Social Responsibility Officer, Diocese of Worcester

Glenda Wheeler, Education Social Worker, Traveller, Hampshire County Council

Jill Wheller, Senior Environmental Health Officer, Basingstoke and Deane Borough Council

Marc Whitfield, Head of Engineering and Environment Services, Stevenage Borough Council

Kanta Wild-Smith, Co-ordinator, National Association of Teachers of Travellers

Marc Willers, Barrister, 1 Pump Court Chambers, London

Nicola Williams, Site Liaison Officer, North Somerset Council

Toby Williams, Planning Project Co-ordinator, ACERT

Caroline Willis, West Cornwall Children's Project, The Children's Society

Tim Wilson, Liaison Officer, Cardiff Gypsy Sites Group / Advisory Group, the Traveller Law Research Unit, Cardiff Law School

John Wilson, Traveller Sites Manager, Avalon Community Enterprise, East Sussex

Viv Wilson, Senior Policy Officer, Chief Executive's Department, Derbyshire County Council

Paul Winter, Co-ordinator, Traveller Education for East Riding of Yorkshire, Hull and North Lincs.

Franqui Wolf, Chair, Friends, Families and Travellers (FFT)

Anthea Wormington, Advisory Teacher, Newham Traveller Education Support Service

Tina Yule, Local Group Director, Friends, Families and Travellers (FFT), Bedfordshire

Appendix 3: Travellers, Gypsies and the Media – A good practice guide from the Commission for Racial Equality

Coverage of race and ethnic issues across the media has significantly improved over the past 20 years. There has been a wider and more constructive exploration of many questions and a reduction in the use of language that is offensive to members of different ethnic groups. However many problems remain. These recommendations are designed to help in dealing with one of them: the way parts of the media report on Traveller and/or Gypsy issues.

Poor quality reporting which exploits or panders to stereotypes can cause much hurt to those about whom the stories are written. By repeating false and negative stereotypes the media can encourage bad practice on the part of those with whom Travellers and Gypsies deal and can validate the expression of language and attitudes which in any other circumstances would be seen as totally unacceptable.

The Commission for Racial Equality has handled cases under the Race Relations Act for Travellers and Gypsies for over 20 years. The number of such cases continues to run at several dozen each year. The majority of these cases involve clear breaches of the Act.

These guidelines are not intended to make the media shy away from covering issues and stories to do with Travellers and Gypsies. Quite the contrary. The CRE and those organisations representing Travellers and Gypsies want to see more coverage in the media but are keen to help the media develop a coverage that is honest and fair, open and inclusive.

Steer clear of exploiting prejudice

The public wants a media that is campaigning, but those campaigns should be built on matters of genuine public concern, not simply prejudices against particular groups.

Check the facts

Go to the experts who can help to set the context. With these recommendations we include a list of contacts of individuals and organisations which can help you with various aspects of your story.[196] Make sure that wherever possible you check the details with a relevant source and don't just rely on expressions of local or popular prejudice. Many allegations are made about Travellers, Gypsies and now Roma asylum seekers from Eastern Europe, but can those making the allegations actually substantiate them?

Don't let your news agenda be driven by the way others are handling the issue

Certain story lines easily dominate media discussion of Travellers or Gypsies while issues of great importance to the communities involved are downplayed or ignored altogether. Don't write about Travellers and Gypsies only in the context of disputes over stopping places, look also at the problems Travellers face.

---

196 The Gypsy Council for Education, Culture, Welfare, and Civil Rights (GCECWCR), the Irish Travellers Project (BIAS, London), the Traveller Law Research Unit at Cardiff Law School, the National Union of Journalists Ethics Hotline, and the CRE Media Office.

Look behind the story line

Don't assume there is only one point of view. Always seek the views of Traveller and Gypsy organisations to se whether or not there is an alternative interpretation or a different and more significant story line to be presented.

Listen to the people you are writing about

This is particularly important when it comes to the terms and language you use. Terms like 'tinker', 'itinerant' or 'gypo' are all highly offensive to those about whom they are used and should be avoided. The terms Traveller(s), Gypsy or Irish Traveller should be used with initial capital letters. Offensive stereotypes (for example 'scroungers', 'dole dodgers', 'bogus asylum seeker') should only be used when they are accurate descriptions of particular individuals and should not be employed to negatively stereotype whole groups.

Don't label people if it is not relevant

Reference to the fact that an individual is a Traveller, Gypsy or Irish Traveller should only be made when it is relevant and appropriate.

Appendix 4:   Letter from the Traveller Law Research Unit of Cardiff Law School and the Traveller Working Groups to the Home Office regarding the Third Review of the Race Relations Act 1976, 4 October 1998.

The Traveller Law Research Unit formerly operated the Telephone Legal Advice Service for Travellers (TLAST). Further to a Conference on Traveller Law Reform held in 1997, we have facilitated the development of specialist Traveller Working Groups. These met this year in London, Birmingham and Bristol to discuss more detailed proposals for reform in the areas of accommodation and grant funding, planning issues, rights, and access to health and education, for Travellers.

   Those attending the Traveller Working Groups have included community development workers, lawyers, planners, health visitors, representatives of the church and of Traveller and more general organisations, local government officers, teachers, academics, members of the media, and equality organisations. These groups constitute the first stage in the process of the development of a common 'platform' for Traveller-related law reform, adapting the successful precedent set in the Republic of Ireland in recent years. The document collecting all the law reform proposals together will be discussed and finalised at a conference in London in February 1999.

   One topic of discussion at some of these meetings was the reform of the Race Relations Act 1976. The CRE proposals for such reform were discussed at length, and the 'platform' felt, on the whole, that the proposals were excellent. It was also determined that:

- in addition to the categories under the heading A Basic Right, 'way of life' or 'social origin' should be added. It was noted that the proposals are internally inconsistent, including a breadth of categories under that section not all of which are synonymous with 'race', and then going on to speak only of race throughout the rest of the proposals. This approach is also not consistent with the broader approach to 'difference' adopted by European bodies and documents (e.g. the ECHR Article 14);
- the CRE maintain that the usefulness of policy and legislation cannot be measured without the use of ethnic monitoring. As they accept at least some Travellers as a 'race' within the meaning of the Act, they should add Travellers to their ethnic monitoring categories and ensure that other bodies do the same.

We hope that you will find such comment useful, and look forward to hearing from you soon regarding these submissions.

Appendix 5:   International documents to which the UK is a signatory

International Convention on the Elimination of all Forms of Racial Discrimination (1966)

Article 2:

1. States Parties condemn racial discrimination and undertake to pursue by all appropriate means and without delay a policy of eliminating racial discrimination in all its forms and promoting understanding among all races, and, to this end:

   (a) each State Party undertakes to engage in no act or practice of racial discrimination against persons, groups of persons or institutions and to ensure that all public authorities and public institutions, national and local, shall act in conformity with this obligation;

   (b) each State Party undertakes not to sponsor, defend or support racial discrimination by any persons or organizations;

   (c) each State Party shall take effective measures to review governmental, national and local policies, and to amend, rescind or nullify any laws and regulations which have the effect of creating or perpetuating racial discrimination wherever it exists;

   (d) each State Party shall prohibit and bring to an end, by all appropriate means, including legislation as required by circumstances, racial discrimination by any persons, group or organization;

   (e) each State Party undertakes to encourage, where appropriate, integrationist multi-racial organizations and movements and other means of eliminating barriers between races, and to discourage anything which tends to strengthen racial division.

2. States Parties shall, when the circumstances so warrant, take, in the social, economic, cultural and other fields, special and concrete measures to ensure the adequate development and protection of certain racial groups or individuals belonging to them, for the purpose of guaranteeing them the full and equal enjoyment of human rights and fundamental freedoms. These measures shall in

no case entail as a consequence the maintenance of unequal or separate rights for different racial groups after the objectives for which they were taken have been achieved.

Article 5: lists these rights and freedoms, which includes political rights and the right to vote, the right to freedom of movement and residence within the border of the State, and the right of access to any place or service intended for use by the general public, such as transport, hotels, restaurants, cafés, theatres and parks.

Article 7: States Parties undertake to adopt immediate and effective measures, particularly in the fields of teaching, education, culture and information, with a view to combating prejudices which lead to racial discrimination and to promoting understanding, tolerance and friendship among nations and racial or ethnical groups ...

A Committee on the Elimination of Discrimination reports annually.

International Convention on Civil and Political Rights (1966)

Article 12: Everyone lawfully within the territory of a State shall, within that territory, have the right to liberty of movement and freedom to choose his residence ... The above-mentioned rights shall not be subject to any restrictions except those which are provided by law, are necessary to protect national security, public order, public health or morals or the rights and freedoms of others, and are consistent with rights recognised in the present covenant.

Article 17: No one shall be subjected to arbitrary or unlawful interference with his privacy, family, home or correspondence, nor to unlawful attacks on his honour and reputation. Everyone has the right to the protection of the law against such interference or attacks.

Article 20: Any advocacy of national, racial or religious hatred that constitutes incitement to discrimination, hostility or violence shall be prohibited by law.

Article 25: Every citizen shall have the right and the opportunity, without any of the distinctions mentioned in article 2 and without unreasonable restrictions:

(a) to take part in the conduct of public affairs, directly or through freely chosen representatives;

(b) to vote and to be elected at genuine periodic elections which shall be by universal and equal suffrage and shall be held by secret ballot, guaranteeing the free expression of the will of the electors;

(c) to have access, on general terms of equality, to public service in his country.

Article 26: All persons are equal before the law and are entitled without any discrimination on any ground such as race, colour, sex, language, religion, political or other opinion, national or social origin, property, birth or other status.

A Human Rights Committee reports annually to the UN General Assembly via the Economic and Social Council.

Convention on the Rights of the Child (1989)

Article 16: No child shall be subjected to arbitrary or unlawful interference with his or her privacy, family, home or correspondence, nor to unlawful attacks on his or her honour and reputation. The child has the right to the protection of the law against such interference or attacks.

Article 24: States Parties recognize the right of the child to the enjoyment of the highest attainable standard of health and to facilities for the treatment of illness and rehabilitation of health. States Parties shall strive to ensure that no child is deprived of his or her access to such health care services. States Parties shall pursue full implementation of this right and, in particular, shall take appropriate measures ... to combat disease and malnutrition, including within the framework of primary healthcare, through, inter alia, the application of readily available technology and through the provision of adequate nutritious foods and clean drinking-water, taking into consideration the dangers and risks of environmental pollution.

Article 30: In those States in which ethnic, religious or linguistic minorities or persons of indigenous origin exist, a child belonging to such a minority or who is indigenous shall not be denied the right, in community with other members of his or her group, to enjoy his or her culture, to profess and practise his or her own religion, or to use his or her own language.

Declaration on Rights of Persons Belonging to Minorities (1992)

Article 1: States shall protect the existence and the national or ethnic, cultural, religious and linguistic identity of minorities within their respective territories and shall encourage conditions for the promotion of that identity. States shall adopt appropriate legislative and other measures to achieve those ends.

Article 4: States shall take measures where required to ensure that persons belonging to minorities may exercise fully and effectively all their human rights and fundamental freedoms without any discrimination and in full equality before the law. States shall take measures to create favourable conditions to enable persons belonging to minorities to express their characteristics and to develop their culture, language, religion, traditions and customs, except where specific practices are in violation of national law and contrary to international standards. States should take appropriate measures so that, wherever possible, persons belonging to minorities may have adequate opportunities to learn their mother tongue or to have instruction in their mother tongue. States should, where appropriate, take measures in the field of education, in order to encourage knowledge of the history, traditions, language and culture of the minorities existing within their territory. Persons belonging to minorities should have adequate opportunities to gain knowledge of the society as a whole. States should consider appropriate measures so that persons belonging to minorities may participate fully in the economic progress and development in their country.

Article 5: National policies and programmes shall be planned and implemented with due regard for the legitimate interest of persons belonging to minorities.